"This is a new, refreshing voice that speaks with complete clarity and understanding about the way people really experience the world. It is a book that is valuable for students and clinicians, as well as laypeople."
— **Faye Newsome, Chair of the Board of Trustees, Centre for Modern Psychoanalytic Studies**

"Recently, the art of storytelling has come into its own, with the popularity of the Moth, and other similar story-telling venues. It wasn't invented by psychoanalysts in the late 19th century, but it certainly was brought to the level of high art as well as science. Unfortunately, when psychoanalysis was brought from Vienna to America, it was coopted by medical practitioners, a tradition that Freud himself objected to, and wrote, "The Question of Lay Analysis," in defense of training psychoanalyst from all walks of life, not just physicians.

Psychoanalytic patients are amongst the best story-tellers we have. They tell the stories of their lives; they ponder the interesting, the painful, the unimaginable (until the unconscious becomes conscious, and all is able to be imagined).

In this new, wonderfully digestible book, Claudia Luiz makes it possible to understand complex principles in an emotional way. It's educative, entertaining, even enthralling, as a good analysis is, to both patient and analyst."
— **Jane G. Goldberg, Psychoanalyst-Author-Holistic Practitioner-Blogger**

"Claudia Luiz understands what leads to mental health, and makes complex psychoanalytic principles accessible to readers."
— **Jane Snyder, President, Boston Graduate School of Psychoanalysis**

"Like her previous book, Dr. Luiz creatively and cogently articulates the inner workings of modern psychoanalysis. She bridges the gap from old to new, modernizing psychoanalysis for our contemporary culture.

This book will be required reading for all my students.

And, since we always remain students in this field, it is an enlightening read for all clinicians and aspiring therapists.

Dr. Luiz blasts through the analytic rhetoric and jargon to bring Modern Psychoanalysis into the 21st century.

Her writing style captivates the reader like a novelist as she teaches the core principles and techniques of contemporary analytic work. Delightful and refreshing."

— **Steven H. Padnick, Long Island Centre for Modern Psychoanalytic Studies**

"An enduring pleasure. Luiz invites us in with her beautiful prose, but what kept me at the table was the feast of intellect, wit, and compassion each chapter provides. I return often for the pleasure of reaching the turn in each tale, in which I can see myself, and all humanity, illuminated from within."

— **Matthew Ponsot, Songwriter, Musician**

The Making of a Psychoanalyst

In this unique and uplifting work, Dr. Claudia Luiz reveals why psychoanalysis is more relevant than ever, perhaps the only discipline currently suitable to help solve the mystery of our emotional challenges.

In gripping stories about people struggling with depression, anxiety, sexual dysfunction, attention deficit disorder (ADD) and more, Luiz brings us right into each treatment where we discover how psychoanalysts today prepare their patient's mind for self-discovery. Following each story, absorbing commentaries acquaint the reader with the theories of the mind that currently guide treatment, and the innovative clinical techniques that are revolutionizing the field, including how Luiz learned to integrate her own emotions as therapeutic instruments for diagnosis and cure.

The Making of a Psychoanalyst is an ideal book for psychoanalysts and psychotherapists in practice and in training, mental health professionals working in social care, and students interested in the evolution of an undying discipline that embodies personal narrative. Anyone interested in knowing how two human beings interact with each other to effect profound change will want to read this book.

Claudia Luiz, EdM, Harvard University, PsyaD, Boston Graduate School of Psychoanalysis, is the winner of the Phyllis W. Meadow Award for Excellence in Psychoanalytic Writing and *Writer's Digest* Best Writer's Website Award. She currently serves on the faculty at the Academy for Clinical and Applied Psychoanalysis, New Jersey. Her blog and website can be found at www.claudialuiz.com. She can be contacted at cluiz@post.harvard.edu.

The Making of
a Psychoanalyst
Studies in Emotional Education

Claudia Luiz

Routledge
Taylor & Francis Group

LONDON AND NEW YORK

First published 2018
by Routledge
2 Park Square, Milton Park, Abingdon, Oxon OX14 4RN

and by Routledge
711 Third Avenue, New York, NY 10017

Routledge is an imprint of the Taylor & Francis Group, an informa business

British Library Cataloguing-in-Publication Data
A catalogue record for this book is available from the British Library

Library of Congress Cataloging-in-Publication Data
Names: Luiz, Claudia, author.
Title: The making of a psychoanalyst : studies in emotional education / Claudia Luiz.
Description: New York : Routledge, 2017. | Includes index.
Identifiers: LCCN 2017015358 (print) | LCCN 2017022156 (ebook) | ISBN 9781315411972 (Master eBook) | ISBN 9781138220805 (hardback) | ISBN 9781138220812 (pbk) | ISBN 9781315411972 (ebk)
Subjects: LCSH: Psychoanalysis--History--21st century.
Classification: LCC BF173 (ebook) | LCC BF173 .L795 2017 (print) | DDC 616.89/17--dc23
LC record available at https://lccn.loc.gov/2017015358

ISBN: 978-1-138-22080-5 (hbk)
ISBN: 978-1-138-22081-2 (pbk)
ISBN: 978-1-315-41197-2 (ebk)

Typeset in Galliard
by HWA Text and Data Management, London

To my analysts

Hyman Spotnitz for giving my life purpose
Eugene Goldwater for the stories I learned to tell
Dena Reed for helping me get married
Joan White for helping me to be in a room with myself
Faye Newsome for helping me know the unthinkable

Contents

Acknowledgments   xi

Introduction to the new psychoanalysis   1

PART I
Introduction to psychoanalysis   7

1 Catrina learns to breathe   9

The twenty-first-century psychoanalyst   25

2 John J and the big surrender   35

The twenty-first-century patient   43

PART II
Key concepts   49

3 Searching for Anita   51

Listening to theories of technique: following the
contact   60

4 The unseen side of Angela   66

Listening to theories of the mind   79

5 Terrell and Rosalia in bed   86

Listening to theories of technique: emotional
communication   105

6 Mitzi's workshop   110

Listening to countertransference   131

x *Contents*

PART III
Putting it all together   **135**

  7 **Mercy gets a tattoo**   **137**
     Layers of listening   159

  8 **Sylvie Spider**   **162**
     The future of psychoanalysis   177

     Postscript   182
     Glossary   183
     Index   187

Acknowledgments

First and foremost, I would like to thank my husband, John Luiz, for taping and transcribing me before I was ready to write by myself, and once I was writing on my own, for showing me how to express an idea effectively. Thank you too, John, for babysitting, cooking, hand-holding and, of course, the endless editing and proofreading. You epitomize devotion.

And second, thanks to my daughters, Zoe and Miranda, whose relationship to "the book" has always been one of solemn respect and understanding.

I thank my family—Paul and Sara Sheftel, my parents, who ignited and inspired my resolve to offer myself in the form of this book, and for giving me the DNA to pull it off. I am so lucky to have fans like them. When Routledge agreed to publish the book, I was thoroughly frightened by the prospect of writing the essays that were meant to augment the stories. So my mother, who teaches psychoanalysis and is herself a great writer, promised me she would write them herself. We spent a year talking about theory every Tuesday afternoon, and on weekends, and many days in-between. By the end of that year, the essays flowed out of me. Great mothers know how to be safety nets. They can provide the wind beneath their children's sails. And mine is one.

My sister and brother-in-law, Gigi and Dave Cebulla, are always there for me. Thanks to my sister in arms, Nika Cavat, for being there with wisdom, insights and editing skills.

Clarice Stone, a family friend who is part of my foundation of belonging, has always watched over me and I am grateful to her for helping me find my agent, Kevin Moran.

Kevin is indeed a wonderful staple in my life. Not only because he is there to ask questions and run ideas by, but also because having someone believe in your mission is ridiculously inspiring. Here's the handwritten communication I received from him on the first advance check from Routledge: "Hey, Claudia, I know this will be the first of many, many more!" What could be more encouraging than that?

I dedicated this book to my analysts, thanking each one for one particular gift, but I would also like to additionally thank Dr. White for helping me realize how much I love to write, and to Faye Newsome for her support and encouragement in the process of producing this book. How energy is freed up for creative ventures through psychoanalysis cannot be underestimated.

I am very grateful to all my teachers. At the Center for Modern Psychoanalytic Studies (CMPS) in New York City, Dolores Welber and Jane Goldberg. And at the Boston Graduate School of Psychoanalysis (BGSP) in Brookline, MA, Eugene Goldwater, Phyllis Meadow, Lynn Perlman, Mary Shepherd ("Boss"), Siamak Movahedi, Jim Morrell, Steve Soldz, June Bernstein, Elizabeth Dorsey, Jane Snyder, Mara Wagner and "uncle" Ted Laquercia.

And I also want to express my deep gratitude to my fellow students at BGSP who I trained with—I learned so much from you, both about my own character and character in general, and I know for all of us the lessons have sometimes been so hard.

Thank you to my friends and readers for their feedback and encouragement, in particular Eva Silver, Elaine Klonicki, Mark Hansson, Nicole DeLisle, Diane Cole, Ronald Pies, Eric Ribeiro, David Fujita, Matthew Ponsot and Laura Ross. Thank you to Tim Wenk for creating "Melon-Ccoly" for me. David Perry was indefatigable in his assistance and advice; I felt the love.

My active fan base, the faithful readers of my advice column "Claudia Confidentially" which ran for so many years in my local paper, changed my life with their enthusiasm and support. I learned to write for you.

I thank each of my patients heartfully and deeply for having taught me about themselves and about myself, about the world, and, mostly, about how emotional experiences work.

To Linda Rode, great thanks for being a wonderful safety net, whose editorial and analytic skills improved this manuscript immeasurably.

And finally, I thank Keith Talbot, who, over the course of many years, sculpted this material. What started as the writing of a dry exposé on change turned into a rich artistic collaboration thanks to his overarching vision, word-by-word analysis and the seemingly limitless reservoir of experiences through which he is able to teach how best to convey a message. This is completely *our* book and, thanks to him, a joy to write.

Disclaimer

All the characters in this book are imagined. Their lives and actions derive from facets of people I have known in real life as well as in my imagination. But make no mistake: the emotional experiences—both of despair and positive transformation—are real.

Introduction to the new psychoanalysis

The relevance of psychoanalysis

I was having an impassioned discussion with a friend in which he was despairingly musing on the current, atrophying state of mental health in the US. "We're losing it," he moaned. "What are you talking about?" I said, forever the optimist. His answer was grim. "Rates of anxiety and depression are skyrocketing," he pointed out. "Mental illness is on the rise. Say what you will about the efficacy of treatment, we're only getting worse."

And yet, I can tell you for sure that the new patients who are coming to me for treatment are more emotionally sophisticated than ever. More aware of their feelings. More attuned and able to face their problems unabashedly, courageously and without reservation. How could there be such a discrepancy between the United States national statistics from the Institute of Mental Health, and my own personal experience treating people in my office?

The answer came to me at a lecture given by one of my beloved analysts at a summer conference on Cape Cod. Dr. Eugene Goldwater was showing snippets from two television segments he wanted to compare and contrast for his audience. One segment was from *Leave it to Beaver*, created in the 1950s, and the other, a 2012 segment from *Modern Family*.

As I'm sure you can imagine, the mother in the 1950's *Leave it to Beaver* episode was an icon of calm. In this scene, her son Beaver had been mischievous, so she and her husband were discussing the consequences as she alone did the dishes, wearing pearls. The father came up with a plan, and she calmly and melodically relented with a simple, "alright, dear."

By contrast, in the segment from *Modern Family* the mother is completely crazed, her kids are saner than she is and her husband is depicted as a bumbling fool. She acts like a total lunatic. She is disheveled, disorganized, regressed… and it makes us all laugh. Because it feels so true.

And this is how I was able to explain to my friend that the rising rate of mental illness in this country is not necessarily indicative of things getting worse. The truth is, we are simply not hiding what we're feeling any more. We're not burying our feelings under explanations. We're expressing ourselves and exploring the consequences. And these changes have necessitated a change in how we conduct psychotherapy, because people are no longer interested in appearing "normal."

Challenging what the statistical data appears to be saying about our society's degenerating mental health brings to my mind what I know about the very structure of any revolution—whether scientific, economic or political—which is that for something new to be built the old existing structure must come down. On the micro level, this can be said to be true for even a standard home improvement project, like a kitchen remodel. Perhaps, what's coming down for us is the pretense of normalcy.

From within the context of the chaos that may be required for any major transformation, as I continued to explain to my friend over dinner, our mental health crisis can be seen in a better light—not because of any hopeless disintegration of mental well-being or because our society is getting worse. All of that may merely be indicative of our newfound freedom to deal with what has always been going on, only now, no longer behind closed doors. The real problem, perhaps, is not that we look worse, but rather that our methods of treatment haven't yet caught up to what society is no longer as ashamed or afraid to talk about.

And that is why I wrote this book. Because I fundamentally believe that we are finally open, vulnerable and emotional enough to become interested in working with our unconscious processes in a new way. What I have charted in this book will, I hope, set forth the methods for working with the unconscious that can perhaps catch up to the tremendous advancements our society has made in emotional self-awareness, in a courageous willingness to confront psychological problems, and in the unprecedented freedom from the stigmas of mental illness, which improves daily a thousand-fold.

The challenge we continue to face in conducting treatment, however, is that people still need to defend against overwhelming thoughts and feelings. These defensive walls can block off entire vital portions of our mind, creating imbalances and suffering. Reality becomes distorted. Relationships get compromised. To some extent we are all—each and every one of us—in some way blind to ourselves. This much has never changed.

Most current therapies, however, simply aren't designed to address the problem of the unconscious: of how intractable defenses prevent neural synapses from connecting the primitive amygdala to the more evolved higher cortex. For our patients to be able to access their higher cortex, think more effectively, and design better responses to the world, means that, eventually, their defenses must come down and reality must become known and dealt with. Once defenses against unmanageable thoughts and feelings come down, we see the birth of what psychoanalysts now call 'mentation.' Still others call it 'a strong ego' and others still, 'a self.'

The way psychoanalysts work with the unconscious today has changed radically since Freud first introduced his interpretive method. *Therapeutic action*, the term used to describe (and hopefully proscribe) psychological transformation in treatment, has completely changed. Psychoanalysts today have evolved as much as the image of motherhood has, as portrayed in Dr. Goldwater's humorous exposé on that beautiful summer day to characterize mainstream America. We are no longer the neutral, objective, un-emotional arbiters of the unconscious, translating for our patients what's going on in the darkest recesses of their most deeply repressed mind.

Instead, psychoanalysis today is predicated not on the analyst's ability to analyze and interpret the unconscious, but rather *to prepare our patient's mind for self-discovery.*

No matter how strong the analytic relationship, or how exquisite the timing of an *interpretation*, it will hardly ever work to create permanent change. The function of interpretation with its corollary penchant for insight is completely antiquated. To put it another way, even if someone can figure you out and tell you everything about yourself, it will not necessarily help. I believe this is why classical psychoanalysis today is no longer seen as an effective method of treatment, because of the failure of the interpretive method and the limitations of simply striving for insight.

But there is still no question that the psychoanalyst's job is to help the patient make the unconscious conscious. Psychoanalysis today, however, is not simply a cognitive experience; it is primarily an emotional one. Learning to work emotionally with mental and energetic systems is the key to providing our patients with a new experience—one which will far exceed that of any therapy that must depend solely upon the patient having a mind, *ego* or access to the higher cortex. In fact, I wrote this book as a set of stories so that you could feel, and not just learn, what the method today is like.

How to read this book

Let me tell you a little about how this book is organized. My hope is that this will help you be a more active reader, and approach the book with many questions, doubts or increased curiosity. The three parts of this book each provide you with a set of stories, followed by essays that teach a particular lesson about what twenty-first-century psychoanalysis is all about.

In the first part of the book, 'Introduction to Psychoanalysis,' I have prepared two stories. The first, about a woman called "Catrina," takes you right into the mind of the twenty-first-century psychoanalyst, and introduces you to the most recent innovations in psychoanalytic history.

Not many people willingly enter into a psychoanalytic experience, however, which is why I prepared the second story for this part of the book, about John J, a man who was plagued by an inability to master his emotional life but who yet had little interest in exploring his own mind.

After this introduction, Part II, 'The Making of a Psychoanalyst,' takes you right into the innovations and current methods in the field. Four stories followed again by essays show you how theories of the mind, clinical metatheory and learning about our own emotions each become integrated into a practice that has as its goal to best prepare our patient's minds for self-discovery.

And finally, in Part III, 'Summary,' I bring it all together. First, I tell you a story about Mercy, a troubled teen, to illustrate how it feels to integrate all the lessons into actual practice. Then, I introduce you to Sylvie, a child with Attention Deficit Disorder (ADD), to convey what I believe to be the incredible promise of psychoanalysis to the future of mental health.

While I have provided you with essays following each story to underscore a specific lesson, examples of those lessons can really be found in almost every story. To help you track those examples more easily, I have included three tools. The first is endnotes for each story, which provide you with the corresponding technical language (or jargon) for what you are reading about—words like '*transference*,' or 'projective identification,' which are very valuable to learn and know. (If they interrupt the flow of your emotional experience of the story, however, please return to them later, once you're done.)

The second tool I included is a glossary. Terms for which you can read a definition in the glossary are *italicized* at the first occurrence in each chapter.

And the third tool is the index. All the endnotes, glossary terms and lessons are cross-referenced in the index so that if you should become more interested in one particular word or phenomenon, like, say, '*countertransference*,' for example, you can look up in the index where else in the book you can read more about it.

Summary

At the heart of psychoanalysis is not only a way of talking to our patients, but rather, a way of being with them. Your ear must be constantly tuned to what they can and cannot absorb; to what they can and cannot change in their thought patterns; to what they can and cannot yet say, despite how obvious it may be to everyone else.

Using your own emotions to gauge these dynamics is at the heart and soul of how psychoanalysis works today. Thinking emotionally is not only how we assess our patients, it's also how we come up with strategies to help them get to know their unconscious. When you look to this book to understand psychoanalysis, therefore, don't look only for what the strategies are, look even harder at what might be required of you as a practitioner to design them yourself.

My mother and father started their own analyses when I was twelve years old, at which time my whole world changed. By the time I turned sixteen, when I started my own analysis, I knew that someday I would become a psychoanalyst. My love for psychoanalysis is so deep and personal, so resonant with feeling—and it is this emotion that I have poured out onto these pages for you. Really, this book tells you the story of my own growth as a person as much as it tells the story of how a psychoanalyst works today. My greatest hope for you, therefore, is that the information and education of this book will bring you not only to a more thorough understanding of twenty-first-century psychoanalysis, but also to an increased desire and means for how to better get to know yourself.

Part I
Introduction to psychoanalysis

1 Catrina learns to breathe

The perfect hair

I could hardly believe it. Why was Catrina calling me for an appointment?
I mean, I thought she was the leading lady, starring in the role of "Mrs.
Absolutely Perfectly Wonderful" in my life. The one, I thought, who had it all.

I had met her at the pre-school where we both dropped off our daughters.
Catrina would sweep in and out of there effortlessly, always exquisitely
dressed. I took careful note of each detail of her outfits: a beautiful trench
coat adorned with a French scarf that complemented her blue-green eyes; a
stunning sweater with a wide collar that cinched at her narrow waist and fell
at just the right length below her hips; and her beautiful leather boots and
straight-edged pocketbooks.

I had probably studied Catrina from every angle, taking in lateral, posterior
and bi-vertical profiles. I had a mix of emotions seeing her. I felt both
inspiration, wanting to emulate her put-together style, and dread because I
didn't really want to make the time for it.[1]

We were just acquaintances then. I knew she had an important role in
the Classical Languages department at a prominent university, that her
husband was a surgeon, and that they traveled to France each spring, where
she probably shopped. She was such a class act. And they had three children.
When I saw her, it made me think that maybe I should keep trying for a third
child myself. A boy, this time, like she had. Maybe I did have penis envy.

But what struck me most about Catrina was her hair. Mine is troublesome.
It always has been. The devout Italian women who raised me used to brush
and wet it down and tie it back so tightly it hurt. By afternoon, I looked as
though I'd been electrified; small ringlets cut loose in a halo of reddish frizz. I
preferred the way I looked in the afternoon but didn't think I was supposed to.
My hair has long epitomized my sense of not being sure of myself, of feeling
guilty for something but not knowing what—of being a stranger even to myself.

Every hair seemed to be in place for Catrina. No flyaways. Blonde. A real
American 1950's bob that curled in a perfect even arc at the bottom. Only
she could pull this off, managing to look fashionable in contrast to the more
disheveled layered looks that most women around town wore.

Now here she was, calling me for an appointment. Weird. Apparently, things had gotten stressful for her lately. She thought it would probably be a good idea to talk to someone. But she was very busy—very "pressed for time"—would it be possible to pop in for an early morning appointment?

Giving her a time, I felt dishonest. She apparently had no idea, when we saw each other around town, that each encounter would precipitate my going down a long list of ways I should improve myself—get a Keratin hair-conditioning treatment perhaps; go on a shopping spree at Bloomingdales, or better yet, in Paris where she went each spring. Become another kind of woman. One I would consistently want to be.

I sat in my chair, staring into space, after I hung up the phone with her. There was some satisfaction in all this, actually. Wouldn't it be funny if I were to become *her* "Mrs. Perfectly Wonderful" now—an emotionally balanced, at-peace-with-herself psychotherapist?

With all these thoughts swimming around in my head, I thought, "I'd better be careful." It could be pleasurable to feel superior to Mrs. Perfectly Wonderful herself. Yes, I admired her, but on the flip side I was scoring so low on how I felt about myself when I stood next to her that it made me feel strangely negative toward her. I'd better not unwittingly act on that. I worried about being motivated to help her, since seeing her suffer could potentially help me feel better about my hair.[2]

If only we could explode all the myths and fantasies that make us feel inferior, the world would be such a better place.

The moment Catrina entered my office, her physical presence, front stage and center, threw me headlong into feelings of awe. She was wearing a silky-looking, baby-blue pencil skirt with a soft white sleeveless ruffled shirt and black patent leather pumps. Absolutely gorgeous. I said, "Good morning" in a neutral way and asked her right away to lie down on the couch. Which I never do. But it helped me feel in control and also kept me from thinking about my outfit, which just didn't feel that beautiful.

"So what brings you here?" I asked.

"So…I've been having sort of a rough time," she said, staring directly out the window where I had hung a pot of geraniums. I was relieved that they were in bloom. We both looked at the geraniums for a little while, and then she started talking again.

A crazed life

In her worst moments, Catrina explained, she had always recited promises to herself, which actually sounded a lot like prayers: "I will take better care of myself. Be grateful every day. Exercise. Let go of petty, unimportant stuff. Invoke patience. Remember what's important. Breathe." The prayers had generally worked for her until one day, a few weeks earlier. Reviewing her prayers right after she woke up, she hadn't felt uplifted. She stepped outside to breathe in some fresh air and invoke the goodness of life, raising her head to the sun, but nothing penetrated. In fact, she felt worse trying to relax, so she decided to get busy.

"That's when I realized that I'm depressed," she said. "That something in me isn't right. I have so much to be grateful for—a great husband, job, kids, house. I have...no reason to feel this way. But I don't know. I do. My doctor's put me on something," she continued, "and it's making me exhausted. We're going to adjust that. I just don't know what's wrong."

"Is something bothering you or upsetting you?" I asked.

"Well, it's the stupidest stuff—totally ridiculous. Like the kids—today Jeremy wanted me to cook him pancakes. I just wanted to go into the bathroom and cry. Like, why couldn't I just make him a pancake? I just felt... destroyed. It's so stupid."

Obviously, Catrina was none too pleased about being bowled over by a pancake. She didn't want to linger over her dismay about it at all. She found her own response intolerable; it never dawned on her to question her perfectionism. She simply saw her meltdown as a failure to be strong.

She moved on to talking more about her kids. They were very spoiled. She had always tried to be good to them, which she thought would make them centered and calm. But now it seemed like nothing was ever enough. There was no end to their demands, and they had *no clue* how hard she worked. She couldn't catch a break.

She didn't blame her kids for being spoiled though. She had, after all, raised them to speak their minds. She said, "I tell my kids, 'I want to know your feelings.' So, I can't very well then say shut up every time they fuss." Catrina wanted to be consistent in the messages she gave her children. She didn't like getting upset with them. It made her feel bad and guilty if she snapped at them.

In fact, most of the time, Catrina explained, she did not enjoy being with her children. "It's gotten bad," she said. "It's not like here and there. I mean, I don't look forward to being with them all the time." Her voice was so soft as she said this, as if she were a little afraid of saying it.

"Do you have enough time away from the kids when you're not working?" I asked.

"Oh, God," she scoffed, "I've got two part-time au pairs. College kids. I don't think I could bring myself to get more help—even if it would help me. That's another story. They have a lot going on in their own lives. Which is good. I want my kids around people who are good role models. But their school schedules are hard to take. I have no choice. I have to be flexible." Catrina was sounding a little detached here, resigned to what felt like inadequate help, which she had talked herself into feeling positive about. She sure had a lot of understanding for everyone. And a lot of patience. It was admirable, really, except that something was so wrong.

"I don't know, it's just such stupid stuff. I have this other stuff—meds—I take because my heart starts racing sometimes, like it's going to jump out of my body. Sometimes I take a painkiller. Sleeping pills. It may be getting to be a problem. I'm not sure. I'm not happy about it. I'm trying to stay positive. I know I should not depend on other people for my happiness. But where do you get it, then?"

"Well, it doesn't sound like you have found the right balance yet," I said.

"Balance?" Catrina said, as if it were a bad word. "Oh, God, that's what my mother and sister are always saying."

"Well, what would happen, for example, if you started saying no to your kids or to the nannies?" I explored.

"I don't think I really want to do that, Claudia. I don't think I have room in my life right now for that kind of drama," she responded.

"*Drama?*" I thought, before saying to her, "So you are damned if you do, and you are damned if you don't. If you don't set limits you run yourself ragged, but if you do set limits, you have too much 'drama.'"

"That's the problem," Catrina said, taking a deep breath. "That is the problem," she repeated, which sounded a little like, "Why do you think I came here?"

"There doesn't appear to be a good, workable option for you yet. No wonder you are feeling depressed."

"Right," she said. "But I shouldn't be. I shouldn't be," she reminded me.

"You don't think it's overwhelming to have to work full-time, manage help and raise three kids?"

"I know people that would kill to have what I have," she answered, which reminded me that I had been one of those people. "I shouldn't be this depressed," she explained. "There is no reason for it. I should be feeling great about my life."

I continued, in the next ten minutes, to assess whether there was anything in Catrina's life that had any "give" because it sounded like she had gotten overwhelmed by all of her duties. Could she, perhaps, set boundaries with the kids or with her husband or try to get more help? Apparently, nothing was possible—nothing. A deadly silence ensued, and I could practically breathe the hopelessness that enveloped it.

Finally, she rescued me from my struggle to find something else to say. "I have an appointment with my OB/GYN. Maybe it's a thyroid problem. I have to figure out how to get stronger. This is just a temporary glitch," she said.

To my mind, the session was not going well. I was filled with as much intolerance as she had for these problems. Why did she insist on boxing herself in with all this stress? Why couldn't she entertain that, practically speaking, there was a way for her to create more balance in her life?

I would have to swim around with Catrina for a while in these murky waters, where she felt stressed, trapped, unhappy and crazed. I had to get away from being the competent, solution-finding doctor, get into her head and enter into her psychological universe to find out what was blocking her from doing what made perfect common sense—relax a little, enjoy life. I geared myself up to tolerate the intense state of frustration and confusion she was in, to stay with her through what she was feeling instead of trying to control it in any way.

Which is when everything between us changed. The enjoyable fantasy, in which she was Mrs. Perfectly Wonderful and I was a project for improvement, fell away. We were in a new zone now: the zone of reality. The zone where we are all perfectly wonderful and, simultaneously, all projects for improvement. This is the zone where we do not shy away from the truth of suffering.

So that is how it came to pass that I stashed away all my advice for finding balance and shelved any other ideas for what might be a viable solution to her over-stressed predicament. I put all practical common sense out of my mind, including entertaining the most obvious confrontation: that her perfectionism and superego were on complete and total overdrive. Here were my prayers: I will not control these energies by talking sense. I will keep tolerating how crazed she is and keep helping her to talk about it, until something happens.

"Catrina," I said, "tell me more about the people in your life." And so, the real analysis began.

Depression

I said very little to Catrina during the next few weeks and asked her a lot of questions about the kids, the nannies, her family. This is what I said to myself: "Tolerate the feelings. Sit with them." This mantra is what helps me do my job: to keep people talking.

This is what I did say to Catrina, "That is not easy." A few times—just to let her know I was on the same page with her. And, now and then, "That's a challenge." Sometimes, as she told me how overwhelmed and depressed she felt, I said, "That's the right feeling to have," which it was. No feeling is ever wrong. It's simply there.

After the sixth session, Catrina looked back at me from the door with a sad smile. She said: "This is helping, actually. I guess it is good to vent."

I thought it was interesting that my having no answers or advice for her didn't frustrate Catrina. She didn't seem at all annoyed with me that I wasn't "fixing" things. Maybe she was relieved that I wasn't going to push her to *do* something like everybody else did. And that I would take the time instead to listen. People are too quick, sometimes, to come up with a clear path—a practical alternative that appears, from the outside, to provide the perfect solution to getting in a more comfortable place.

But to the crazed person, either the "better" place is not more comfortable or getting there can't happen. Catrina felt guilty for feeling so crazed. She didn't feel entitled to being miserable; it made her feel weak and guilty. Telling her it was OK to just talk about what was going on, and that it would lead to something eventually, was all she needed for now.[3]

I continued to be tempted to provide solutions that would relieve Catrina's suffering. But...when you can accept, get comfortable and feel at peace with the nature of a seemingly hopeless situation, when you can listen to how terrible it is and bear the suffering…eventually, something will give. I have faith in that.[4] Even though you never know quite when, exactly, something will give.

Indignation

My simply listening to Catrina was proceeding nicely. I learned that a lot of things were upsetting her. She told me that some nights she fell into bed without even brushing her teeth. She had lost her sex drive, felt no joy around the kids and wondered if the beauty of her children's early years was going to be completely lost on her. She had sex with her husband once every month or less, but it was very hard to relax and rev up. Sometimes it was just uncomfortable.

Some of the upsetting things in her life were long-standing and familiar: her husband didn't care if they celebrated their anniversary; her mother seemed to care more about Catrina getting a promotion than about any of her daughter's feelings.

As our sessions progressed into the summer, it started to get hot out, and one day Catrina came in to her session in a very heated state.

"My mother and sister are both telling me to say 'no' to the au pairs taking vacations again," she said, "because I didn't make it to my nephew's second birthday on Saturday. Like he would remember that I wasn't there—he's TWO! I had to run the errands I couldn't run on Wednesday because the au pair couldn't work that day. So now my family's mad at me! Can you imagine? Where were they when I needed them on Wednesday?"

Catrina had clearly been a little edgy in her conversations with her mother and sister, and I was glad about that for her. We all need people we can be edgy with when we are crazed. This is one of the best reasons to stay married: to have someone other than yourself to be edgy with. Catrina's relationship with her husband didn't allow her to be that way with him so her sister and mother were the ones she permitted herself to get aggravated with.[5]

"They act like I'm stupid," Catrina continued. "They say I'm too insecure—and that's why I don't tell my nannies to do more. Can you imagine? That is the most ridiculous thing I have ever heard in my life. It just makes me so mad. You know why they're trying to put me down? Because THEY feel insecure. I would love to see them work as hard as I do. I don't sit around waiting for things to happen, I make them happen. *I make things happen.* I would like to see my sister do even one-tenth of what I do."

"You work very hard," I corroborated.

"I am not afraid to work," she continued. "They say I should ask for more. I am not a passive person like that, whining my way through life. They say the same thing about my husband—that I should ask him to do more. Are they kidding me? Do they really think Jack is going to come in the kitchen, out of his study if he's working on a paper, to wash dishes? That is the most ridiculous thing I've ever heard. They don't even realize how important he is.

Honestly, they act as if I am stupid. Can you imagine? They're telling me, 'Just say NO!' They have no idea how crazy it would make me to start a fight in the house with Jack or the sitter. I have the three kids to take care of, and now I'm going to start squabbling with my husband over doing chores? It's beyond ridiculous. I don't have time for that. I have bigger fish to fry and so does Jack. Do they think he got to be where he is because he came home and had squabbles with his wife over nothing? It takes ten minutes to do the dishes! That's not the kind of stupid house I want to have. I—unlike them— have a nice, productive home. Do you want to know what would happen if I started making waves and lost my nanny, Claudia, would you like to know?"

"I know," I said, understanding that Catrina couldn't say no to her nannies or ask for help from her husband. Catrina's indignation was growing by the second. This was totally new, seeing Catrina so angry. This was not the same woman I had been getting to know—who had been so depressed, who had felt so weak and disappointed. This Catrina before me now was filled with righteous indignation. Her family failed to see what was so evident to me now: she wasn't stressed, depressed and overwhelmed, she was unrecognized for being important.

How could Catrina's family not understand—or see—how well she kept her life together? Why was it that all they could see were the things that she was doing wrong? There was no comfort in this family; nobody who understood her or knew her; only people putting her down. No one was ever there to urge her on, to tell her, "You are so great." All they communicated was, "You are missing out on life. You do too much."

She went on: "You know, if I did what my mother and sister said and started creating waves with Jack and the nannies and pushing back on the kids and creating all that drama and started a revolution in my house, Gaston would pounce on it."

"Who is Gaston?" I asked.

"Oh. Gaston is my colleague at the French department. I guess you could say he's my nemesis. My competitor. I probably haven't mentioned him because that's the one thing in my life that's not upsetting me. Sort of. But anyhow, he is just waiting for the opportunity to see me stumble—being a mother and having this job. Just waiting for it. And I am never going to give him that satisfaction."

This was the first I had ever heard of Gaston because Catrina had only talked about her "problems." Funny how people can go to a therapist to talk about their most private problems, totally overlooking what can turn out to be the most important details of their lives. Now, we were getting to the real stuff.

This, by the way, is why it is so good to have patients like Catrina who are content to just lie on the couch and talk, rather than imagine that you are going to solve their problems within a six or twelve or twenty-four-week timeline, with specific goals. Things come out when you talk only for the sake of talking—details that might not seem important, but which really are. And I'd just hit the jackpot.

The importance of Gaston

"Why is Gaston out to get you?" I asked.

"Oh, Lord—we have been competing for research money, awards and nominations for years. He is something else, that one." As she talked about Gaston, Catrina had tremendous energy in her voice.

"He wants to chair this meeting and steer the research in his own direction. If that happens, I swear, I am going to blow a gasket." This was such a new side to Catrina.

"He's done it before. I know how he pushes himself into what I'm working on. And since he's done it before, he is going to do it again. We were competing for a small two-hundred-thousand-dollar project. And I was supposed to be the primary researcher. This was a couple of years ago. Gaston got some theorists from Paris involved in the project, and, of course, they won it. I'm working under him on that. I can't let that happen again. I have to get my name on some more papers, or he is going to continue to place me under himself again and again. We do the work; he takes the credit."

After a quiet minute, Catrina returned to the original problem. "I still can't believe that my sister would call me *insecure*. Do you get it?"

"No, I do not," I said and meant it. After this last animated detour about Gaston, I had seen the side of Catrina that bespoke power. Hence, the jackpot. This woman, contrary to what I had thought previously, was not someone meek who didn't like to face confrontation or set boundaries or say "no." Actually, she was someone who didn't want to deal with family problems because she imagined that she had much bigger fish to fry.

"Don't my mother and sister realize that I can't afford to get into skirmishes with my nannies or get caught up with all of these other stupid problems? Have they ever offered to come over and babysit if I had to work or maybe to drive the kids somewhere. I mean, my sister doesn't work. I am supposed to attend a stupid baby party? Does the baby care? Do you know what I just realized? SHE is insecure. She is talking about herself. My problem is, I'm OVERWHELMED, not 'insecure.'" Catrina took a deep breath here. This plot was seriously thickening.

"Why does your sister put you down so much?" I asked.

"Because she hates me, that's why. Because I have it all and she doesn't. She's jealous. I am the smart one. My mother, our mother, never had a career. She just took care of us, me and my sister, and she always wanted us to be big successes, and I am the one that did it, not my sister. I don't limit myself. Never have. I believe there are no limits to what I can do, and I live by that every day. And now they hate me for it. That's why they keep telling me 'do less, do less.' Of course my sister wants me to do less. Then I wouldn't be the success that she is NOT. And in fact, I'll tell you something—the better I do, the more she puts me down—the more she keeps telling me, 'do less.' Like hell! She *wants* me to be vulnerable. She *wants* me have the kind of stupid drama in my life that she has with her husband and her kids. They argue all the time. Where does it get them? They are probably the reason why I'm so depressed."

"Yes!" I said, not so much because I was agreeing with her, but more because I was finally getting a sense of what was going on in her head.

Now I finally understood. Here was the reason that Catrina could not integrate more balance in her life: she didn't want it. Balance, in her mind, meant having to admit she needed help. It meant being weak. Getting "balance," in her mind, was like having to admit defeat.

So Catrina had pride. She wanted to feel invincible. That would be her way to get revenge on her sister and mother for treating her with so little respect. Maybe, if she got to be more important, they would realize it and regret putting her down. Catrina was angry at herself for not having the energy she needed to expedite this plan: win over Gaston, gain importance in the family.

But her frustrations with herself only fueled her desire to be even more self-reliant. Catrina derived a lot of pleasure and strength from being better, doing more, and appearing to be strong. She wasn't going to give that up for balance. The only problem was, did she have the strength for it?

Well, if Catrina needed to feel important and strong, to keep fighting and competing in her department, to find the strength to keep things running without lumps or bumps at home, I would certainly not make the same mistake her mother and sister were making by telling her she was doing things wrong. I would not suggest a better way. I would not doubt or challenge her need to feel important and take everything on. I would never tell her she was trying too hard to be "perfect." Doing that would alienate her from me. She needed to feel important and strong—the way she felt at work, but not at home. And if that was what she wanted, that is what I would help her with.[6]

Strengthening

Of course, helping Catrina get stronger and do more, reasonably speaking, may not have been the optimal solution. Trying to do everything, to be perfect, and fight inner demons that take the form of mean mothers and sisters, isn't really healthy.

But when we get overwhelmed, the path of good sense and reason is not always the road that can be taken. The path that was *possible*, in this case, was the one that I was taking: the one that didn't set me in opposition to Catrina, but that would help her to do more of what she wanted—be better, more important, stronger. My goal was to align myself as an emotional ally. To establish my standing as a soul mate and trusted confidante.

It is always good to become welcome in a person's mental house. That is how you gain the footing that you need to help the person, eventually, to change. As I entered into Catrina's personal universe and stayed by her side, I asked questions like: "Have you thought about whether you're on the right vitamin?"[7]

"Hmmm," she said, "I hadn't thought of that. Maybe I do need to look at that. That is a really good idea." I was on the right track.

I thought of something else: "What about getting regular massages to release some of the tension so you can take more on?" She really liked these ideas. This was the kind of support she was lacking; the kind of respect she didn't get from her family who just wanted her to find balance by doing less and saying "no" more.

We spent weeks talking about different things that she could do to get stronger so that she could manage things as competently and seamlessly as she needed to: moving ahead on every front and keeping her house calm, assessing what was working and what she needed to pay more attention to.

I said things to her like, "You just feel too alone," which was true. It comforted her. She felt understood. I wasn't criticizing her way of doing things.

I started to genuinely believe that with enough support, strengthening and coping strategies, Catrina would be able to get on top of this crisis and resume her usual high level of functioning. I soon forgot that I had even wanted her to find balance originally; I was really getting into supporting her.

It is fun becoming a cheerleader/soul mate when you find the right path to walk alongside someone who is being challenged emotionally. This is my favorite part of my job—*joining* my patients on the path they want to be on, walking alongside them. When this happens, we can't wait to be together—it's so fulfilling, so comforting. Everybody thrives. It's exciting to imagine where we are going to go to next.[8]

I had fully entered Catrina's universe and was now sharing completely in her vision of how to be in the world: fight to be strong, do not create drama, remind yourself that you are important. At this point in the treatment, Catrina felt truly heard.

A crack in the foundation

One day Catrina came in through the door and didn't make eye contact. Once on the couch, it took her a while to start talking, which was unusual. Something heavy was on her mind.

"I don't know," she started, "I just don't know." And then, she grew silent.

"What's up?" I asked.

"I...oh...I don't know," she said again, slowly.

I could see she was in some kind of zone. This is not uncommon for patients who lie on the couch when they are in therapy. People don't get into these spaced-out zones as often when they are sitting up and facing their therapists. On the couch, people space out much more easily, which lets them wander into parts of their minds they probably would not be able to venture into (or stumble upon) with a more directed conversation. We may have come a long way since Freud, but, for me, using the couch is still fantastic. I waited.

"Why is all this stuff so important to me? Why do I need to keep everything together so much?" she asked.

"What thoughts are you having?" I answered. I was surprised that she would ever question herself.

"I don't know. I'm in that place again where nothing matters. Sometimes I wonder what it's all for. Is becoming the head of the department what I want? I don't know if it's what I want. I don't know if I even care if anybody thinks I'm losing ground at work," Catrina said. Being strong and important wasn't working for her today. This was strange. I felt a little disappointed, actually. We had been having so much fun with the "strengthening" project.

"I didn't sleep a lot last night," she said. "Tomorrow will be better. I'm in that dark place again. It's okay. I know what this is. I know it's normal—you've helped me with that. I am just feeling a little weak. I don't have any energy today. I wish sometimes…I don't know…that I didn't have to spend each day fighting so hard to keep things together. I wish I could relax a little more sometimes."

"Well, it's hard to sustain that feeling with little sleep," I said to Catrina. And then I added: "You can't feel invincible every day. Nobody can. Even the most important person in the world feels this way, I'm sure."

This was becoming therapeutic for me. You see I had no problem being sub-perfect and unimportant. These feelings could throb within me as loud and strong as the bells pealing in St. Peter's Square in Rome, and they were so familiar and intrinsic to my existence that I could still move on from them and get on with my day. Would Catrina ever reach a point where she could be happy on the days that she lacked the feeling of importance? My hair insecurities were really not so bad compared to what Catrina's insecurities did to her.

I was hoping that Catrina would start to question her foundation of needing to be strong and important. I wished she could have a revelation or that I could give her an *interpretation* like: "You have never felt truly loved just for being *yourself*. You can only feel worthy if you *do* everything."

Or: "Screw feeling important and competent! Forget what anybody else thinks of you…you need balance!" These walls of competency Catrina needed to erect everywhere to feel strong were so exaggerated. It seemed she had to prove herself every single, blessed second of the day. It was like she needed a feeling of *extreme* importance. Importance on steroids.

But I did not say anything, because it would have come from a place in me of wanting her to get rid of the foundation she rested her life on. That foundation was that she should manage everything alone and not make waves.[9]

But I could see that Catrina's need to feel important was breaking down. It wasn't working for her all that well anymore. Still, the dissatisfaction wasn't yet enough for her to decide to loosen her defenses even more. In fact, after a good night's sleep, she was back to full-throttle importance, as defended as ever.

That's how the next week began, and Catrina's doubts about being so competent had all but disappeared. Things had quickly settled back into their usual patterns. That small feeling, "Why do I have to do all this?" was gone. She had renewed strength to tackle the challenges of a new day, keeping things in order. She had gotten swept up in the pleasure of achievement again.

But not me. Seeing her so depressed and depleted reminded me that her way of life was pretty crazed. My supporting her way of manufacturing feelings of competence and worth was starting to feel like a strain. I was no longer enjoying helping her do everything. This was a good omen. Whenever I grow tired of supporting an old foundation, it's always a sign that the patient is also not benefiting from it enough, that its use has been outlived. I was having less fun in the sessions. I could feel a change. The question now was how—and when—that change would manifest.[10]

A real break

It was on a day that Catrina came in, looking bouncy and energized, that I found a new wrinkle to her story. Almost as soon as she was on the couch, she started talking about one of her children, Jeremy the pancake boy. He really was fussy and was becoming more upset on several fronts. It felt to me like the boy was begging her to slow down and pay attention to his feelings. His insistence on being served pancakes for breakfast every morning seemed to be a little too intense—there must have been something behind it, a feeling that he could not articulate except through this yearning for a big-deal meal.

"What if you didn't cook the pancakes for him? What if you told him he's not to fuss—that he can't always get what he wants?" I asked, exploring Catrina's thoughts despite my nagging pity for the child.[11]

"Oh, *meltdown*," she said. "I'd rather get up earlier and cook him the stupid pancakes. If he misses the bus because of a meltdown on Tuesdays, I'm screwed."

"You're going to get up *earlier*?" I said.

"What else can I do?" she answered.

"Sounds like you're going to have to get up earlier," I relented.

"Yeah," Catrina said and grew silent.

"What's wrong?" I said, after a few minutes had gone by. "I'm just so tired," she replied, and all the energy had gone out of her voice.

"I'll bet you'd rather stay in bed," I said.

"Yeah," she said. "I'm not sure I can do this." The next thing I knew, she was crying. I had never seen her cry before. I didn't even notice it until she grabbed a tissue. This was very unexpected.

"Sometimes, all I think about is staying in bed," Catrina confessed.

"Well...what would happen if you stayed in bed for once?" I asked her softly. "Are you not allowed to catch a break? Would that be so terrible?" Gently, I pushed against the walls of competency. "Could you allow yourself to feel tired and weak for an hour or two?"

Catrina took a deep breath and held it. For a long time. I was thinking, "BREATHE!" Finally, she let it out.

"You know," she said, "if I didn't get out of bed one day...I would...I'd just...I'd...I think I'd never get up." There was a long pause here. "I think I'd say no to *everything*. [long pause] I would just say no to life, to the kids, the job, my husband—stay in bed and never get up again. I...I wouldn't get up. God. Shit..."

Catrina started crying hard at this point. Quiet, uncontrollable sobbing.

"I think, sometimes," she continued, "I just want to die. Jesus Christ." I listened, the lump in my throat growing.

The crack in her foundation of competency was becoming dangerous. She was experiencing a lot of pain. It was as if, meandering along her purposeful, important life, we had come to a huge clearing overlooking a great valley; and there she was, staring into the abyss.

I could feel how scared she was. I said, very matter-of-factly, "I don't know anybody who hasn't faced these feelings at some point in their lives. Had moments when they wonder if life is worth living. Of wanting to die. It's normal."

"Really?" Catrina said, breathing hard. "It's horrible. I can't stand it."

"Well, we all come to the feeling in our own time," I said.

I, myself, had faced this desolate abyss for the first time when I was just sixteen, which is what had led me to begin my own analysis. I remembered how, when I had first started treatment, I couldn't stop crying. Session after session, I cried from beginning to end.

It is so amazing, when we arrive at these deep and dark places, to experience the power of having someone by our side who is not daunted. Who can say, "*It's only a feeling.*" It is so good to be with someone who is strong and unafraid. Who seems convinced that it's okay—that we are exactly where we ought to be.

If Catrina could know these feelings and stop pushing them away, perhaps she could design a life that wasn't driven by a fear of them. Speaking your fears—if and when it comes your time to see them—to someone who is not afraid to be with you when you meet them, strips them of their power to destroy.

Change

We were making progress, Catrina and I. I thought I understood the case: Catrina was fighting against deep feelings of emptiness and the secret thought that nothing mattered. Her entire foundation of competency had, perhaps, been erected to counter the swelling tide of feeling that she didn't want to live. But the desire to give in to those feelings was catching up with her, and her way of coping with the feeling was growing old.

When we outgrow familiar ways of operating in the world, we become unhappy. We need to replace old foundations of belief and behavior with new ones. But, before we can do that, the old foundations have to come down. We don't always know if we *want* our old foundations to come down. Sometimes we get caught in this in-between place of dissatisfaction and discomfort—neither here nor there as far as doing something different or staying the way we are.

Autumn had arrived, and the leaves were falling. For Catrina, it was a time of hunkering down. The university where she worked had opened its gates, and she had put together her fall wardrobe in preparation. She seemed less undone. Her despair had quieted, and she was steadying herself for the onslaught of responsibility, which was energizing her.

Catrina was less upset by her own impatience with her children and the nannies—our conversations had helped her accept the feelings more. And, after all, we had noticed some new places in her mind she hadn't even known were there.

I'm not sure why one morning I asked her this particular question, but it was dawning on me how alone Catrina was, living in a world where people could not be trusted to say the right thing, do the right thing or provide her with much help. I asked her: "How would it be if anyone other than me ever found out how vulnerable you can get?"

"Oh, trust me, I have had plenty of people who would *love* to see me be vulnerable. In my own family, trust me. *Trust me*, I know that people would just love to see me with a little mud on my face. I've known that for a long time—since grade school. Trust me."

What was it with this "Trust me"? She had said it *four* times.

"I learned a long time ago not to trust anybody," she added.

I realized that Catrina got excitement from her mission of competency, in part, because she felt like she lived in a dangerous world, sort of like a war zone. She was fighting for respect and feelings of importance, which, when she could get them, felt like a "win." Something she had conquered. For her, this feeling was probably as good as the feeling of being loved. Admiration is a powerful drug.

"You know," she explained "not to sound vain, but when you're attractive—forgive my sounding arrogant—things are not that easy for you. People aren't that nice to you. They either envy you or want to kill you because they think you have everything or they don't want to be friends with you. I am not afraid of that. Women can have whatever feelings they want about me. When I was a kid, I was beautiful, and I swear, people discriminated against me. They tell you beauty is an advantage. Well…it is and it isn't. People want to knock you down. They don't think you get scared or feel vulnerable. They think they can be mean because they don't pity you ever—there's no compassion. No one cares about you. I decided a long time ago, screw it. I was going to be the best I could, and if people were going to keep me at arm's length, that was *their* problem. I didn't care anymore if I intimidated anyone or if they were jealous or envious. If people were going to be aloof and distant with me—try to put me down—that's what they were going to get *from me*."

Well no wonder I'd felt inferior in her presence. My feelings of inferiority, it was turning out, had not only originated from my own hair insecurities, they were also coming from *her*.[12] She needed, expected—and perhaps wanted—people to feel inferior to her so she could feel stronger. It was too bad that the good feelings it gave her came at so high a cost. Ironically, gaining strength was depleting her.

I could see now how the competency foundation had gotten built. It was fun and felt good to keep people at a distance and compete with them.

It would have made it so much easier on me from the beginning if I had known that being in awe of—and insecure—near Catrina was practically a requirement of being exposed to her. It's a good thing I didn't mind feeling insecure, or I would not have been able to treat this competitive woman. My willingness to feel insecure fit perfectly with her need to feel important. The sessions were becoming progressively more therapeutic for me; Catrina's analysis really was helping me to feel better about my hair. We were, I realized, an excellent match.

This new twist, Catrina's need to out-compete people, filled out the picture. This was a reason for her emptiness, and it explained why people did not sustain her or bring her happiness. She was aggressive, scared and fighting for her life. I had to respect that her exhausting tactics came from her strong life drive. I guess you could say that she was fighting, struggling to feel alive. The respect I had mustered for her extreme need for competency was real now. I saw now how Catrina was built to feel like a winner. She just needed a new way to get there.

Balance

Summer had come around once again. Since the winter, Catrina had completely stopped taking anti-anxiety and depression meds. When you can speak your story, it no longer scares you. It no longer felt overwhelming that sometimes she did not want to live, or that she lived in a competitive world, wanting to outdo people to get some good feelings about herself. It was all natural, normal and acceptable.

She came into one of the early summer sessions wearing a beautiful pair of patent leather sandals, her toes painted a gorgeous shade of pink matching the T-shirt she was wearing that had lovely soft ruffles down the front. Her light grey trousers made her legs look even longer. I was thinking how much I loved the subtle pink when she said: "There are a couple of things that I should—and probably could—start saying no to. I was thinking—if the au pair doesn't like it, she can leave. I can interview other people. If Jack doesn't like that he might have to do a morning drop-off at the school, I'm going to have to put my foot down. I don't care." And then, she laughed. Perhaps, she was delighted or surprised by how out of character this all was.

Wow. Was this "balance?" This was unexpected. She went on, suddenly serious: "You know, if the sitter wants to take that morning yoga class and

I can't go in to those morning faculty meetings because of that, so what. I should take that class with her! I think I could make some phone calls—make some headway on how to write that proposal anyway. I'll bet I could outsmart Gaston anyway...The department can live without me for a few mornings. Nobody is going to die." Well, I was very glad to hear that. I was very, very glad to hear that nobody was going to die.

Postscript

Catrina was to stay in treatment with me for many years, building new foundations of connectedness and trust to replace the old foundation of competency that had been slowly killing her. She kept coming back with new problems, like how to connect more with her children and get to know her husband, whom she loved but wasn't very close to. She continued to seek help with how to ask her family for what she needed, requests that her family responded to—interestingly enough—with love and support. It seemed like people weren't always out to get her any more. The world, and she, had changed.[13]

THE TWENTY-FIRST-CENTURY PSYCHOANALYST

Perhaps you're wondering why, in writing a book about the making of a twenty-first-century psychoanalyst, I would begin with a story about my hair. Or why, given the severity of the anxiousness and depression this character was experiencing, I would recommend vitamins. Why, you might ask, did I not spend more time directly exploring the roots of Catrina's perfectionism, addressing her oppressive superego, helping her to understand herself or at least questioning her need to self-destruct?

It may surprise you to learn, because the treatment seemed fairly relaxed, that absolutely everything that transpired was carefully strategized. Behind the scenes of this treatment, I was operating with a cogent theory of the mind and an explicit theory of technique.

Before I explain what was going on theoretically behind the scenes of this treatment, let me explain what the challenge has been to this field in the past half-century. This will provide some context for what I was doing in the treatment as well as introduce you to some of the most recent clinical innovations that are revolutionizing psychoanalysis.

The problem facing psychoanalysis is this: We can no longer expect our patients to have the capacity to think rationally and respond positively to traditional interpretations. The character of Catrina is a perfect testament to the difficulty: here we have a stunning and accomplished woman—psychologically sophisticated, brilliant, and self-aware—and yet, completely under the spell of unconscious processes that could not be touched by interpretations or ideas alone.

For Catrina, the unconscious struggle was about an unmet need to feel "important," which culminated in a powerful need to prove herself and, worse, to outdo anyone she could in order to attain that feeling. These unconscious struggles prevented her from having satisfying connections with people that she could depend on her or who might have been able to help her. However, the defense of perfectionism did protect her from having to come to terms with both her rage about negative experiences she hadn't yet reckoned with, and the ensuing destructive impulses, which were masking an even deeper underlying depression. To defend herself from feeling disturbed by her own destructive aggression, Catrina projected that aggression onto other people whom she imagined wanted to bring her down.

In fact, Catrina experienced her mother's and sister's well-meaning advice as negative. She was convinced that rather than caring and worrying about her, they were unconsciously trying to bring her down, to undermine her importance, to undercut her competitive edge and otherwise diminish her power. Unfortunately, their well-meaning efforts only stoked the fire of Catrina's ruthless ambition, as their advice ironically made her more convinced that people were out to get her. For her, this was an unfortunate distortion—and one that epitomizes what happens when people are in the grips of an unconscious struggle.

The problem with defense mechanisms like Catrina's perfectionism is that while they may protect us from having to admit into our consciousness disturbing wishes and impulses, they become completely compulsive. In other words, we lose our capacity to discern choices when we are driven by unconscious motivations.

Catrina, as a result of this, fundamentally believed that she had to manage everything and run herself ragged. She was fully invested in this narrative, and before she entered treatment, she didn't recognize that there could be any other explanation for what was going on in her life. Even as she drove the people around her crazy, she firmly believed she was lovingly pinch-hitting for everybody else by doing everything herself. You will see with most patients coming into treatment that they have the feeling that they are cornered into their current circumstances by forces of destiny, and they are unable to identify or take advantage of any other, possibly better, options. In fact, you may even see this in your own family when a person—whether it's a significant other, parent or sibling—insists on a version of reality that you believe has absolutely nothing to do with what is really going on.

When we are under the influence of defensive mechanisms, we simply can't entertain any ideas that might differ excessively from our own. This is what is at the root of all unhealthy narcissism, small or large: an inability to discern or recognize any truths—whether they be thoughts, feelings or ideas—that are outside our own consciousness.

Everywhere we turn, whenever our narcissistic tendencies are influencing us, the world reflects back to us our own unresolved unconscious dynamics as we project our distorted narratives onto people, who then respond accordingly. Ironically, Catrina, who was looking for feelings of importance from her family, repeatedly induced feelings in them that she was acting foolishly. In turn, their reactions confirmed for Catrina that they were trying to bring her down. Freud called this vicious cycle the *repetition compulsion*, and it is a phenomenon that we often perceive in our patients. To put it another way: it's how we set the wheel of karma in motion.

We become narcissistic when we defend against thoughts and feelings that are too painful or unbearable for us. When we are so busy trying to block things, we can't entertain many other options. Instead, we engage all energy in the preservation of our version of the truth, which feels infinitely better. We can't empathize with others, get outside our own perspective or discern choices when we are defending against thoughts and feelings, and we develop major blind spots as parts of ourselves are blocked to us.

This is why, despite the tremendous wealth of psychological education currently available about dysfunction and mental illness, and despite our increasing emotional sophistication, self-awareness and acceptance, people still persist in being dominated by unconscious dynamics, unable to do things better. It is why parents and children become estranged, why divorce rates are so high, why we fail, remain unhappy, and maybe even why there is war.

Defense mechanisms put us in intractable positions that preclude our ability to discern, believe in or persevere towards better choices.

For therapists, so many questions arise from this challenge—how do we handle other people's defense mechanisms? What can we do to impress upon our patients that they are almost completely under the sway of unconscious motivations, driven by unseen forces that are hindering their ability to experience choices? How can we help them recognize what they're doing wrong? How can we show them that life could be so much better if they could only listen to other people and at least consider what they say?

For decades, the search for answers to these questions—under the rubric of "What constitutes *therapeutic action?*"—gave rise to an untold number of journal articles, conference proceedings and entire books dedicated to charting the precise genesis of change in a patient. Therapeutic action was mainly centered on the psychoanalyst's ability to correctly analyze the patient's unconscious motivations, and then to interpret that understanding to the patient with such exquisite timing that the interpretation would prove effective and meaningful. Most of the discussions around therapeutic action that you will encounter in the literature focused on the nature and timing of delivering the interpretation. More recent literature has extended this by examining the ideal state of *transference* in the patient for the delivery of insights from the analyst.

Ultimately though, providing insight as a means of cure will falter. Only a very small number of patients can absorb insights. Even for those who are willing to absorb and integrate an outside person's version of their life—and ready to consider and make the effort to change—there may be no enduring impact.

Advances in neuroscience finally started to reveal the core of the problem. The regressed states of consciousness that psychoanalysis had been challenged with for decades were described by the neuroscientists as "activation of the Autonomic Defense System (ADS)." In the presence of ADS, when patients are in states of anxiety or depression, for example, synaptic activity to the higher brain—where reason, planning and the ability to discern choices prevail—is severely compromised. With these insights, the problem gained new clarity as the evidence was uncompromising: when we have emotional reactions stemming from primitive feelings that aren't even at the level of consciousness, we cannot think well.

The implication for psychoanalysis, as a method designed to reveal the unconscious, was that an entirely new set of innovative strategies would have to be developed to help our patients get to know their hidden thoughts, feelings and impulses. Ultimately, this challenge is what led to the incredible innovations in clinical methodology that hold the key to how we currently practice psychoanalysis. Instead of being direct purveyors of insights and interpretations delivered to our patients' consciousnesses, analysts realized that we would instead have to learn how best to prepare our patients' mind for their own self-discovery.

Preparing the mind for self-discovery

From the minute a new patient walks through our door, it is good for us to have on hand a set of operating theories of the mind that can explain how and why people conjure their reality. These theories will fuel our curiosity and fascination with the mystery of the patient's condition. Without them, we would just be swimming in a quagmire of emotional agitation or confusion. In addition to a theory of the mind, having an operating theory of technique will challenge us to proceed like scientists, investigating consciousness. All of these theories, which we call 'metatheory,' arm us for the journey into our patient's mind.

Let us now turn to the story to illustrate how metatheory works:

1   *Structural theory* informed me that it would be fruitless to try to influence Catrina's perfectionism or the lack of balance in her life. Whenever I am confronted by patients' thoughts and behaviors that defy logic, I am never tempted to fruitlessly defend or argue against them, because I know this is not a good way to work with the unconscious. People need their defenses until they have something better to replace them with. If you try prematurely to free them of those defenses, you may become witness to mental breakdowns.
2   *Drive theory* figured into my thinking, as I began to recognize that Catrina's lack of joy, as well as her fatigue, were symptomatic of her libidinal energy being drained, probably in her effort to keep her aggressive impulses and wishes in check. I hypothesized that her libidinal energies were being almost entirely consumed by the need to sublimate and channel her aggressive energies via exhaustion-inducing levels of perfectionism and her unabating need to outdo others.
3   *Object relations theory* informed my thinking about Catrina's internal object representations, which is to say, the pictures of people she carried in her head.
4   *Conflict theory* was later applied in this case, as I became aware that Catrina had an intrapsychic conflict. There had to be some pleasure that she was deriving from the relentless striving for perfectionism—and all of that would have to become conscious to be grappled with.

My clinical techniques would have to address all of this metatheory. If I were to adequately prepare Catrina's mind for self-discovery, I first had to help liberate some of the libidinal energy that was being spent preserving the defenses. Without a loosening of those energies, she would not be able to move forward.

With regard to her conflict, I would have to explore the unspoken sides of the conflict—how much she enjoyed her perfectionism and her impulse to outdo people—until she could land upon the things she hadn't yet spoken. Only then, I postulated, would she be able to know what she was fighting against, and then be able to decide to let go a little.

Finally, I knew that a new form of mental organization would have to be built so she could be helped to loosen her grip on the existing maladaptive one and thereby get to know herself. A new structure would depend on my ability to help strengthen her *ego*.

This solid grounding in theory helped me guide the treatment because the four theories of the mind that were operating in my understanding of the case (structural theory, drive theory, object-relations theory and conflict theory) informed what would be required to help prepare her mind for self-discovery.

Sufficiently armed with theory, I knew exactly where and how to begin clinically. Let me now illustrate how my understanding of Catrina informed the design and implementation of a cogent set of interventions.

Because I understood that Catrina would have experienced any initial questioning as an affront to her perfectionism, which would only have heightened and strengthened her defenses, I did not, at first, explore Catrina's mind at all. Not even a question about why she had to work so hard. Also, from a drive theory perspective, I recognized that she was already very overstimulated as a result of her perfectionistic compulsions.

Since she was in this high tension state, I wanted to create a calm environment. My drive theory perspective also alerted me to the fact that I would have to help normalize the aggressive components of her thinking, so that she would not have to defend so much against that set of feelings— her desire to outdo people and her antipathy toward them. In so doing, I postulated that I would be helping to free up some of the valuable libidinal energy she was employing to maintain defenses against knowing the degree and depth of her aggressive tendencies.

Therefore, when Catrina described her anger at her family and co-worker, I joined her vigorously, remaining in total agreement with her view of things. In real life, people do not tolerate either negativity or unreasonableness very well. In analysis, she would be having the rare experience of someone being on her side, without being challenged that her view of things might be distorted.

By joining Catrina, and thereby strengthening her ego and liberating her libidinal energy, I was employing not only a theory of the mind, but also a clinical technique to help me work towards the goal of preparing her mind for self-discovery.

Later in the treatment, when Catrina described a recent, particularly stressed out morning for her, when her son asked if she could make pancakes for him—an incident that set her into despair—I did begin to use some *object-oriented exploration*. I asked, "What if you didn't cook the pancakes for him?" This question marked the beginning of a new phase of treatment, during which I included, alongside my joining techniques, some benign exploration. Even this minimal exploration, you may agree, would have frustrated her at the beginning of treatment, when she didn't want another person advising her to resist trying to do everything.

After still more time had passed, Catrina arrived to a session having regressed to a weary, depressed state. This time I used an *ego-oriented question*: "What would happen if you stayed in bed for once?" This was a much more invasive type of exploration. It addressed a hidden aspect of an intrapsychic conflict for her, which was the feeling that she might never want to get out of bed.

Ultimately, when Catrina did reveal her unspoken fear of not wanting to be alive, I was able to normalize those feelings by stating nonchalantly that such thoughts were natural. This reassured Catrina about her impulses, further liberating libidinal energy that was previously being consumed trying to ward off the disturbing effects of such thoughts. Again, this gradual exploration is what paves the way for the patient's self-discovery.

So far, I have not yet described any techniques that reflect any new approaches to psychoanalysis. I have only described what has been intrinsic to psychoanalysis for the past half century: basic metatheory; a set of solid joining and exploration techniques and supportive communications; and finally, a good and increasingly stronger therapeutic alliance.

But here now comes the real, and most important question: How, exactly, did I know when and how it would be appropriate to join, to ask an *object-oriented question*, to use ego-oriented questioning or to make a supportive communication?

The answer to these questions is what has brought psychoanalysis to what I believe are the two most exciting innovations in the theory of technique to be discovered in recent history: the '*contact function*' and '*emotional communication.*' Both of these innovations are founded upon this one, uncompromising truth: to assess and intervene effectively with Catrina, I had to use my own emotions.

The contact function and emotional communication

The dual concepts of the contact function and emotional communication cover the two basic components of all successful treatment: first, being able to correctly assess the patient, and second, being able to design a customized clinical treatment plan based on that assessment.

I used my emotions to assess Catrina immediately at the start of treatment, quickly surmising that she was extremely agitated. There is no real way for us to assess the level of agitation or disturbance in a patient without the use of our own emotions. Our emotions really are the best instrument we have for gauging and measuring our patient's emotional state. The more tension, agitation, confusion or disturbance we experience in the room, the greater the pathology is likely to be, at least in that moment.

When I started pushing against Catrina's defenses by asking if she really had to make her son pancakes, I was again using my emotions, by knowing at that point that she could handle such a question. Later, the ego-oriented question I asked, about what would happen if she stayed in bed, was again based entirely on my emotional understanding that she was ready to talk about it. In fact, that understanding also led me to modulate my voice, as if to communicate, when I suggested she stay in bed, "Aren't you tired? Wouldn't it be nice if you could relax a little?" As it turned out, she was very tired. So tired, in fact, that she might not want to ever get out of that bed.

What I was doing, in using my emotions as instruments to guide me as to how to be in the room with the patient, is an example of *'following the contact.'* When we do this, we consistently follow the patient's lead, by closely gauging and assessing both the feeling in the room and the patient's preparedness to think about things. The guideline of following the contact not only dictates what to talk about with the patient, but also the tone and tenor of our communications.

Working in this way, mindful at all times of the emotional climate in the room and the patient's emotional state, means that all of our interventions become, in essence, 'emotional communications.' That is to say, our interventions are not designed, as they were in classical psychoanalysis, only as ways to promote insight or otherwise influence the patient to employ higher-brain functions. Instead, the interventions of twenty-first-century psychoanalysis are designed mostly with the intent to address the emotional state; to liberate libidinal energy, strengthen the ego, promote expression and help the patient find words for their experience.

When we can follow the contact effectively, by listening to our emotions closely to guide what will be comfortable for the patient to talk about and by using emotional communication to promote continued talking, our patients will become increasingly more able to say new things to us. It is in this speaking that we become witness to therapeutic action, as I will discuss in greater depth in Chapter 4, 'The unseen side of Angela.'

The patient's self-discovery, whether in the form of a simple, totally natural realization or a highly cathartic unearthing of an unspeakable thought, happens when our patients can finally say things that have not been said aloud before. Then, we become witness to therapeutic action.

And so it was that finally, in that gleaming moment that Catrina declared that she was going to soften her schedule—when she said, "I don't care," and laughed as if it was the most natural, ridiculously obvious thing in the world—I knew that she had replaced her defensive structures with something far more sustaining: a good relationship with me, a deeper understanding of the previously unspoken workings of her own mind and a new resolve to feel alive.

Conclusion

The twenty-first-century psychoanalyst is put to the test by this struggle between our patients' conscious need to feel good and do better and the unresolved unconscious dynamics which stand in the way of all that. No longer the arbiter of 'normalcy,' trying to alter our patient's behavior to suit an ostensibly arbitrary normative standard, the twenty-first-century psychoanalyst does not concern herself with changing a patient's behavior in any way, barring, of course, intervening to prevent the patient from injuring herself or another person. Even when an explicit command is issued, the goal is not to change behavior but rather to continue to prepare the patient's mind for self-discovery. I might have, for example, recommended that Catrina get more babysitting if I felt that would have been supportive of her ego or good for the therapeutic relationship. I would not have made the intervention, however, simply to normalize her behavior. We're not interested in behavior as psychoanalysts. We're always working with emotions, preparing the mind for self-discovery.

Emotional communication works with everyone. We can truly dispel the outdated notion that psychoanalysis is a form of therapy just for the 'elite,' such as the upper middle class. In fact, we can treat the widest possible variety of people, regardless of their sexual orientation, religious affiliation, social class, gender identity, relative pathology or level of education. Absolutely anyone and everyone can become dominated by unseen psychological forces that seem to mysteriously prolong suffering, and it is in that suffering that the twenty-first-century psychoanalyst applies herself, without any regard for working the patient back to any standard of normative behavior. If anything, we can help our patients become quirkier, because then you are not defended or afraid to be yourself, and yourself may be unique.

We can truly work with everyone and anyone when we become curious about their unconscious.

If the twenty-first-century psychoanalyst's primary instrument for assessing, diagnosing, planning and executing emotional communication is our own emotions, then we have to know those emotions extremely well. This is the most important feature of psychoanalytic training—the individual analysis, supervision and classroom discussion—and where all treatment starts and ends: with your own emotions. Now you know why I opened this book by talking to you about my hair insecurities: first, you have to know yourself.

Of course, this is also one of the great benefits of becoming an analyst; as I treated Catrina, I realized that my own inadequacy was illusory. When we become psychoanalysts, we are confronted over and over with the fact that as a species, we construct realities that are often illusory. Our patients, as we ceaselessly resolve our own resistances to being in the room with them, always take us to new levels of understanding about our own consciousness, about our own distorted ways of seeing the world and seeing ourselves, so that we too can flower and blossom to new states of consciousness in which we can enjoy being in our own skin, and come, on our own journey, to feeling attractive, competent, intelligent or alive.

In Part II of this book, I'll be giving you a full, guided tour of the clinical method. But before we get to that I first want to tell you more about the twenty-first-century patient. Catrina was a wonderful case in that she was interested in exploring her unconscious, and very happy to spend her sessions with me free-associating. Most twenty-first-century patients are not like this, though. That is why, in the next chapter, I will be introducing you to John J. He, like most patients today, was under tremendous pressure to solve his problems, with little if any interest in exploring his unconscious. And as psychoanalysts, we do have to help people with their immediate problems.

As I will try to illustrate for you, even in these cases we are always seeking to prepare our patients' minds for self-discovery, always following the contact and making emotional communications that will pave the way for the day when, finally, a patient can start to wonder if something is going on that they don't yet understand, something that may still be unconscious.

Because if there is one thing that has not changed since the days of Freud, it is that every psychoanalyst still wants to have a patient who is ready for real analysis to begin. So now, let us examine what it takes, exactly, to travel on this emotional journey that goes into the making of a psychoanalyst.

Notes

1 This is what is known as the *'subjective countertransference.'*
2 When you are a psychoanalyst, it is a good idea to know all your negative feelings, impulses and wishes (*countertransference*) well. This is, in fact, your best insurance against acting unwittingly upon unacknowledged, repressed feelings.
3 The technical term for what I was doing with Catrina by trying to enter into her world rather than disagree for her way of managing herself, is called 'joining.'
4 Joining strengthens the ego.
5 The technical term for not behaving maturely with our family is 'being regressed.' We work to promote *regression* in treatment, using the couch and allowing the patient to talk freely, because it makes it easier to diagnose and work with emotional problems.
6 This is what is known as 'joining the defenses.' Once we recognize defense structures and start to unravel the mystery of their function as a form of creative adaptation, we appreciate their value and importance. Eventually, the patient will be able to replace the defenses with better adaptations.
7 This question was an 'emotional communication' that conveyed my respect for Catrina's defenses.
8 This may be considered a *'countertransference resistance.'*
9 It is vital that we become aware of our *countertransference*, no matter how negative, counterproductive or irrelevant. This is to insure that we have a good handle on our subjective countertransference, which is what minimizes the risk of contaminating the treatment with subjective elements.
10 This is how the twenty-first-century psychoanalyst uses her own emotions, or countertransference, to gauge the patient's own relationship to their defenses. In this case, entertaining the idea that Catrina's defenses were maladaptive again was a sign that she herself may be approaching a softening of their place in her psyche.
11 This is the first time in the treatment I actively explore Catrina's defense and whether she can push back on her perfectionism, no doubt because of the induced feeling that the defense was becoming overly inconvenient.

12 Sometimes, we mistake our subjective feelings for feelings induced by the patient. Or else, feelings we think belong to the patient are really ours. Becoming a psychoanalyst requires less of a clear picture of where the feelings originate from than it does a willingness to explore and investigate their origin. We form hypotheses and then test them against the data the patient eventually provides.

13 Change is also called 'therapeutic action.'

2 John J and the big surrender

The farm boy

John J had only recently turned twenty-eight. He became my patient on a cold winter night because of some things that were disturbing him. His face was expressionless as he told me this, looking down at his shoes. He was engaged to a woman he had been with for some time, but when he went away on business, he liked to get drunk and have sex with different women. He thought he should probably stop, he said, wringing his hands. He didn't know why he did it. He and his fiancée had been together for a few years, and she was a nice girl. He didn't want to hurt her.

They had a name for John J at the company where he worked, which he did not appreciate: "that bull in a china shop." In his mind, this was uncool. The problem was he liked to tell it like it is. If he thought an idea was foolish, he said so. He thought he was just stating his educated opinion—he had an MBA—wasn't that what they were paying him for? To make things work?

He started to shake his head and chortle at this point. He couldn't believe how people acted sometimes. Men weren't like this on the farm where he grew up. You worked together there toward a common goal. There wasn't any time for "stupid shit."

But after his firm's human resources department advised him to talk to a coach through the employee assistance program, he decided that "maybe I could use some help with all these foolish people playing mind games."

How to become a better man

John J wanted to become a "better man," and I was actually psyched about helping him. Self-improvement, as you yourself may know, is quite uplifting—at least initially. But, barely twenty minutes into the hour, I completely lost my enthusiasm for this better-man project. Let me try to trace for you what happened.[1]

"OK, I'll give you some background," John J said, leaning so far forward to engage me that he put his elbows on his knees, "The thing is, we didn't argue when I grew up, right? It just didn't make sense to. If you didn't do something the way you were supposed to on the farm, you could get your hand mangled in the equipment, you know? Lose an arm or something. That was the bottom line—survival."

"Yeah, things were simpler there—very cut and dry. In the morning we all met at the barn, and we all agreed on what had to be done. We talked, you know? And then we knew what to do for the day. Simple. We just went about what had to be done, and we did it. Everybody worked together. There was absolutely no room for any stupid shit there—excuse my French." John J glanced up at me to double-check that I wasn't offended by his swearing. I said, "Right."

He nodded and continued: "Now at the company, nobody works together like that. Just the other day, I thought I was getting along fine with someone, and next thing I know, she sends an e-mail to my boss. She said something about things not getting done. What is that? Instead of talking straight to me. Made me look bad. Everybody is out to get everybody there."

"Then there's the people who are nice. But they complain like babies. It's just…so messed up. The way it is there, is like…even if I know more than the next guy, it doesn't matter. If he's above me let's say, or even below me, I'm supposed to sit things out and pretend an idea has value even when it doesn't. Really. No, I don't know if I can play this game. I worked hard to get here—I thought I could do it, and I was told I had some talent. But I don't know now."

"And my fiancée—I might as well bring that up, too. She is just…so confused. I mean, she's great, don't get me wrong, that's why I don't want to lose her. She is a really nice girl. If she found out what I do, God, that would be it—it would be over. She's going crazy planning the wedding. She wants a big wedding, but then again, she doesn't. Her father wants her to have like 300 people, but it's all got to be his way. So then she says she just wants to have a small thing in a restaurant. So like, every night she has me going to a different venue. Until she decides. I'm telling you [and now he sat back on the couch], I'm just about this close [and he held two fingers close together with hardly any space between them] to telling her point blank—*just make a fucking decision.*" Then, silence.

"It wasn't like this on the farm, I'll tell you that. I used to be on the wrestling team. Yeah, every Friday night I'd wrestle. My family would come, my friends…cheering, clapping. Yeah. The women…" And he looked at me with a half-smile.

As far as I could tell at this point, John J had two sides to him: one of raw, undiluted instinctual energy and the other that managed to tame himself with self-control and an MBA. Of course, we all have John J's two sides to some degree—who hasn't struggled to keep his or her hostility or perhaps lust in check. But in his case, the amperage of his drives was just ridiculous. The main thing was: John J wanted my help becoming what he called a "better man."

This would be frustrating, at best. City life was so different from what he knew. We were far away from what he had had; from the cheering at Friday night matches from fans, his family, the women. There he sat, this champion of a man, a small pot belly emerging from his pale grey, wrinkled suit. I didn't want to help him become a better man; I wanted to help him go back to the farm to get built up again. Have some fun. Tell it like it is.

The stalemate

Things hadn't always been so perfect on the farm though, John J said, reading my mind on some level. He began studying the rug as if deciphering some complicated pattern in it. But then he started to relay a story. One night, he started telling, just after graduating with honors from high school, he stepped out and got drunk with his buddies. Then, he came home and, thinking he was in the bathroom, took "a real long piss" that hit the TV. His father woke up and became ballistic, punching John J until he knocked him out.

John J figured he had better leave the farm early for college after that, so he packed up and headed out the next morning. But he didn't blame his father for what he had done, since, after all, he had ruined the new TV. After a little more silence, he looked me straight in the eye and repeated that he could see his father's point—that's how it was on the farm. I could tell that he had searched his mind as to whether or not there was more to process about the incident and decided that no, there really wasn't.

A part of me registered reflexively that this must have been an emotional trauma for John J: to be brutally beaten by his father and to leave the farm in a state of disgrace on the eve of making his way out into the world. Or if not traumatic, at least in some way pivotal. But John J had told me that he thought most therapists were "too touchy-feely" so I didn't press him; he was more concerned with the assholes at the company.

Here is what John J did want me to understand about the farm: it could be a dangerous place, the way storms in nature are. But it was also, on the whole, a desirable place to be—uncomplicated, straightforward, and definitely simpler than being at the company. He missed that life.

And so I asked him, "John J, are you sure you want me to help you become a 'better man' in this life? Don't you think it's going to kill your spirit?" He had an answer for that: "Well, I can't go back and just be the kind of guy that rides his motorcycle over the hills all day with his buddies, drinking vodka for breakfast. I've worked real hard to get here. I want to move forward."

So now we had it. Both John J's farm life and his company life had the same bleak emotional terrains. He was not truly happy or alive in either place. Except, of course, when he was getting cheered or getting laid. This explained why I had lost my enthusiasm for helping him become a "better man" in either place: he felt bleak everywhere. Feelings are contagious, and I had caught his.

I wasn't in a *totally* bleak state, mind you. Not when John J described the times he acted like a bull. One night, he told me, shaking his head with a half-smile, he had hooked up with *two* women. At the same time. Yes, John J had the potential to be a force, I could see that—and those jolts of energy, even though he wanted to tame himself out of them to become a better man, at least showed signs of life.

But all these signs of life truly weren't working for him. He wanted to stop being a bull and womanizer. Where would all that energy go to next, I wondered. Did he expect to "better man" himself into a complete abyss? I needed a little more time to figure out why, when he felt alive and like a bull, it wasn't working for him. It seemed as though he had a secret self.

"John J," I said, "why don't you lie down on the couch here and tell me the story of your life—it helps me get into things a little better." "Nah," he said with a slow drawl, "I'm good." And with that he drew himself up for a casual stretch that became completely awkward since he couldn't quite execute it. I should have known that John J wouldn't take the couch; what was I thinking? I had completely forgotten who I was talking to. This man was not yet ready for that level of surrender.

Fix it and forget it

John J and I had certainly stumbled upon an unfortunate stalemate in the treatment. I wanted him to talk freely so I could get to know his inner landscapes, and he wanted to set an agenda, solve his problems and become a better man. Fix it and forget it.

Now certainly, we were in agreement about one thing: John J and I both knew that something wasn't right. *Houston, we've got a problem.* But where we differed was that whereas I wanted him to delve into his inner world, he just wanted to solve the problem. He believed that if he could just borrow my psychological way of thinking and my mindset for a few quick sessions, he might very well succeed.

This struggle between John J and me is representative of the struggle that will usually emerge in any treatment:[2] a part of us has no problem delving into our emotions where we feel, process and analyze things, but another part of us doesn't want to delve in there at all. It's not comfortable there—especially when it's negative. We want to do what John J did: try to be practical and fix things. We think: if we can just be practical and reasonable, use our common sense and stop indulging our emotions, we can move ahead. We want to drive the boat; stay in control.

John J didn't think about his emotions much. He was certainly interested in *learning* something about the workings of emotional life, but only insofar as it would inform him as to how, exactly, he could get back to business and keep things moving.

Unfortunately, when people get out of balance emotionally and do things they themselves may not even fully understand, trying to coach them with solutions and common sense can be like painting over mold. Practical solutions often can't cover a deeper problem. Emotions can't be controlled just because we may want them to be. We can't always get into a better mindset, no matter how much we might want to, consciously.

Sometimes our thoughts keep going over upsetting things, retelling a tragic story; a sad or painful feeling lingers. Maybe we can't sleep; we're racked with worry—or envy or anger or frustration or despair. Or we begin to do things we can't even begin to understand, like John J did.

In fact, I don't know anyone who, in the face of certain idiosyncratic situations, hasn't been hit by a mild but perpetually recurring 'fight or flight' response. Even as we recognize that we are perhaps worrying unnecessarily, ruminating too moodily or feeling angrier than we should, we can't always move effortlessly and productively through the feelings.

At these times, we are drawn like magnets to some different force within ourselves we do not yet understand. We may then fight against knowing more about our inner world, believing the solution is to simply build our narrative and leave it at that. Sometimes, we get stuck in a strange no-man's land, neither here nor there, suspended between being magnetically drawn to an internal chaos we don't yet understand, and an impatient attitude towards the thoughts and feelings. We may feel defensive or agitated, and the disturbance is like quicksand, drawing us in while we feel powerless.

Pre-analytic patients, who are busy building defensive narratives and don't have the luxury of being curious because they're in a chronic state of fight or flight, need help initially simply to feel a little calmer. To surrender to free associating on the couch would require some hope that comes with knowing that there's something still inside you that you cannot control, which you would be well-served to get curious about. Most people, however, believe they can get things in control.

To surrender to the couch, patients need to hope that it will lead to something, then they have to have enough comfort to get curious, and once all that is in place, they can hopefully find a question. Once they have a question, they can stop searching for a magic pill, and work instead to search for answers by free-associating.

I wanted John J to surrender, to be confused about the forces that were overtaking him and leading him to be the adulterer; the "bull." I wanted him to take the couch and talk about whatever came into his mind. But he didn't want to. I had to admire him, at least, for making it to my door. He did know something wasn't right. For him to have even called me, as I am sure you can appreciate, was huge.

We are collectively much less reluctant to deny and push away our problems these days, thank goodness. We have evolved so much. But we are still reluctant to surrender to just talking about ourselves without aim. So while there are far fewer restrictions than ever on admitting to being unhappy—to being stressed, overwhelmed, addicted, neglected, abused, angry or dissatisfied, for example—we still haven't been educated as to how getting more curious about these states of mind can be fruitful.

Education about optimal states of emotional well-being—in books, on television shows and on the radio and the Internet—are, ironically, one of our worst enemies when we are overwhelmed and lose our balance. Because the knowledge of how things should be—happy, enlightened, balanced, healthy, loving, wise, educated, grateful, in shape—even while useful and necessary, makes us feel inadequate and even hopeless when we fall so helplessly short of being able to get there.

And the standards as to what's "best" that are set before us these days are bigger than ever. They affect every aspect of our lives. They give us hope, and they are certainly worth aspiring to. But in light of unconscious dynamics, those goals appear to be *outside* ourselves, as objective goals to strive for. And when our patients are under the spell of unconscious forces, they can't make it over to those goals; *they just can't get there*. We have to hold in our minds patiently the knowledge that once we can help our patients feel a little calmer about their real-life predicaments, and once we can educate them about the mysteries of the unconscious, they may surrender to using the couch and free-associating in search of an answer to a new question.

John J, in the meantime, had a good ol'-fashioned solution to the emotional problems he was encountering. "Teach me," he begged on the night that he became my patient. But he was plainly quite uncomfortable with his emotions. He approached his emotional challenges the same way he would approach a tractor. Figure it out, fix it, ride it. And so, our lessons began.

The lessons

Each week, John J came to my office and sat on the edge of my couch eagerly—a model student.

"So who's on your roster today, John J?" I'd ask, and he was ready. First, he wanted to tackle his boss. John J and I took the boss apart; he was a man who needed to feel powerful, but imagined he was being disrespected. To succeed, John J would have to act more deferential toward him, give him the feelings he needed. "Do you believe I have to eat this shit?" John J said. He would need a lot of patience for this asshole.

"Oh, pleeeease, what the fuck?" he said at one session, which featured a co-worker, a man who was competitive and hostile. John J was going to have to watch his ass with him.

"God help us and keep us all," he said reverentially at another session, which featured his confused fiancée who was at the mercy of her father, a wealthy financier who wanted to control her every move. "I should just friggin' get her to elope," he said, and we laughed. We were becoming friends. This is how his nervous system was slowly getting calmed in treatment for the event of a possible future psychoanalytic experience.

Actually, John J seemed to be getting the hang of emotional things, but it was a practical matter, and still not an emotional one. Beyond his generalized impatience and disdain for each person on his roster, I didn't have a sense of how John J really felt about anything or anyone. He had long learned to shelve his feelings; they were impractical.

Certainly, John J was learning some useful psychology. He was learning to recognize behavior patterns and identify character types, including what made them tick and how to deal with it. And he was enjoying that. "Women are a whole other species," he noted, reflectively.

But I was feeling that after six sessions, he would be gone. Six was the magic number John J had in his head for what constituted a successful course in therapy. Not surprisingly, it was the same number of sessions that his company had given him to work with the corporate coach he had met with before he came to me. My insurance patients usually get double that; their magic number is often twelve.

I do get upset sometimes about the limits. It's not only the insurance coverage, it's the personal commitment to exploring your own mind with a trained professional. It takes time. I want to stand on a mountaintop and shout out to the universe: "Allow your mind to wander where it will. It will take you places, I promise. There are new methods for mastering your inner worlds. Stop setting goals and trying to reach them. Stop solving. Start evolving!!!!"

I wanted to say to John J: "TALK!! Just LET yourself!!! LET yourself!!!!" But instead, I just sat in my big red leather recliner and waited.

The tourist

By session five, I was really starting to feel antsy. I knew that we were approaching the finish line. Only one more session to go, and still no interest in more treatment. John J would leave the sessions with a little jounce to his walk though, like "I'm nailin' this thing."

I wanted to tell him: "Baby—it's gonna take a lot more than six lessons for you to become a 'better man,' for your powerful urges to take you to better places, for you to be able to plan and think strategically through your emotional wastelands and war zones, for you to feel whole instead of feeling dazed and confused. You're just a tourist here in the emotional world of my office, going on a little-baby guided tour."

I even fantasized about making an intervention. "John J," I could tell him, "you may not know this, but you are on the brink of despair. If you don't someday connect the dots between your audacious behavior and some unseen forces within yourself, then your impending marriage—as well as your professional success—will continue to be under threat of your wild impulses. Even just a small fissure in the stone wall you have built around your emotions, John J, could cause the entire structure to fall down. That's why they call it a 'breakdown,' sir."

Hey, a new treatment modality! Prophet-of-doom-prognosis-therapy! No, that would not be friendly or nice. Very John J-esque though—tell it like it is.

Maybe, I continued to fantasize, I could try a gentler approach: "John J, you know…there's a lot more to learn over here about your emotions. I can guarantee that if you spend a little more time here, just lie down and relax on my nice long couch, say whatever comes to your mind and tell me the story of your life—that you will find your own answers to all the things you don't yet understand about why you do the things you do. I promise you that you'll discover what to do with what it is that roils within you."

But I didn't say any of that, because I thought it would scare him. He was already dealing with a lot. Instead, I sat on my hands and was quiet because I knew intuitively that John J didn't want to stay and talk more. For whatever reason—and I still had no idea exactly why—it made him horribly uncomfortable.

If I, standing on the threshold of his mind where he had opened a welcome door to me, tried to sell him something he really didn't want, he would surely slam the door on me. I know from experience that it is always better, once you've made yourself a welcome guest in someone's mental house, to keep it that way. Becoming friends is huge. That way, you're guaranteed an invitation back when your company inside is wanted. The time wasn't right yet. I had long ago learned the golden rule for how to work with resistance: you follow the patient wherever they need to go.

The question comes

So session six came, and John J went. He shook my hand real hard, thanked me, and made his way down my brick path and into the night. I often stare out of my window after patients leave, watching couples embrace or studying someone's gait to gauge their mood. John J looked determined. At least we had that—even though I have to say I did regret that his surrender wasn't big enough.

It was a few months later that the phone rang in my office at ten o'clock on a Tuesday night. John J's name showed up on the caller ID and I picked up the phone from the extension in my bedroom. "Doc," he said. He was crying.

"John J, what's happened?" I asked.

"She left me," he said, "She found out. Somebody texted her a picture of me in a room with a woman. It's over. The father said he's gonna get me fired. I don't know, Doc...why is this happening?"

I took a deep breath, and said "I'm so sorry this is happening John J. Well...we have to figure out why. That's what we have to figure out. Will you come in next Wednesday?"

John J said OK, and we set a time.

At last, I thought, John J could finally surrender to the analysis and start examining the forces that churned within him. We had a question: "Why is this happening?" And now, the real work could begin.

THE TWENTY-FIRST-CENTURY PATIENT

John J, an attractive, intelligent man on the brink of a total breakdown, epitomizes the twenty-first-century pre-analytic patient in two central ways: first, he was plagued by unresolved thoughts and emotions that he knew he should get help with, and second, he had little if any motivation to face them.

I'm sure the tale of John J is not unfamiliar to you, and that you can either identify with aspects of his character or know of someone exactly like him. But I want you for a moment to think of him not as an actual person, but rather as a metaphor for a particular state of consciousness that is in avoidance mode, that is in a chronic, low-level state of fight or flight. This condition can even occur when patients have made a commitment to being in analysis, but their need to feel better suddenly exceeds their desire to get better and they want immediate direction as opposed to long-term analysis. It can also occur when disturbing feelings loom much larger than any real ability to cope with them, and treatment feels threatening.

Before the mind has been sufficiently prepared, talking about even conscious problems can be too difficult. I once had a patient who had been traumatized by a sexual encounter with an uncle, and it took her five years before she was able to speak to me about exactly what had happened. To respect the patient's pace with regard to when—and how—they are willing to talk about thoughts and feelings, the analyst has to be able to work pre-analytically at times.

Pre-analytic patients typically present real-life problems and don't usually have any questions yet about what may be happening unconsciously. The analyst, therefore, has to be willing to engage with those problems directly, rather than insisting on exploring what the patient has not yet shown an interest in, and which it may therefore be too difficult and premature to start examining. When patients look for real-life solutions to their problems, and want to talk about other people in their lives and otherwise focus on practical matters outside the realm of their inner thoughts, the analyst has to be willing to serve as an educated advisor, a consultant working cognitively on an explicit problem.

Perhaps you are wondering why I didn't suggest to John J that I could best assist him if he would just take the couch and free-associate, so that we could better understand why he continued to do things that could potentially destroy his chances of success—both in love and in work. In fact, in the early stages of this treatment I actually did suggest it, but to no avail. During any pre-analytic period, such as here in John J's experience, it's simply too hard for the patient to study his or her own mind.

And yet, despite some patients' obvious resistance to psychoanalytic treatment, the main tenets of twenty-first-century psychoanalysis still apply: even with people who do not under any circumstances want to focus too hard on their own minds, we always *follow the contact* and make sure, with our *emotional communications*, to meet the patient where they are at emotionally.

The analytic patient, on the other hand, typically has a question they want to explore, one that may be as general as, "Why does this keep happening to me?" or one specific as "Why do I get triggered by this particular feeling or dynamic?" When we work with a patient who is ready for analysis, we can then become fully attuned to what may be unconscious in the patient. We can then analyze *transference* and resistance and try to figure out how to prepare the patient's mind sufficiently for self-discovery.

With the analytic patient, therefore, we are monitoring tension levels in the room, thinking about how to either gratify or frustrate the patient sufficiently to foster continued talking. For example, too much gratification, and not enough frustration through questions or emotional communications, would not foster continued talking. With the pre-analytic patient, however, we are not monitoring tension levels in the room at all. Instead, we are simply making sure at all times that the analytic environment is sufficiently positive to ensure that the patient will want to continue coming to sessions. I am always making sure, with the pre-analytic patient, that there is enough dopamine in the room.

To illustrate the difference in action between how I might work with a patient who is pre-analytic versus an analytic patient who is willing to free-associate on the couch, let's look at one, common circumstance: a patient bringing a gift of a muffin to a session. These examples demonstrate how I would think about and analyze the muffin with different patients who are ready for an analytic experience, monitoring frustration and gratification levels in the room:

1   With Tilda, an analytic patient with an impulse disorder, I might say, "It would be better for the treatment if you didn't bring me things to eat." This would certainly be very frustrating to Tilda, as setting boundaries with impulse-ridden patients typically is. It would also model for the patient how to set boundaries and, perhaps, create an environment safe from destructive acting-out. This patient might feel reassured that her analyst is not afraid of the patient's potential anger. Through the transference, a lot of great conversations could be had about frustration, boundaries, rage and much more.

2   To Elsa North, a depressed analytic patient who has been in treatment already for five years, I might say nothing initially about the muffin. Instead, I'd listen for any kind of symbolic communication in her dialogue, like about feeling emotionally starved. If there was such a communication, I might pose an exploratory question like, "Is that why you brought me the muffin, Ms. North? Because you want to make sure I don't feel emotionally starved?"

3   Tom Black was an analytic patient with a lot of unexpressed anger. If he had brought me a muffin, and I felt it had a hostile connotation, I might use the opportunity to see if I could facilitate the expression of his anger directly. So I might say to him, somewhat stridently, "Why are

you bringing me this muffin, Mr. Black?" This could potentially frustrate him sufficiently to allow for the verbalization of some of his feelings of resentment and bitterness towards people—and that might give me the chance to work with them in the moment.

When you are working with analytic patients, you are never simply applying a prescribed set of interventions to match a specific behavior or resistance. Instead, everything has to be studied and responded to according to its specific emotional meaning and in accordance with a determination about the current structure of that person's mind. You do this by exploring the transference, by staying attuned to the process of helping the patient speak their mind out loud, by monitoring the frustration levels in the room as to what the patient can and cannot yet tolerate, always using our own emotions to assess the emotional environment and design the right emotional communication or form of exploration.

Analytic patients somehow know, intuitively, that you are doing something analytic, and they can stay with the process. If I had made any of the above interventions to John J, however, he surely would have left treatment. That is why if John J had brought me the muffin I would just say, "Thank you!"

If I was at all hungry, I might even add, "Would you mind terribly if I ate some now?"

The difference? With the pre-analytic patient, I am not working with transference and resistance. In fact, the transference with a pre-analytic patient who is only just starting treatment is usually very shallow, meaning it has not yet been invested with *projections*, fantasies, longings, wishes or fears. There is nothing loaded about it. Typically, the transference between a new pre-analytic patient and their therapist is as simple as: "I'm a nice person, you're a nice person and the rest of the world is not so nice." It's the same transference you might have to any relative stranger helping you professionally such as your banker, hairdresser or dentist. It is the transference of normal social interaction, without any regressed components. In these cases, to treat the muffin gift as anything other than what it is, a gift, would be, for the pre-analytic patient, just plain weird.

So if I am hungry, and I want to eat the muffin, doing so communicates to the pre-analytic patient that I am willing to enter into a nice relationship. This willingness explains why I might answer my work phone at ten o'clock at night, as I did with John J in this story. Pre-analytic patients are introducing you into their lives gradually, and, if you can, it's nice to be available at the time of those invitations. Nor do you want to prematurely invite them into something they didn't sign up for. Until you both agree to explore a question by free-associating, you simply help them with the problem at hand whenever possible.

I actually did have a pre-analytic patient who brought me a muffin once, and I'll never forget it. I was a little hungry and thirsty when she brought it. She was a very narcissistic person, whom I had been introduced to at a social event, and I knew she had little emotional awareness of anyone around her. So I asked her if she would mind terribly if I made myself a cup of tea to go with the muffin. She followed me into the kitchen gladly, and I enjoyed a nice second breakfast. Working with pre-analytic patients can be very relaxing. She was very glad, I'm sure, that I was symbolically so willing to ingest her, and flattered by the intimacy so rarely extended to her.

Let's not forget that even in our work with pre-analytic patients, we are always following the contact and responding emotionally to establish a lasting connection. Sometimes this will lead to landing on a question worthy of analysis, and sometimes it doesn't. But long gone are the days when the analyst projected an air of neutral impartiality, making sure not to express any emotion. Instead, it's our willingness to enter into a real soul-to-soul connection that creates the optimal environment for starting a real analysis, should a suitable question worth exploring arise.

This willingness to enter deeply into what feels like a real relationship with the patient does present the risk, for both the patient and analyst, of falling into patterns of emotional contagion and *induction* that catch us unawares. Perhaps, it is a meeting in public in which there is a spontaneous hug, after which the patient reports feeling violated. It may occur after a period of time, perhaps well into the treatment, during which the analyst becomes unable to listen any longer to the patient's complaints, falling into a trap the patient has lain to recreate their feelings of early neglect. Or maybe it happens when a certain patient continuously falls under the radar, and the analyst forgets to write him or her into the appointment book—on multiple occasions. But these transgressions, when framed by the analysis as "enactments" of unconscious patterns, are just more grist for the mill. In fact, enactments can become the most powerful means of accessing, *in vivo*, what could not be talked about before. As such, these experiences elevate the analysis beyond a cerebral process of shining a spotlight on experience, and become instead the actual arenas of experience where the drama of the unconscious unfolds and the chances for reparation and connecting to hidden feelings grow exponentially.

Transitioning pre-analytic patients into an analysis, in fact, can often happen on the heels of an enactment. It can also happen when the patient wants to leave treatment, at which point the analyst can invite the patient into a deeper experience by asking, "Should we keep talking about why this keeps happening to you?" At other times, a question may come up for the patient naturally, as it did for John J, who ultimately had no choice but to question what was happening to his life. As soon as there is a question on the table worth exploring, the analysis can begin.

When John J came back into treatment and finally took the couch, entering into that sacred zone where *regression* is reached so much more easily, and where it becomes so much more possible to study the unconscious, an awkwardness fell like the night's sky over the room. He had no idea what to talk about.

When this happens, I always give my new analytic patients an instruction, which is to talk about six things: their transference to me; their thoughts about being in treatment; possible goals for the future; memories; dreams; and any waking fantasies. "Talk about as many of these topics as you can in one session," I recommend. With this injunction, the patients can busy themselves with an assignment, and temporarily forget that they don't really want to face themselves.

Psychoanalysis is kind of scary for the pre-analytic patient. Years ago, if I was at a party and anybody asked me what I did for a living I'd actually be afraid to tell them. The mere mention of the word 'psychoanalyst' would seem to make people squirm or even physically recoil, as if I was either going to mentally undress them or tell them things about themselves they'd never want to know.

But now, I like saying "I'm a psychoanalyst." It's fun. First of all, it's interesting, and second, I like talking about it. If I get any kind of deer-in-the-headlights look back, I just say, "Oh don't worry, I only analyze people if I get paid large sums of money for it." Since nobody likes to pay large sums for anything, that lets them off the hook.

But admittedly, I'm always analyzing everybody, and in many ways, when you become well versed in how to use your emotions as instruments for being with people, it does provide you with a voyeuristic lens that can be quite illuminating. I know of analysts who even analyze their pets. But for now, let's stick to people. Whether our patients will come in pre-analytic or ready to explore their minds, our welcome mat is always out, and we will always meet them at whatever point they're ready to begin.

Notes

1 At first, we have our own subjective appraisal of a problem. Soon, inductions from the patient alert us that our initial appraisal is too shallow.
2 The term for the conflict between wanting to get better but not wanting to delve into painful thoughts and feelings is what we think of as 'resistance.'

Part II
Key concepts

3   Searching for Anita

Ward B

I was still in my early twenties by the time I had taken enough courses to be eligible for the clinical component of my psychoanalytic training: seeing chronically ill patients on the locked wards of a state mental hospital. Which is how I found myself on a fine midsummer's day, walking the dingy halls of Ward B, searching for Anita, a fifty-four-year-old paranoid schizophrenic, assigned to me for observation. She had been living in and out of the hospital most of her life.

There were no offices available so we would have to meet in a hall lined with chairs. She had been told I was coming and was waiting for me in the next hallway, sitting on a hard plastic chair clutching a deflated handbag and staring into space. I took the chair next to her. We didn't speak for several minutes until she asked in a startlingly loud voice, "Are you my best girlfriend?"

I wanted to set the record straight about who I was: a student observing psychosis, not her best girlfriend. But introducing reality was technically not a part of just 'observing.' I was not supposed to correct perceptions or provide any information about myself that could potentially taint the process of observation. So I just said, "Sure," and we remained in silence for a little longer.

Anita wore mismatched clothes with pants that rose high above her distended belly. She walked stiffly, which, I would soon learn, is how most people on the chronic wards move from years of being heavily medicated. She was wearing bright red, garish lipstick, badly painted on, and had only two or three teeth, which made her talk with a lisp. This, in combination with how loudly she spoke, made her appear to be drunk.

I was somewhat repulsed by Anita, although I would have been slow to admit it, because it didn't seem pertinent, and who likes to admit to their own negative, judgmental character? It is absolutely amazing, when it comes to observation, how much we believe is inadmissible or irrelevant to our thinking without realizing that no thought or feeling is ever irrelevant when it comes to doing psychanalytic observation. This is what I want to show you in this story about starting one of the very first levels of psychoanalytic training: how we learn to get past an elemental awareness of what we think and feel to something far more complex, useful and encompassing.

Observation

I was frustrated and, quite honestly, a little lost, sitting there with Anita on that first day. I wanted at least a clipboard; some sort of rational treatment plan to guide me or make me seem "professional"—anything that would distance me from the growing confusion and awkwardness I felt, sitting like a patient in the ward, secretly anxious that someone walking by might assume I was Anita's best girlfriend.

But what was required at this level in my training was simply to observe, and "observation" had its rules. You had to sit with the patient. There was no treatment plan and no goals. You could ask three questions that were designed to be neutral in nature,[1] perhaps about the food or the accommodations, but nothing too intense. Hopefully, you would be able to engage the patient in some kind of dialogue that would inform your understanding about psychosis. Yech—I hated that word, it scared me.

Pretty soon, Anita walked away, which set the pattern for how our sessions would go every week for the next two years. We would sit next to each other, one or the other of us would ask a question, and then, after between five to seven minutes, Anita would walk away and I would sigh with relief and go home. Before long, my two years were up. I had logged enough hours at the mental hospital to qualify for my oral examination, mostly by hanging around the nurses' station just long enough to stretch the hours so I could fulfill the time requirements.

I eagerly presented my observations before a panel of distinguished faculty members and fellow students, expecting that they would approve and advance me to the next level of training so that I could finally transfer out of the mental hospital field placement. I set about describing Anita in as much detail as I could: how she looked and acted, a thorough account of the range of feelings I experienced sitting with her, a well-researched medical history and description of her general preferred behaviors and modes of communication. The presentation was well organized, well documented, and had a lot of information about the etiology of Anita's illness and its general characteristics. I thought I had delivered it pretty well. I knew the presentation had to have an emotional and psychological component, so I described my feelings too: repulsion, emptiness, loneliness. I thought my awareness of these feelings rounded out the presentation nicely.

I felt excited as I left the classroom for a few minutes while the faculty deliberated on my presentation. Within minutes, I was asked to come back in. As I sat down, I noticed that the faces around me looked grave. Sure enough, the verdict came in and it was "FAIL." My presentation, I was told, was lacking in "depth." I was horrified, partly because I had no idea what more depth was required. Was it a matter of providing more details about Anita's behavior? Or more background on schizophrenia? Did I not report accurately enough my own awareness of how I felt while sitting on the ward? It was a complete and total mystery to me. All I knew was that I had apparently not observed enough about Anita. My observations, unbeknownst to me at that time, were simply too elemental. What I had done, I would soon learn, was not yet "real" observation. But in the meantime, I simply could not believe I hadn't passed. This was truly one of the most thwarting experiences of my life.[2]

My sad relationship to the history of lay analysis

I decided at this point that I had to leave psychoanalysis; I had had enough. I began applying to business schools. Unless you had an MD, psychoanalysis, at this time, was not strategically a great career choice anyway. Political power struggles had worked for decades to keep psychoanalysis as a subspecialty of medicine and, later, of psychology and social work as well. Those of us who weren't MDs were classified as "lay analysts." Now, Freud believed in lay analysis—he didn't think having an MD was a requirement for doing treatment. But even so, without an MD you couldn't become accredited as a psychoanalyst in the United States.

So for me to have suffered the indignity of failing the fieldwork externship, when staying in the program wouldn't even earn me a doctorate or a master's degree in psychoanalysis, was beyond frustrating. All the psychoanalytic institute really had to offer, if I now chose to stay, was a "certificate"—a certificate that would not even enable me to earn a license. At that time, a full lay-analytic education would not entitle you to accreditation, a license and, therefore, an ability to take insurance and build a practice.

In fact, friends had told me they thought I was crazy putting all that effort, money and time into a certificate that didn't yield either a degree or a license. Especially given that completing the whole program was even harder than getting a doctorate at an accredited school. The psychoanalytic certificate training program requirement, in fact, was daunting: eight courses each in psychoanalytic theory, human development and history as well as a long list of research courses. Full completion of two clinical internships under continual supervision—the fieldwork placement and then another two years at the school's in-house treatment service. And then, of course, a doctoral thesis. After that, as was the case for admittance to any new level in the program, a rigorous oral examination involving a full faculty panel would have to be endured. All this, in addition to 350 hours of individual analysis and 50 hours of group, for a *certificate*.

This was no easy ride. Eventually, the Massachusetts Board of Higher Education did award the institute I was studying at authority to grant masters and doctoral degrees. I now have a PsyaD, a psychoanalytic doctorate. The school, the Boston Graduate School of Psychoanalysis, was actually the first in the country to have been awarded the authority to grant psychoanalytic degrees, a hundred years after Freud first spoke in the United States at Clark University.

But prior to that, anybody interested in psychoanalysis usually got accredited degrees from other disciplines. Even I had gotten a Master's degree in Education from Harvard University, despite wanting to study psychoanalysis alone. What I am trying to convey is that the only reason anyone continued studying in unaccredited programs like the one I had just failed the fieldwork component in, is that we believed in the clinical method. This belief was usually personal; most of the people in the training, I believe, had benefitted from their personal analysis and knew from deep experience that psychoanalysis provided a solid means for getting better.

Without question, psychoanalysis had been less a practical career choice for me than it had been the only thing I could imagine doing with my life; it had been in my life since I was still a tween. My mother had gotten into analysis right when I turned twelve, when, for the first time, she started talking to me by my bed each night, like about my day. We had truly never before talked like this.

I began my own analysis only a few years later with an analyst who is now of great renown, Hyman Spotnitz, who, when he invited me to study with him, removed any shadow of doubt from my mind as to what I knew I would someday become. The emotional connectedness and understanding that I had experienced with him and with my mother and father was all I needed to help me reach that deep knowledge about what my future held in store.

But now, in my mid-twenties and ten years after that promise to Spotnitz, the fieldwork failure caused me to doubt my impractical choice. I asked myself if this could have just been a childhood dream? Was I really cut out for it? Clinical fieldwork was so difficult, and I was having such a hard time learning how to do "observation" that I questioned everything. I started to doubt my commitment to lay analysis, and to doubt my abilities and my purpose. That is how hard it is to learn how to do observation. Reflecting on my training on the whole, without question, "observation" was one of the most difficult things I have ever had to learn.

But, as I would eventually learn, "observation," at the level I am now going to describe to you, could very well be the most vital component of the training. Developing the skills of observation that integrates into the experience of observing absolutely everything you think and feel is what the entire investigative method of psychoanalysis really revolves around: the better you get at it, the further you go.

What I was about to learn would take me way beyond the elemental levels of simply watching and interpreting, which is a very straightforward activity with a discrete beginning and an end, a starting point and a conclusion. The observation I was about to learn would put me in an endless, timeless stream: one idea leading to the next question, leading to more watching, leading to more awareness. What I would eventually learn would finally take me way past feeling and knowing the same thing over and over. Your powers of observation increase exponentially when you learn to integrate your own emotions into what you see and hear as you search for answers and develop new questions. It is what takes your scientific inquiry off of all potential dead-end roads as you constantly find new things to be curious about and to explore. This is what I was going to learn, and what I want to show you now.

Because I didn't yet know the wonders of what lay ahead of me though, I took some time off from observing Anita and waited to hear from the results of my applications to business school. By a fortunate twist of fate, I did not get in anywhere. My head hung low when I resignedly returned to the psychoanalytic institute for lack of anything better to do with my life. As I entered the building, I spotted my supervisor going up the stairs to the library, and I called out to her glumly, "I didn't get in."

"Good!" she called back jubilantly, with a broad smile, "That's wonderful!" It was the greatest vote of confidence I've ever had.

So I returned to Metropolitan State Mental Hospital for a fifth semester, confused and frustrated, wondering what was going to come of being on what felt like a complete and total dead-end road.

Beyond mere awareness

Sitting with Anita, I had never felt so bored and impatient. This time, almost immediately, she walked away. This set a world record for the brevity of our session time. "Pathetic," I thought sadly as I made my way out of the hospital with the rest of the afternoon stretching out comfortably ahead. On the ride home, I felt guilty for feeling so happy about getting away from Ward B so quickly. I felt strangely grateful to Anita for walking away and making my choice to leave so easy. She was doing me a favor.

But as I thought about that, I wondered: did Anita know how much I didn't want to be there? That was an interesting question. Somewhat horrifying since she wanted a best girlfriend, and I thought she was a freak.

My new question made me slightly more interested in going back to Ward B the following week. I had found the thread of a barely discernible idea that at the time seemed completely absurd to me, but that I could nevertheless pursue. I had nothing to lose by seeing if there was a relationship between my feelings and her abrupt departures. Anyway, I had to make something creative up about our relationship, if only for the damn oral presentation committee. Something had to give.

The next week came and I entered the ward, took my place by Anita's side, and tried not to think about all the places I would rather be and all the things I would rather be doing. As I sat next to her, she didn't move for quite a while. Then she turned toward me, and my familiar dread returned; I wanted to get away from her. Sure enough, she got right up and walked away.

So maybe she *did* know what I was feeling. I had read somewhere that some schizophrenics, because the boundaries between their conscious and unconscious minds are so thin or even non-existent, can sense what other people are feeling. Sometimes, from what I'd heard, they can even appear to be psychic.

Later that week, meeting with my supervisor at the school, I told him what had happened; about my discovery that maybe Anita could sense my dread about being in the mental hospital.

"Why do you dread it so much?" he asked.

Thinking that I was making an obvious remark, I laughingly said, "I guess I prefer 'normal' people!" But he didn't laugh with me.

"What is 'normal' to you?" he asked.

"Oh, you know," I said, "just...not crazy!" I couldn't find the words to explain it.

"Well, maybe you can help me understand what you think is not normal?" he asked.

"Oh, *not* normal?" I said, "not normal is like...different. Struggling. Not...happy. Can't function like other people? You can't think straight."

As he helped me to talk more about what normal and not normal meant to me, it became clear that in my mind normal meant being undisturbed by difficult emotions; it meant being upbeat and able to get on with your life in a practical way. Normal meant not having emotions that made you feel twisted, so twisted that you might feel like a freak.

I didn't want to feel like a freak. Because inside, that's how I felt sometimes. And it was horrible. I didn't want to open myself up to that.

"Why not?" my supervisor asked. I started to cry.

I told my supervisor that I had, at times, felt like a freak. It scared me. He nodded and said: "I think you understand more than you know about this case. About why people have to push parts of themselves away." This was encouraging.

Coming into focus

I felt different the following week as I approached Anita. It was as if the whole ward had come into sharper focus for me, as if my vision had gotten better or I had gotten taller. I did not mind being there as much. "Anita," I asked, "what did you have for lunch today?"

"Eggs," she said, not looking at me.

"Are they any good here?" I asked.

"They're better at the halfway house," she said.

"What house is that?"

"That was the house I lived in. They had good eggs. It was in Boston. You would like it there."

"Did you have a best friend there?" I asked, and with that she got right up and walked away.

I told my supervisor what had happened, and he took a piece of paper and drew a circle on it, saying "This is a person." Then he drew another smaller circle inside of the first circle. Pointing to the smaller circle on the inside, he said, "This is the ego. Anytime you ask anything that is about a 'you,' it's an 'ego-oriented' question. Emotional. The zone of the ego is what you want to stay away from because it's too intense for the schizophrenic who we don't even think of as having an ego. So that's why we stay outside the zone of the ego when we explore things during observation with schizophrenics. You can ask about the person—the object-oriented 1 zone, like, do they like peas. But not about a feeling."

Then he circled his finger around and around the larger circle, expanding his circles outward. "Ask about things out here, outside the zone of the ego," he said, "this is the 'object-oriented 2' zone—completely outside the person—it's even more neutral."

The following week, I flubbed it. I said to Anita, "Sorry I asked about your best friends at the halfway house, Anita." Within half a second, she was gone. I realized I didn't need to make apologies. That was addressing feelings—hers and mine. It was too ego-oriented.

More and more, I began to understand what the "zone of the ego" was and to figure out what topics of conversation would make Anita stay or walk away.

I started to get to know her—not that I knew much more about her really—but to sense what made her comfortable. If a question was too close to the ego—either too emotional and personal or, on the opposite spectrum, too neutral or distant—she would leave. If I betrayed awkwardness or discomfort, she was gone.

Being with Anita was almost like trying to hold an umbrella in the wind, trying to find the right angle and height to hold it at so that it neither inverted nor collapsed. Searching for the right way to hold the umbrella of comfort with Anita, I had only the use of my emotions as a gauge. My own emotions—of calmness or of tension—became powerful barometers, guiding me as to what would be good or not good to say or to ask so that the observation would go smoothly.

Once I had dealt with what I was afraid of and had taken care of my own discomfort,[3] I could use my emotions to sense what would help us to keep talking. Slowly, through my feelings, I was learning who Anita was. And of course, she continued to get up and leave if something I said didn't feel right, guiding me as to what she could and could not tolerate.

Soon we started talking about food, patients, the nurses, the furniture. One day she told me about a sister who she thought was still alive. And then one day, she asked me, "Do you have a boyfriend?"

"No," I answered, uncomfortably, because I'd been worrying about this very question. That was a pretty *ego-oriented question*. I noticed that it made me want to walk away.

Finding Anita

The more closely I observed Anita, the more I learned that my negative feelings could actually assist me with my observations, instead of just providing the backdrop of unpleasantness that I had just accepted as part and parcel of having to sit in Ward B.

The freer I became to acknowledge my feelings toward Anita, the more I was able to observe not only what she did and how she acted, but also what she might be feeling and experiencing. It was almost like studying something invisible between us instead of just seeing her concrete form, or my own being.

I realized, in studying my own feelings of repugnance, that the repugnance was at the essence of Anita. I started to observe how often and how strongly I had the feelings. I grew to understand, through my feelings, how accustomed Anita must have become to feelings of having been neglected, unwanted, abandoned and abused. Perhaps I could use all the feelings I was finally courageous enough to admit into my consciousness and get comfortable with. I just had to reinterpret them so that they would inform me about the case, so that the dread and repugnance that had originally led me to turn away from Anita could become informative.

Wanting to shut out my feelings of repugnance—of disgust, horror, boredom and judgment—had shut my heart and mind to Anita. Once I could admit to and explore my emotions, understand which ones came from me and which ones came from her, I could regard them as information. I was learning how to use and understand emotion. I could decide what I wanted to do and learn from what I was feeling.

To get more information about Anita, I started to talk to the hospital staff not only about the history recorded in her chart, but about the gossip they'd heard about her. Her off-the-record history was heartbreaking. Not only had Anita been neglected and abused since early childhood, but also some of the younger patients had raped her more than once. She had been beaten several times, and two infections had gone unrecognized until she was on the brink of death.

My feelings, once I was willing to observe them in a new way, became my friends, avenues to better places. Anita stopped feeling like such a freak to me. And at the same time, I became more accepting of those unwanted parts of myself; I stopped being so afraid of feeling like a freak.

Graduation

Six months passed, and one day Anita announced, "We're going to the cantina today." The cantina was a canteen in the inner sanctum of the hospital, where only the patients with special dispensations went, and it was completely unsupervised by any office personnel. We were released from the locked ward, and I walked behind Anita through a seemingly endless maze of abandoned hallways and corridors, down into the bowels of the building until we finally reached the unlocked, windowless canteen. We sat there, silently, along with maybe fifteen other patients.

Nobody spoke at the cantina. Some people rocked, some smoked. I surrendered to the world of the surreal as my thoughts whirled uselessly around me. Anita ate potato chips and looked at me, contented. "Want one?" she asked in her loud voice, smiling her toothless grin. I didn't want one, but she didn't mind. We were best friends, after all. And then our session—a full hour and a half—was up.

The next week, when I got to the hospital, she was gone. I learned that a room had finally opened up for her at a halfway house that she had been waiting a few months to get into, because she'd gotten better. That trip to the canteen had been my farewell graduation party.

Here is something important that I learned in working with Anita, which has served me well whenever I have found myself at an emotional dead-end, confused or humiliated, filled with dread perhaps, or overcome by negative forces more painful than I thought I could bear: there is a way to get beyond mere awareness.

I learned through Anita how to follow even the most seemingly irrelevant threads of emotion by getting curious about them. If in times of confusion you can do that, and search to understand yourself or someone else more deeply—using as many people as you can to help you—then you may also graduate as I finally did, with honors from my fieldwork placement, to the next phase of your life.

LISTENING TO THEORIES OF TECHNIQUE: FOLLOWING THE CONTACT

In 'Searching for Anita,' you are on the ground level of psychoanalytic training, with a student analyst in search of herself. I remember the first two years of that clinical internship well—the dread, revulsion and fear that churned within me every time the deadbolt locked behind me after I entered the ward. Once, I even had a fender bender on the way to the mental hospital to see Anita. I felt so unbelievably distracted and detached.

It was only after I was able to process and accept my feelings that I could begin to observe Anita in an engaged and positive way. Before that time, my observations had been perfunctory as I objectified Anita and stalked her from afar. Connecting to our own feelings as analysts is a fundamental requirement for successfully treating patients. Without the intentional use of our own sensations, thoughts and emotions to inform and guide the treatment, we cannot know how to keep patients in the room long enough for them to get better.

Anita really had it right when she asked me if I was there to be her best friend. I was. If you hold in your mind the image of a best friend, you think of someone who is fully attuned to you, who you are thoroughly comfortable with, and who may even be a mirror for your soul. This is what patients require emotionally of their analysts if they are going to allow them access to their most private and unwanted thoughts and feelings with the ultimate goal of discovering their own unconscious: a soul-to-soul connection. It is imperative that the analyst knows herself well enough to enable that connection to unfold.

Achieving this kind of connection with our patients requires '*following the contact.*' To follow the contact, we work hard to bring into the treatment questions, thoughts, ideas and an attitude that respond to a need in the patient. Some patients may need more stimulation in the form of questions, *interpretations* or observations. Other patients may respond better to lowered stimulation, including silence or *object-oriented questions*. In this story, Anita was uncomfortable with ego-oriented questions which felt too invasive. Schizophrenics usually do not have an "I" as a reference point, so they cannot manage lines of questioning that assume an *ego* is operating. Any questions about friends, thoughts or feelings, therefore, would make her walk away. Instead, Anita needed to sit next to me in companionable silence, and to talk about food, places and any impressions that were happening outside the self.

The mandate to ask patients three object-oriented questions is every beginning student's introduction to doing treatment. It arms the student with a way of observing patients that is minimally invasive to the patient, as well as minimally stimulating for the student, while facilitating an initial connection. Ultimately, however, once the student analyst learns how to follow the contact, a connection can be made with a new patient in any number of ways. Some new patients may activate the analyst to more verbal activity through their silences, eye contact or questions. Other new patients may seem to need little if any stimulation: they may talk incessantly or seem either very agitated or extremely relaxed, inducing in the analyst a calm or non-imposing response.

The analyst's attitude while conducting treatment has historically been conceptualized as one of adopting a neutral stance. A neutral attitude, however, could backfire if misconstrued by a patient as a sign of disinterest or even that they are being judged. Therefore, I prefer to think of the twenty-first-century analytic attitude as one of '*analytic transparency.*' The concept of transparency better conveys, to my mind, the need for the analyst to be in the room with the patient only as a vehicle for the patient to connect back to herself.

When we follow the patient's contact, even if we appear emotional, personal and engaged, we achieve transparency. We are focused on how to stay at the patient's level, emotionally, cognitively, intellectually and stylistically. We hover in the room with evenly flowing attention, registering every nuance of the patient's presence, so as to become as attuned as possible to how they think and what they need from us to be comfortable and keep talking. It may be that we register the experience of the patient by how they relate to us—whether they look us in the eye or avoid our gaze. Perhaps we use impressions that don't even seem relevant to what is happening in the moment—an analyst may become suddenly hungry or get a headache or experience some other bodily sensation. At other times, the analyst may register an impulse to become very active and start giving lots of advice or weaving a narrative, acts which might reflect the patient's own difficulty with feelings in the room.

With Anita, I experienced an enormous measure of repugnance and dread. The first thing I had to do, to keep her sitting next to me for more than a few minutes, was to overcome my resistance to experiencing that dread. Interestingly, my supervisor never brought my resistance to my attention. I was never warned that I was probably going to fail my oral presentation, or that I was working with Anita in an evasive or shallow way. Only when I was sufficiently motivated and prepared to explore my feelings did my supervisor help me to talk about them. He too was following my contact, as I was learning to follow Anita's.

By the time I became interested in exploring my dread, I had developed an excellent relationship with this supervisor: I trusted him. He not only understood my feelings and complimented me for having them, but he also gave me hope that they would help me understand the dynamics of the case. In fact, Anita had suffered a lifetime of abuse and neglect, life circumstances which explained her descent into madness and her need to escape reality. Her dread of a potentially toxic connection was understandable, as was my dread of having to be with her, which may have been induced. In short, I was having the right feelings, which ultimately could inform my understanding of the case.

Psychoanalysis is first and foremost a method of research into the psyche, and learning how to follow the contact is what makes that research possible. When we can follow the patient and go with the flow of their mind—rather than work to redirect, correct or otherwise change it—we make it possible for their mind to gradually unfold. Then, we are able to study how their energies and thought processes are organized at the deepest possible level. In a sense, the analyst is like an espionage spy who must retain their anonymity at all costs so they can enter as deeply as possible into the system they are trying to uncover. By following the contact, we are guided by our patients as to how to interact with them.

Let's say, for example, that we have three patients, all of whom have the same presenting problem: losing their temper with their child. One patient may explain the problem and tell you that their own mother yelled a lot and they don't know why. Their open curiosity invites hypothesis formation, and together you embark on a "What could it be?" journey of exploration. This would indicate that the tensions in the room are minimal. The problem may even be solved in a few sessions if the patient realizes that losing her temper has roots in a lack of learned organizational systems or if she can learn to ask for help from another adult. This patient has sufficient cognitive ability available to apply their mind to the problem. Very little mental preparation is required to help this patient understand the unconscious workings of the mind and for her to become more mindful and effective as a parent.

The second patient, however, may describe the same problem in a completely different way. She may avert her eyes and reveal a tremendous amount of shame about how often she yells at her child. She can hardly talk about it. This patient is not ready or interested in problem solving. She may really be talking about a much deeper problem: shame. In this case, you would not jump to exploring hypotheses or problem solving. Instead, you would have to spend more time preparing the patient's mind for self-discovery by asking non-invasive, object-oriented questions about the children, the marital relationship and other less tension-producing topics so that you could build a comfortable relationship. Sufficient ego strength would have to be built before the patient could talk openly about her relationship to shame.

More challenging still might be the third patient, who may not even be aware that his yelling is abusive. He may weave a narrative for you that makes it clear that he feels like a victim of circumstance: that other people are acting badly and that he can't get them to stop. This level of distortion and denial would indicate that this patient is unable to entertain another person's perspective. The lack of compassion results from his being unable to access large quantities of thoughts and feelings. It could take years of treatment before that patient could locate blocked off emotions within themselves and make it possible for him to connect compassionately towards anybody else.

Following the contact makes it possible to know what your patients can or can't yet tolerate talking about, and how to intervene with each of them in a way that ensures the most comfortable experience for them, so that they can continue experiencing the sessions positively and continue the conversations and the analytic work. By integrating emotional impressions, assessing the tension levels in the room and by employing a certain level of intuition, the analyst becomes more and more comfortable in following the patient's contact and thereby entering more and more deeply into the patient's thought systems so that they can best be analyzed. This course of action creates a therapeutic environment optimally suited to self-discovery.

When we follow the contact, we also convey respect for our patient's defenses. For the third patient in the examples above, following the contact would have meant *joining* his feelings that he is a victim, while helping him to stay calm. Defenses serve an important purpose in keeping our patients' minds organized, and thereby preventing too many disturbing thoughts and feelings from entering prematurely into consciousness, where they could be overwhelming. Even though defenses may often appear inefficient, impractical and unreasonable, we have to respect the role they play in maintaining psychic equilibrium. Anita had to conjure a fantasy that we were best friends in order for her to sit with me. Without the function of that fantasy, she could not tolerate being near me.

Therefore, we always work to preserve the patient's methods of emotional insulation—their defenses, including delusions, *projections* and psychological distortions—as we follow their contact. This is also why we no longer use interpretation to remove, lift or break through defenses, since we understand their intrinsic role in preserving mental organization.

Patients need to have a lot of analysis to replace defenses, either with an ability to tolerate feelings or with a genuine desire to engage in real, connected relationships with people. Until emotional tolerance and a desire for emotional connection are built, the important role of defenses in maintaining mental organization cannot be overestimated.

Our respect for defense structures means that we no longer, as analysts, push beginning patients (or students) towards understanding. We never try to convince them of a reality that they may not yet be ready for, or to explain their unconscious to them. The use of interpretation in psychoanalysis has been radically limited to finite moments in treatment when the patient not only has learned to express and tolerate a lot of feelings, and therefore has sufficient ego strength to know themselves, but also to when the analytic relationship itself is so stable, and so much trust has been established, that the analyst has earned enough influence to make possible the patient's willingness to see outside the compelling power of their own repetitive narrative, and they can entertain the possibility of seeing things in a new way that reveals their own unconscious. Later stories in subsequent chapters will provide illustrations of how this happens.

During the initial stages of treatment however, we simply prepare our patient's minds for analysis. To prepare the mind, a soul-to-soul connection with our patients must be developed, by following our patient's contact long enough for them to stay in the room with us and keep talking.

Anita was certainly right in ascertaining that I was there to become her "best friend." Since I had not been mandated to do therapy around her or engage with any of the other activities behavioral therapists usually worked on with her—such as smoking, eating, making art—Anita understood intuitively that I was there to develop a different kind of connection with her.

If we can achieve 'best friend' status with our patients by learning how to create an environment which places no demands on them and that can tolerate their gradual unfolding, they learn that they are in the room with someone who can be totally attuned, comfortable and easy to be with. In this type of emotional environment, patients can become relaxed and feel safe enough to venture into conversations that are new. At that point, we see shifts in conversation as new ideas and feelings that previously had to be repressed begin to dawn on a new consciousness.

Failure, unfortunately, is truly one of our best means of learning what a patient needs to stay in the room with us. It is what alerts us to what is happening with our own emotional radar, and it is what teaches us best how to use our radar as far as what can and can't be talked about. When a patient leaves treatment, like when Anita got up and walked away from the chair next to me over and over again, it is because we fail to create an environment they can tolerate. These failures make it possible for us to study the interventions we made as well as our own states of mind and levels of discomfort. Failures can motivate us to open up to emotions we may have been blocking. Once we open ourselves up to those thoughts and feelings, we can invite the patient to stay with us and hold that space comfortably.

Your own analysis is ostensibly the most important component in becoming an analyst, and the best place to start analytic training. Treatment failures subsequently attune you further to the nature of your own emotions. You learn which emotions may stem from your own unresolved issues, and how they inevitably get projected onto your environment as you study why a narrative you put forth might not resonate with your patient. You learn which emotions, even when they stem from your patients and get induced in you, are tolerable or intolerable for you. You learn which emotions are most challenging for you, and which ones are most difficult for your patients. The more familiar you become with sensing and processing these emotions, the better your chances of staying in the room with an ever-widening range of patients and finding words to say to them that will ensure continued collaboration. The more experience you gain in the playground of emotion, the greater the likelihood that you will arrive at that magical place every psychoanalyst dreams of where something is spoken which has not yet been said; where an emotional experience is had that has never been had before; where the unconscious can be revealed and energies that have been blocked are finally set free.

There is perhaps nothing harder than learning how to resonate with a person who is suffering from psychosis or, for that matter, from any level of emotional disturbance that results in distortions of reality or pervasive negativity. It can be upsetting, painful and even thoroughly disturbing sometimes. But the disorientation, the disconcerting absence of reality-based thinking, and the unforgiving requirement that you surrender yourself completely to the world of sensation are all truly what prepare you to be in the room with a wide range of disturbances, and to stay the course with patients no matter how mentally disorganized or regressed they will become. As soon as you can do this, the chances for a successful analysis become instantly improved and you will be on your way to a very exciting research adventure.

What is particularly exciting about psychoanalytic treatment is that each one of your patients will set you on the course of a unique adventure since no two people are alike. Every time a new patient walks into your office, you are faced with uncertainty, confusion and an ever-changing landscape of disturbance. The one constant you can expect and enjoy is having a cogent method to guide you. The method of following the contact and adopting a stance of analytic transparency sets you on the right course of research adventure with every new patient. The better you become at being with each patient in the right way, the greater the chances you will be able to conduct your scientific investigations and eventually help that patient arrive at self-discovery.

I believe that our 'friendship' is what brought Anita to a new level of consciousness. When patients are moved to halfway houses after having lived in a ward for chronically ill people for so many years, it is because they are deemed capable of interacting with others well enough to make it in the outside world. I don't believe it was any coincidence that Anita's life took such a positive turn on the heels of our deepening relationship, culminating in what was essentially our goodbye party in the bowels of the building. I had searched for over three years for how to be with Anita. But it was only after I had found myself that it was possible for us to finally become best friends.

Notes

1 Neutral questions are also known as 'object-oriented questions.'
2 When we fail to resonate or emotionally understand a patient, it is known as a 'countertransference resistance.'
3 My own feelings with regard to Anita are known as 'subjective countertransference.'

4 The unseen side of Angela

Two Italians in a pod

Angela sat straight and tall. She had a mistrustful and distracted air about her that seemed to convey: 'I don't really care who you are, what you think, or what you're going to say to me.' She looked tough, but at the same time, vulnerable. When she did catch my eye, there was something very solemn and piercing in her look.

Dressed plainly in loose grey slacks and a black sweater, Angela had a sexless quality about her. She was neither masculine nor feminine, just nondescript, and looked to be in her mid-thirties. "What brings you here?" I asked.

"Well, I have to tell you from the start that I don't really *need* therapy in the sense that there is anything really *wrong* with me," she explained. I would learn later that in fact she had been in therapy twice before.

"I'm not in any crisis or anything like that—I'm not a sick person or anything—there's no mental illness or even any real problem. My sister suggested I do this. What I was hoping for was more like support dealing with some people around me...that make things very difficult for me."

She looked at me to see if I was going to buy her story. I nodded. "I'm by myself now," Angela continued. "My parents have passed and my sister lives far away. She's the one who said I should go to therapy, like I said, but she thinks it's because our mom died. I'm at peace with that, always have been. Now my dad's gone too and...I don't know, it seems like I probably *should* need therapy. So anyway, I thought—why the heck not. Things aren't that easy for me anyways and...I don't know...I have nothing to lose, right?" And she laughed at this although the laugh held no levity. It was a way of telling me without self-pity that, literally, she had nothing to lose. Angela said she had little to her name—no spouse, no children, no home, no pets. No, wait, she did have two girlfriends and an old red car. But from the way she put it, these were not riches.

"Who is making things difficult for you?" I asked at a pause in the conversation. By the way, I rarely ask new people about themselves directly. I prefer to ask them about the other people in their lives.[1] Especially with Angela, I did not sense that she particularly liked to talk about herself. It's always easier for people to talk about the people around them.

"I'm going to tell you honestly," Angela replied. "I know you have won some awards for your work, and you went to Harvard and such—you look like the kind of person who would have high standards. And I personally am one of these people, such as yourself, with very high standards—maybe too high. The problem is, doctor, that I am living with people around me that are just so…such…*idiots*. You know?" I nodded approval.

But secretly I was thinking, "Oh, boy. High standards? Me?" My writing awards were lucky by-products of massive procrastinations; I was avoiding growing my practice after my kids were in school. It never ceases to amaze me how people sculpt each other, so often inaccurately. You can never know how people are going to see and experience you—it's bewildering sometimes.[2]

I had an impulse to say to Angela, "Oh, those awards were not a very big deal," so she could see that I don't particularly like to think of myself as a person of extreme excellence, looking down upon a sea of lesser beings. I started shifting in my seat uncomfortably. But I was there to *follow* Angela's impression that I was an ambitious high-achiever, not to *correct* her.[3] Why was I so uncomfortable with the persona she was sculpting?[4]

I sat in my chair toying with the idea of being an intimidating award-winning doctor with high standards of normalcy who could function the way Angela would want me to. It would actually be really great. At that time, early in my career, I often fantasized about being considered a respected authority, someone who could hold up an excellent standard of normalcy with a concrete path for people to follow like many successful self-help gurus. But how could you ever become such an authority when your only standard for anything was to search for unseen dynamics? This was the problem with psychoanalysis.

"I am curious about those earrings, Dr. Luiz," Angela interrupted my reverie. "They remind me of earrings my Italian grandmother used to wear."

"Oh, really?" I said, feeling my ear to remember what I'd worn and finding the ones with pearls with little diamonds over them. She was wearing small gold hoops with a little diamond. They looked similar.[5]

"You're Italian, right? With a name like Claudia?" I laughed because this was just so perfect—my having actually been born in Rome because my parents were stationed there when they were still going on tour as musicians. Her fantasy and my reality had meshed in a way that added even more flavor to the persona she needed me to be. I smiled.

"I knew it," she said, looking satisfied with herself because she was really feeling glad that she had found what she'd been looking for: someone cut from the same cloth as she with extremely high standards.

"You are very smart to have your own business," Angela continued. "You know, after my mother died, even though I was only five, I had to take care of my father when he was dying. I didn't get the benefits of a good education. I barely made it. Otherwise, I would have done what you did—go to Harvard."

"Instead," Angela explained, "I learned how to type so I could work secretarial jobs, and that's how I got to be office manager, over the years, learning a little bit about everything—finances, phones, catering, human resources, you name it. I always get work with these small startup companies where I get to do everything. They would be dead without me. But the problem is—I am sure you can appreciate this—I am surrounded by such ridiculous people, totally incompetent, oh, my God."

"Oh, dear," I said, as if I knew exactly what it felt like to experience other people as idiots. This was going to be a whole new ride for me. This woman did not judge herself at all; she only judged what would appear to have been every other person in her life, minus, at least for the time being, me.

The universe of idiots

There were a large variety of idiots in Angela's world, as I was to learn over the course of the next few years. There were incompetent idiots, who fumbled and stole office supplies. There were leadership idiots who had the wrong vision for the company and squandered money. There were relationship idiots who could not get out of bad relationships or were screwing up their kids. There were idiots in her building, on the streets, in the office, in her family, here in the United States and certainly abroad. If her father, after whom she modeled herself, had not been cremated, he would be turning over in his grave.

Angela's righteous indignation was absolute. I had never met anyone who could be so completely free of self-doubt, so completely certain of her own moral, ethical and personal values and opinions. Most interesting about Angela's assessment of her difficulties with the general incompetence of the universe is that she understood cognitively that her standards were "probably" too high, as two other therapists before me had tried to explain to her.

One of her past therapists had been very aggressive about it. This therapist apparently did not understand, as Angela did, that if a person acted like an idiot, it was not worth knowing them. And the other therapists did not understand, as Angela did, that Angela's father had given her his high standards, and he should be respected. Angela had had a very good relationship with her father. She honored his memory; he had raised her. Her mother had died young, when Angela was only five.[6] And there was nothing much more to say about that apparently. But they came first. Not some stupid therapist's opinion.

The experiences with the prior therapists gave me a clue as to what had not worked for Angela: *interpretations* and insight. She had felt so misunderstood. She didn't need "fixing" as far as I could tell. I would just wait and see what she might need from me, if anything. For now, it was simply support from someone like her: excellent, strong and Italian. Viva Italia!

And thus our therapy continued, with Angela on the couch providing me with weekly diatribes on the general incompetence of humanity at large, in honor of her father and the memory she would keep of him always, until the day, it would seem, that she would die. She knew exactly who she was and exactly what she needed: a better set of friends, more people around her who had a better work ethic and a new car. She was wrong on all counts, however. What she really needed, we would discover, was entirely different.

Pockets of indignation

Things were going along smoothly. Angela and I were both enjoying my getting to know the full spectrum of her indignation. I was comfortable not saying much; there was little need to—I felt like the completely right fit for Angela so she was comfortable just talking. Things were not easy for her; she felt very alone, and sometimes, I think, she liked to come in and talk just to hear the sound of her own voice since she had no one else to talk to. And her own voice was company enough for her as far as I could tell.

Angela's consternation with the world was pervasive. She would find even small things to get upset about, like: "Why do people not wear deodorant and then raise their arms on a crowded bus?" This upset her a lot.

I regarded Angela's "incompetence" observations in this way: they were neat little pockets she could stash all her negativity into. Her "standards" helped her to identify and zero in on distinct pockets of incompetence and stupidity that she could then vent about. After she had dumped her negativity into one of those "pockets," she felt better. While the vents provided her with relief and organized her disturbance, they prevented her from having relationships.

Instead, Angela was fueled by little judgment radars that were seeking incompetence in the world, as if she woke up each morning telling herself, "Let's see what I can find to get indignant about today." Then, she'd find a pocket, and enjoy experiencing all that negativity *outside herself*. Without those perceived frustrations, and with no way to vent, she would probably have experienced complete mental chaos: rampant internal agitation—steam in a kettle with no escape valve.

I understood, over time, why she had fired the previous therapists who had suggested that she lower her standards. She needed those standards, however negative or faulty they might have been. They provided structure. They kept her mentally organized because they provided a target for her frustrations, and a justification for venting them, so she didn't have to carry all that pain inside.[7]

I respected Angela's standards, just as I respect every patient who comes to me with a painful story, painful feelings, frustrations, memories or worries. Angela's perception of an inadequate, frustrating world safeguarded her sanity. It filled her with the only sense of well-being that she had ever known, preserving the memory of a loving father who, she believed, had he still been alive, she could have had a relationship with.

We all need structure for our energies. The stories that we have about our lives provide that structure, and we can't always talk ourselves out of the negative ways we view the world. A 'positive attitude' can create a lot of despair and mental pain and suffering if your negativity has not yet found a proper home. No, you cannot and should not always talk yourself out of feeling negative. In Angela's case, being negative was very positive in helping her to feel mentally organized and, thus, preserve her sanity.

So this is why I stayed with Angela quietly and patiently, without trying to "fix" anything, through her never-ending diatribes on the general ineffectiveness of humanity at large, and why I never tried to help her see things in a different way. I had hope—hope that I also hope to generate in you—that sticking closely with the patient's way of thinking will help prepare their mind for self-discovery.

Impatience

One day, somewhat unexpectedly, Angela's complaints started to wear on me. She came in to the office in a particularly agitated state, very upset with a man in her office. He had been on paternity leave for two weeks already. His wife, who had apparently suffered some complications from her caesarean section, needed him at home for another week.

Angela was disgusted. "Why should the office have to pay the toll for this man and his wife's decision to have a baby?" she said. "It was *his* choice to have the child, not anybody else's. Therefore, *he* should take responsibility for it," she insisted, poking my couch viciously.

Angela, in her role as office manager, had adamantly denied this new father, who was "obviously" trying to take advantage of her, more time off. But then her boss had overruled her and given the man an extra week of paternity. Angela was outraged. *Outraged*! This was a terrible mistake. Now everybody in the office was going to start making excuses for why they should take more time off. They would all try to overrule her. Her life was going to be a living hell from now on.[8]

Angela went down the list of who was now going to take advantage of what, and how she would end up doing more work because everybody knew that she had no life; that she would always be there to pick up the pieces and help out everybody who had a life.

Angela was once again the victim of her need to feel superior. But she had finally picked a topic I could not agree with her on. I remembered that I had been terrified to be alone with my first newborn baby after my husband's slim two weeks of paternity leave at home. Those fourteen days had passed by faster than a blink. Lord, if I'd been Angela, I would have given that poor father *three years* of paternity leave.

I had reached the point where I wanted Angela to chill out; the tension, and her anger, was starting to get old. I wanted to say: "Listen, Angela, what else is new? So what? Aren't you getting tired of the indignation? Just tell your boss to delegate to someone else. Don't you see how you design more torment for yourself?"[9]

"Well," I said gingerly, "should you tell your boss that you're going to need to hire a temp for a few weeks?"

"Come on," she scoffed. "Get real. Like that's ever going to happen. I did joke with my boss, 'OK, well, guess I'm going to get take-out again for a few late nights at work.' But you know what he said? Nothing. No, wait. He said, 'Well just don't order from Lombardo's.' Why not? Why shouldn't I order from Lombardo's? Because the entrees are $20? I'm not worth $20?"

There was no helping Angela to see how she designed her own sorry destiny; to her, there was no way to make things better. I felt like arguing with her, but it's not my job to get trapped by my own ethics and restlessness and biases and frustrations the same way she was. Besides, even if I did act on my frustration and start telling her what I thought (like "speak up for yourself! Order from Lombardo's! Hire a temp!"), she would probably fire me out of indignation just as she had the other ignorant therapists.

Now we were both stuck in the torment of an unfair, frustrating world. I had gone beyond understanding and respecting Angela's character; now I could feel what she felt. I had fully entered into her emotional universe. It was a very frustrating place. It made you want to scream. When I get to the point where I really feel what my patients feel, I start to white-knuckle my recliner. It isn't pretty. This is where the job gets hard.

Before long, the hour was over, but something had changed. I was having a hard time tolerating all this frustration. Whenever, after a few years of feeling agreeable, you grow restless, it always means something is about to change.

Restlessness

My impatience with the frustrated feelings Angela kept bringing into the room gradually intensified to a measure of dread that I would start to experience the morning of the day that Angela was due to come in for her session. It was like wearing a pair of shoes that was too tight. I started wondering just how long I would have to follow her around in her little toxic, angry universe, where people were just trying to cheat the system and manipulate things to their own advantage, and where, come hell or high water, the grand martyr of Angela had to toil to set things right. How long would we have to continue to believe that the world was such a twisted, unfair place? I started to sigh more, to say things like, "I know, people are…something else."

One particularly hot day, my little window air-conditioner was acting up. As soon as the temperature rose, it would fire up with a loud groaning, moaning buzz. And then, after the room had cooled a bit, it would shut down with a lurch. An awkward silence would then ensue, as if a loud person had just left the room, creating an unwanted intimacy.

As I kept adjusting the air conditioner to avoid the lurch, I started feeling cranky. I felt supremely annoyed with John, my husband, for not fixing this problem, thinking, "Why can't he help me more?" and plotting the changes I was going to make to the marriage. I was completely in sync with Angela because, at that very moment, she fired me.

"I've decided to quit therapy for a while," she said. The switches were getting crossed in my mind as I made my way back to reality—was she also mad at John about the air conditioner?

"What?" I said, "Why? Why now?" After all, she had not really improved or changed in any way. Were we anywhere near termination?

"Well," Angela explained, "I don't really think I've improved or changed in any way. I think it's time for termination. It just feels like the same-old, same-old. I mean, how long do we keep going with this? It's not that I don't like being with you—I do. We agree on a lot of stuff, but to tell you the truth, I think I'm good now. I don't see what else we can do."

"Aren't the people around you still difficult?" I responded weakly.

"Yeah," Angela replied, begrudging me the point. "But is that going to change? I mean, so what? I don't know if I really need therapy for this. It's not going to change. Nothing is ever going to change, so what's the point? I don't really have friends or anything. I still don't have anybody to really have lunch with. And the new car has turned out to be more expensive than I thought so...I don't know. I'd like to come visit you. Maybe we could have cappuccino or something sometime."

I was trying to get a grip on this incredible shift in the treatment and was at a loss for words. Angela was quiet too, for a long time, until I finally asked, "Why have you stopped talking?"

"I don't know what more to talk about," she answered. "I don't see where it's getting me. I've been coming here for over four years now, and all I do is talk. I still feel the same way. Nothing in my life has changed."

It's always upsetting when a patient wants to quit before you think that you are done. I used to find it devastating when I first started doing treatment. Especially when I was a student, when each and every patient was a precious commodity for research, a requirement for graduation.

"It's just resistance to treatment," my supervisor had explained when one of my best patients started threatening to leave. "The best things in treatment often happen in light of resistance," she added.

"When you hit a resistance you're at the epicenter of a core problem or intrapsychic conflict," she taught. "Everything that's hidden and intolerable will show up in the resistance," she had said. So I had known for a long time that if you can work with resistance and resolve it, that is almost always where you will see *therapeutic action*. Every time you encounter a resistance, you encounter this gleaming, golden opportunity for self-discovery.

One thing was for sure: a new negative path had certainly become revealed here with Angela. I had to explore what she was thinking, to go down this new path and investigate everything on it. What was happening here?

Certainly, Angela had never spoken to me this way before. This alone was a powerful change; her dissatisfaction with the world had finally landed on *me*. Now that what usually happened in her life was happening between us, I could respond to her frustrations in a new way. I had to get her to keep talking in order to see—now that her negative energies were directed toward me—if I could do something with them to help prepare her mind for self-discovery. Everything that was bothering me fell away—the air conditioner, John, the heat, my frustration: I was riveted.[10]

The extension

I said, blaming myself so as not to threaten Angela in any way, "I haven't helped you enough to change, have I?"

"What?" she said, sounding surprised. "Well, I guess that's true, but then again, there was nothing to change, I guess. I guess I thought things would get better. Why? Did you think you could help me?"

"I don't really know," I responded. "I have to think about that more. Did you have any ideas about it?"

She had a ready answer for this, which she delivered after an almost imperceptible snort, "Well, you don't really say much, do you? You don't really do anything."

"What should I have done differently that might have helped you more?" I asked.

"I don't know. Sometimes I wonder if you're not just collecting a paycheck while you relax and enjoy yourself back there. What are you doing back there? Making out your shopping list?"[11]

I swear I almost snorted too, thinking, "Lord Almighty, I have been sitting with you for almost four years, fighting the universal laws of attraction not to be brought down by your negativity. Pleeeeease don't tell me I haven't done much. I HAVE NEVER NEGATED YOU! I have stayed by your side traveling for years through these horrible negative wastelands with you! Following you around, joining you in your bleak and angry little world, agreeing to be the haughty and exacting Italian you have always wanted me to be, only to arrive at this moment—the moment we can finally get some work done—when all you want to do is get rid of me? I haven't helped you? You should have paid me TRIPLE just for staying in the room with you." I noted my indignance and didn't say any of this, of course. I thought to myself, "Stay the course. Do your job. Follow her thinking." The feelings I was having, in essence, were just more information as to the emotional dynamics of the case.

She interrupted my thoughts. "Sorry, did I offend you? Or am I right?"

"I haven't been doing enough?"

"I just think I need to stop coming," Angela reiterated, pulling away from the conversation, as if my inability to disconfirm her "shopping list" idea was proof enough to her that that is what I had been doing during our time together.

"But why now?" I repeated since, after all, we were only just getting started.

"I just told you," she said, getting more impatient. "It. Is. Not. Helping."

"But you haven't even told me yet what would help you," I argued. This really made her mad.

"OK, so now you want *me* to tell *you* how to help me? So is THAT what I'm paying you for?" she asked.

"Well, yes, I know you are paying me to help you, but I need a little help sometimes," I explained, "if there's something I'm not getting here."

"Um," she said after a while, sounding tense. "Are you listening? You never exactly probe into anything. Your questions don't really get to anything. You never really give me *advice*...or tell me if I should be doing something differently. I hear people in therapy have revelations, insights, they change, they get guidance. What is the point of my coming here each week and just complaining? If anything, I think it's been making things worse. You're just letting me stay in the same place."

Now, keep in mind: she had fired two therapists before me who had been very active in trying to get her out of that same negative place. Yet I was the one ostensibly keeping her in this negative place? Wow. But this is how things work in psychoanalysis. Our patients not only project their negative impressions on us, but also blame us for their own limitations. It's not unlike what happens in marriage. I was certainly a mirror for Angela now, and she was sick of her own complaining. And so, de facto, she was sick of me.[12]

"Do you think I'm too negative?" I asked her, to see if she had any thoughts about how stuck I was in this negative place.[13]

"Yes, maybe that's the problem. You always tell me that the people around me just don't get it—but what good has it done me? You've never helped me get people to do anything for me." I could see that Angela had a lot to contend with as far as *my* negativity and high standards were concerned.

"Well, I had no idea I wasn't helping you," I pointed out to Angela. She sighed deeply here, as if to say if she had all the patience in the universe, it would not be enough.

"What would you like more of?" I asked.

"Well...some advice, maybe?" she said, thinking that she knew what she wanted. Of course, she had no idea what she wanted. But remember: none of us knows what we need and want when we are under the sway of unconscious dynamics. We may think we want or need something, but that is only a thought. Actually, if we have never seen or experienced what we think and want before, it can be hard to know what, exactly, it is. All we can know is what starts to dawn as to what we don't want. That feeling can then guide us to discovering something new, just as Angela was doing with her new complaint against me.

"I'm tempted to say," Angela began, sounding a little bitter, "that if you haven't figured out yet that you are not helping me, then this is not going to work any more."

"Are you feeling hopeless?" I asked because I certainly wasn't feeling hopeless now. There was finally some emotional action in the room.

"Well, I don't know about hopeless," Angela said in an exasperated tone, clearly miffed by my interpretation. Boy, she was really seeing me as incompetent today.

"But you have to admit that my life hasn't changed much."

Except, I thought silently, that you are finally telling me what I'm doing wrong.

"Would you be willing to help me figure out how to help you?" I asked.

Angela didn't seem to like this proposition much. Don't forget, she couldn't stand inept people, which became as clear as ever with her next sentence: "SO YOU'RE TELLING ME I SHOULD PAY YOU, SO YOU CAN GET MY HELP? Listen, this is stupid. This isn't working any more," she said. And with that, she sat up and started gathering her coat and bag.

"Listen," I explained to her, gearing myself up for the sales pitch I usually give people who are feeling hopeless, to generate some hope in them about continuing with treatment when these difficult paths open up, "if you can help me figure out why this analysis isn't working, that would be very good for you."

She was still suspicious. "I don't know," she said, her voice thick with doubt.

"Have you ever had anybody in your life willing to work with you? Don't people usually try to thwart you or ignore you or abandon you?" I asked.

"Yes," she conceded.

I continued, "How about taking the couch again and giving me another five minutes?" She cooperated, thank goodness, because I find it hard to do this work face-to-face when I'm dealing with these heavy, confusing emotions.

"Listen," I explained, closing my eyes, "How many people have made you this offer, in your life, of trying to figure out what would help you? At least, I am willing. In fact, this might turn out to be a very good experience for you, helping someone to become a better person." Angela had to concede this point.

I continued with my sales pitch: "What do you have to lose? You are still unhappy. Do you have another analyst lined up out there to start all over again with? You have invested over four years here—why not take it a little farther?"

Then I threw in a little guilt: "Don't you owe it to me after all these years to give me a chance? How about another six months?"

Begrudgingly, but perhaps with a little faith restored, Angela decided to stay in treatment for another three months. Now we would start in earnest, working on my becoming less negative and more practical, more active and involved—everything she should become. Angela felt a little bit like a caged animal, restless and trapped. But getting rid of me, I knew, would never be what could free her.

The hidden story

A few weeks went by as Angela and I worked on modifying my therapy methods to be less negative and judgmental, and more helpful and active. In one particular session, Angela was talking about a very disorganized and incompetent female employee who had not returned any of Angela's e-mails. Totally exasperated, Angela had spent more than a half hour getting all the e-mails together for her boss, in preparation for a meeting. I asked her how I should help her with this problem. She said, "How am I supposed to let this not get to me?"

I agreed, "How can you? This woman is impossible. She is incompetent. How else should you expect to see this?"

She said, "I don't know," and seemed dejected. She did not yet have another way to see things. There was no new paradigm to replace her old one. We often tire of our perceptions, of our old ways of structuring our energies. But we can't yet come up with new, more satisfying ways to see things that feel real. Angela did not yet possess a means of thinking that could replace her defense of superiority and finding ineptness everywhere.

I thought about waiting to see if she could maybe come up with a new way to help me see things differently, as a way to stretch her own mind. Maybe I should have waited longer, but I'm impatient, and I didn't want her to get too frustrated with me. So after a few minutes, I decided to give her a new way of looking at things: "Maybe this woman didn't return your e-mails because she's anxious. Sometimes people get disorganized if they are anxious. Maybe we can try to understand her by learning about how anxiety works."

I began talking at some length about the relationship between anxiety and ineffectiveness in people. Angela didn't respond. "Did what I say make sense to you?" I asked. "I don't know," she said and paused for a long, long time.

Finally, she sighed and said, "I didn't hear a word that you were saying. Sometimes your voice just goes too fast and rumbles over my mind like a train, and I can't hear any of it. Your voice is like a freight train in my head sometimes—it just goes too fast and it's like…riding over my mind."

"Oh," I said slowly, "I'm talking too fast." Angela didn't respond. I had blocked her energies with my lecture, rather than helping her to explore hers. I felt inept.[14]

"What's keeping you silent?" I finally asked. I was at a total loss for how to help this woman. This was such a confusing, difficult place. I felt like I was rocking on the precipice of something without quite knowing in what direction things were going to fall.

"I don't know," Angela said, "I don't really want to tell you that I can't hear what you are saying because…then you're going to go back to saying nothing again. Which is useless. Then we're just going to be right back to where we were. Nowhere. I don't know…" and Angela turned her head to the side and stared at the wall.

Nothing I was doing was right. Being with me, for her, was like getting water from a stone. She had no idea what she needed. I had no idea what she wanted. We were both completely clueless. This work feels so messy, sometimes—so unclear.

I said, stating the obvious, "I have not found the right way to be with you yet." At this, little rivers of tears started to flow soundlessly out of the sides of Angela's face, which she brushed away immediately, with an impatient hand.

"There is nothing you could say that would be right for me. There is nothing you can do," she said. I took this to mean that Angela's dissatisfaction with me was just too hopeless. But then, she added, "It's me. I'm just…I am uncomfortable."

She said these last few words in a soft voice that did not betray the rivers of tears still flowing from her eyes. She seemed to be in a place of total clarity, having finally achieved presence and calm with what she was feeling in a way that had never been possible before. She had found the hidden story, and knew now what it was: *I am uncomfortable.*

Angela had finally experienced something new after I had said to her, "I haven't found the right way to be with you yet." My wanting to help her had sufficiently prepared my mind for the discovery that may otherwise have been far too painful to make because of how lonely Angela was, living in a world of inadequate people. Even though I was so inadequate and incompetent, and things were so hopeless and so difficult, and so frustrating, I had not given up. I had kept trying. I hadn't left her. I had insisted that we stay in the same room together and keep trying no matter what. I had been there through the worst dissatisfaction and impasse; I had not lost hope.

Pet peeves

It had been a four-and-a-half-year quest to arrive at the hidden story that Angela was uncomfortable. Now, she was free to expand her experience of the world. She was tired of the anger. She no longer needed it to define her; she could have a new feeling.

When the petty problems of the office came up, they didn't get to her in the same way any more. Now she could say new things in the face of a grievance that previously would have sent her into paroxysms of martyrdom and subsequent irritation, like: "I don't have time to worry about this stupidity," or "I'm not going to let this ruin my day."

Angela no longer had to experience the world in the same way, and could stop herself from getting too frustrated with people when she wanted to. And then, she found a way to channel her usual way of thinking to a much bigger problem: she discovered a local animal shelter that served as a refuge for abused animals who were being cared for by an entire cast of big-hearted volunteers, all of whom shared her propensity for seeing ineptness in the world. She couldn't believe how cruelly those animals had been treated, and she developed relationships for the first time with like-minded people who also enjoyed complaining about many of the same things.

And over time, Angela would become even more relaxed at the office and develop even more solid friendships with the people at the shelter who were just as outraged and in need of love as she was. She would adopt a dog, call him "Leo," which was short for Leonardo, and tell me endless stories about his capers and their mutual escapades. Angela had finally found some happiness.

This is how therapeutic action works in psychoanalysis, by helping our patients be prepared to know what is in their unconscious so they can then go on to create a better life. The fact that Angela never married, that she may have been gay, that she never went back to school or made a lot of money is inconsequential. As psychoanalysts, we are never working towards a standard of normalcy that rests somewhere outside the patient's sphere of interest or knowledge. All we are interested in is helping remove the obstacles to self-knowledge that are required to design a constructive, satisfying life. In Angela's case, it was to learn how to enjoy people, and to love an animal who had had a history of neglect.

But back to our three-month contract. At the end of the sessions, Angela said something new in the last five minutes. "We're really all alone in this life," she said. "Nobody is going to make things better for us. We have to come to terms with things ourselves."

"So true," I agreed, "life is a very, very lonely place."

But in saying it out loud, the room felt less lonely. And then the session was over.

"Well," Angela said, standing up. "See ya next week."

"You betcha," I said matter-of-factly, quickly adding, "glad to hear it." And I was.

LISTENING TO THEORIES OF THE MIND

It was such a simple, quiet statement: "I am uncomfortable." Hardly what you would consider as a grand, cathartic moment of revelation, signaling the ultimate lifting of lifelong repression and ushering into consciousness of long-forgotten memory. Nowhere in this statement did there appear to be any specific insight into the unconscious, either—no sweeping revelation that you might think would have the power to create a change in character. But in fact, all this is exactly what you saw because this is what twenty-first-century revelation often looks like: natural, quiet and completely understated. In fact, these three small words, "I am uncomfortable," each marked a moment of gargantuan change.

To understand why, exactly, such a simple statement was so profound, let me talk to you a little about psychoanalytic theory, starting with the concept of 'repression' itself. As I'm sure you are already aware, repression has always been thought of as the phenomenon of pushing down into the deep, hidden recesses of consciousness a painful memory or traumatic event—something that, it was originally believed, the analyst could brilliantly unearth and rescue from the dark shadows of repression into the light of consciousness, thereby freeing the patient from the shackles of illness. I am always surprised to learn that most people still think of repression largely in these terms, as a single event, memory or set of circumstances that has been banished from consciousness. But repression doesn't exactly work that way.

In fact, it is not only specific memories or discrete traumatic events that get repressed from consciousness, but something far more general, like an entire set of unwanted emotional impressions, such as feelings of anger. Or of being frustrated or sad or lonely. These more wide-ranging and less specified experiences may be composed of emotions, longings, wishes, impulses or fears. For the purpose of brevity, let us just call them thoughts and feelings. So repression may not necessarily occur as the result of a single traumatic event or set of circumstances, but perhaps result more often as a gradual process of prohibition against intolerable thoughts and feelings, an internal process that may even take years to fully effect.

Somewhere along the continuum of one's childhood then (if not even before, in the DNA passed down genetically), if any thought, feeling, impression or set of sensations was not experienced as safe or desirable or comfortable, it would get repressed. And then the creative process of developing defenses that could serve as effective gatekeepers to the repressed content would begin in the form of designing convenient narratives, however distorted or exaggerated or downright untrue. The more dangerous, threatening or unwanted the thoughts and feelings, the greater the need to repress them and, then, defend against them with sometimes very elaborate narratives that can really miss the truth. This is how we develop blind spots: to avoid feeling and thinking about things we can't tolerate.

Thanks to advances in our understanding of genetics and what can happen in early life, our thoughts about the concept of repression have undergone a seismic shift. We have come to recognize that since many of the problems we see in treatment may have originated in preverbal stages of development they may even predate memory. Pre-oedipal problems, as they are called, will therefore not usually carry with them explicit memories that can become vividly accessed through a process of cathartic revelation. Instead, we have implicit memories, which we "remember" emotionally through how we may re-experience them; the patterns that developed in early life can become re-experienced in the here and now via *projection* or behaviors that are puzzling. For example, we may imagine someone is out to get us because we are unable to locate, within ourselves, our own aggressive feelings. When we work psychoanalytically to unearth the hidden thoughts and feelings behind the projections or puzzling behaviors, we are therefore actually working with them in the here and now, and most particularly if and when they show up in the feelings the patient reports having for us (in the *transference*).

In this case, for example, Angela's mother had died when Angela was very young—only five. Rather than process her grief and despair at that time however, as a child Angela had probably simply tried as best she could to keep living amicably with her father and sister. Children don't always understand what is happening around them. And when they don't, they make up stories to make sense of things. Sometimes the stories are misguided; children often blame themselves for circumstances out of their control. While some children are very uninhibited about their feelings, talking easily about their perceptions, stories and feelings, others are easily deterred from expressing them, particularly in families where there is chronic or prolonged crisis. Angela's sister, who had referred her for treatment, understood that Angela had been through a lot and hadn't processed it. It was only Angela who could not connect to her early history.

The pervasive feeling Angela had that people around her were inadequate—which grew progressively and ultimately found an elaborate narrative in the form of all the "idiots" around her—was how these early repressed feelings were showing up in the here and now and in the transference. And that is exactly when and where we have to work with them psychoanalytically—in the here and now.

As an aside, you may notice that I have not devoted any single chapter entirely to the concept of diagnosis, talking about it in significant detail only in Chapter 6, where I explain how twenty-first-century psychoanalysts listen to their own feelings as a main source of information about the severity of any given patient's condition. Diagnoses like 'schizoid,' or 'bipolar' or 'clinically depressed' are useful categorization schemes, but more important is conceptualizing any illness along a continuum of how the patient is managing their thoughts and feelings. This includes first, an ever-shifting assessment of their relative ability to talk about difficult things, as measured mostly by the degree of emotional tension in the room. Second, the analyst assesses the degree to which the patient may or may not seem to experience reality according to their own internal set of truths. Ultimately, all pathologies carry with them a set of narratives which the psychoanalyst must respect and understand. I cannot emphasize this enough: for patients to get better, the patient's mind has to be sufficiently prepared for self-discovery.

Angela, for example, had repressed that she was "uncomfortable." Instead, she constantly created narratives for people's ineptness and stupidity, which explained how she felt, so she would not have to re-experience the discomfort. Behind the frustration her narratives justified, she was safe from knowing about her disturbance. What Angela unearthed, then, when she said, "I am uncomfortable," was huge. It heralded a newfound ability to connect back to and reintegrate the parts of herself that she had lost in the process of repression, and which had led to her alienation from people she chronically experienced as toxic. Once she could finally know her own feelings, and speak them out loud, she was released from the defense of anger at the world. This was, in essence, a form of awakening. This is how the unconscious becomes conscious.

Operating from within this new model of repression, where what becomes excluded from consciousness is a whole set of unwanted emotional dynamics, we can no longer reconstruct for our patients a particular story or event about themselves that they seem to be missing.[15] The patient, for the analysis to work, has to connect back emotionally to the missing experiences. When the patient is able to reclaim the lost parts of herself emotionally, by both feeling the lost experiences and discovering a new narrative for them, we become witness to the lifting of repression, or what I am calling 'self-discovery.'

In the process of reconnecting with the parts of the self that had to get repressed, the patient's choice of words is key, infused with a meaning that we may never fully understand. I can't say I really knew what "uncomfortable" felt like for Angela, or what it meant, except by my own feelings of frustration and disturbance in the room. One patient, for example, reported realizing he felt "stuffed," to describe what I would imagine would be a clogged, depressed state. While we may not know, exactly, what these words mean for the patient experientially, it doesn't matter. What matters is the patient being able to locate, within herself, something she had not talked about before, and re-experience it emotionally. Language often gets reinvented and infused with new meaning, each patient creating, ideally, their own unique poetic lexicon for their own emotional experience.

Sometimes, the analyst may certainly feel and generate meaningful words for the patient's experience even before the patient does, like, "you were trying to keep people from hating you." In these cases, if the patient can resonate with the analyst's version of what may have happened to them intrapsychically, they will experience the same feeling of revelation they might have if they had found their own words. The analyst's interpretation, at these times, comes from a place of emotional knowing. In this case, I might have said to Angela, "I can't seem to find a way to help you feel comfortable." I didn't, only because I wasn't completely sure her *ego* could manage it. Again, we use our own emotions as instruments to gauge whether or not a patient is ready to know themselves, and whether it is fitting or not to lend them our own words.

In this story, Angela found the words for her unspoken feeling state herself. Whoever finds the words for the unspoken feeling states first, however, whether it be the analyst or the patient, is not important. What matters is that the words be infused with the lost emotional experience. That makes it then possible for the patient to have available all of their thoughts and feelings. By landing upon the previously unspoken thoughts, feelings and narrative, patients are helped to finally become whole, and they are then able to design better ways to respond to life.

Now that the profundity of Angela's simple statement has hopefully been revealed, let's turn again to how we can best prepare our patients' minds for such revelation. Thinking in terms of metatheory is key for the analyst to understand what patients may need from the analysis to prepare them to connect back to the unspoken parts of themselves and start on the path toward self-discovery.

If Angela presented differently, or if she had had a different history, like for example if she had been emotionally blocked and not as vociferously angry, I might have held a *drive theory* model of the mind in my head. To that end, I would have wondered why her libidinal energy was so bound up, keeping the aggressive energies in check. I would have wondered what I could do to loosen the energies, perhaps saying something to Angela, when nothing worked, like, "No matter what I do, you just spit me out!" An *emotional communication* like that might have led her to more expression of forsaken feelings. So too could I have said something provocative like, "How could I have helped you more when you didn't want to hear from me or anybody?"

If heightening and mirroring the frustration in the room had led to unblocking some of the pent-up feelings, Angela would have experienced a shift in her drive energies, with a diminished need to waste precious libidinal energies to keep the aggressive energies in check. Facilitating these shifts in energies, with well-timed emotional communications, is perhaps the most powerful and effective means of preparing the patient's mind for self-discovery.

From the standpoint of *conflict theory*, had Angela been able to entertain even the faintest notion of how unreasonably negative she was toward people, I could have addressed the unspoken side of her conflict by asking, "What would your mind do if you didn't have so many people to enjoy hating?" This could have helped her to explore why she hung so tenaciously to her negative narratives.[16] Exploring with our patients their addiction to certain feelings that no longer serve them can help them discover their unconscious attachment to suffering. I did not think in these terms with Angela because she never showed any evidence of insight into herself, which is required for patients if we want to help them explore their unconscious motivation.

In this case, I prepared Angela's mind for self-discovery by holding in my mind an *object relations* model of the mind. Constant in my thoughts was the idea, as I struggled to find a way to help her be more comfortable with me, that she did not have a positive picture of me in her head.[17] That is, a representation of me (or anyone else) inside her head that she could count on to be comforting or helpful. In trying to help her in whatever way I could, I was pushing against the boundaries of her internal impressions and offering to see if there was any way I could be less inadequate and perhaps even less toxic for her. As we explored this possibility together, I was studying the degree to which practically anything I said was perceived as inadequate and fruitless. From this relational perspective, I held in my mind the image of a crying baby, whom I was trying as best I could to hold comfortingly.

We choose a theory of the mind to guide our treatment, and design a set of emotional communications on the basis of that theory, largely by using our own emotions when in the room with the patient. I have heard analysts talk about their patients in terms of the theory of the mind that patients conjure, like "oh, that's my Jungian patient!"

It is mostly our emotions that alert us as to what the patient can and cannot yet say. In this case, my emotions alerted me to Angela's fragility, and to the need to place the onus upon my own ego to create a relationship that would make it possible for her to get better. My own emotions alerted me to what model of the mind would be most fitting as I investigated her response to my interventions. I knew that I felt motherly and protective toward Angela. I knew she did not need more help venting and that provocation would be deleterious. I believed she would benefit from knowing that I would try to stay attuned to her no matter how much she complained about me. In a sense, the moment we meet the patient's dynamics and emotions in a session is the moment that the right model of the mind comes to us. We operate from that model not because we are wedded to it as a result of our training, but rather because the patients elicit in us a mode of operation that is best suited to preparing their mind for continued progress in speaking.

Without any operating theory of the mind, I believe it would be very difficult to feel confident delivering an emotional communication or intervention. Having a foundation of theory gives structure and purpose to our emotional communications and imbues them with a sense of purpose the patient can sense. This contributes to their feeling safe and promotes continued deep conversation.

This is also why it is so important for you, as a student, to study a wide range of theories of the mind, and to know the basic tenets of as many schools of thought as possible since Freud—*Modern Psychoanalysis*, Existential Analysis, Jungian Analysis, the Object-Relations school, Ego-Psychology and more. Different patients will elicit different theories, and your interventions can borrow from a wide range of approaches. The theories you learn will, in essence, serve as tickets to the consciousness of different patients. The more tickets you have, the more places you can go investigating the unconscious.

Of course, after this signature session, Angela did not become a completely different person. Even at her job as a volunteer at the animal shelter, she could still enjoy finding people wholly inadequate; she and her new friends enjoyed nothing more than to rant together against how badly other people treated animals. Analysis does not cure us of our preferences or our basic personality, only of their destructive potential. Now that Angela had discovered the root of her negativity, she could figure out how to enjoy it with others.

I remember the first few years that patients started exposing me to their negative transferences: canceling sessions or perhaps becoming confrontational. It would fill me with dread and insecurity. Even on that unbearably hot, humid day in the middle of summer when Angela decided it was time to find me inadequate, before I reconnoitered and realized what was happening, I felt aggravated.

I could immediately switch gears because I could remember intellectually that the moment negative feelings arise in the patient toward the analyst, the treatment potential grows exponentially. Now I feel completely riveted and excited by these moments—on full alert with all of my creative and cognitive capacities lined up and ready for action. I truly feel moved now when my patients' negative feelings toward me emerge, knowing that they are a by-product of my deep and intimate connection with them. Often such feelings are reserved only for the patient's closest immediate family members, like a mother or a spouse.

With a solid grounding in metatheory, and always with a view to using your emotions as instruments to gauge where the patient is at, you can view the moment when patients finally bring their deepest unresolved thoughts and feelings into the transference as a cause for genuine excitement. It is knowing the theories of the mind that anchors you to hope, and to continuing to invite the patient to unfold no matter what.

Notes

1 The term for asking neutral questions is 'object-oriented questions.'
2 The process by which people sculpt an image of you out of their own classification and categorization schemes is known clinically as 'projection' or, in this case, when the patient is identified with something they believe they see in you, '*projective identification.*' The phenomenon itself is known as '*transference.*'
3 The clinical term for allowing a patient to enjoy their perceptions, however inaccurate, is called 'joining.'
4 My discomfort with Angela's projection of me is what is known as a '*countertransference resistance*' because I was resisting entering into the world Angela inhabited intrapsychically.
5 When patients create an image of the analyst they can identify with or that is familiar to them, it is known as the 'narcissistic transference.' This is an optimal transference environment to do analysis because it reflects that the patient feels comfortable in a familiar emotional environment.
6 Early trauma can lead to fixation at the level of development when the trauma occurred, if basic needs cannot be met. Angela may have become fixated at latency, and not be able to progress to more mature levels of development, because of the need to repress and block off feelings. Until trauma can get worked through, energy is required to defend against the traumatic events. Once the trauma is

worked through, and energy is liberated for growth, the personality can progress to more mature levels of development, which promise greater potential for mature relationships and a more mature way of experiencing the world.

7 Angela's need to seek out inadequacy is what is known as a '*defense mechanism*' because the indignation preserved her mental organization and precluded her from having to experience painful longings, or other emotions she still needed to repress. The typical diagnosis for this particular set of defenses and alienation from other people is known of as 'schizoid personality disorder.'

8 Angela's feeling that people were always out to get her is technically known as 'paranoia.' While not flagrantly psychotic (Angela didn't fear she would be murdered), paranoia nevertheless has as its primary characteristic a generally inaccurate appraisal of negativity occurring outside the self, which is how the personality projects its own negativity to the outside world. Paranoia makes it possible for the personality to stay organized: by perceiving the locus of negativity outside the self, the paranoid person is justified in discharging negative feelings against an imagined offender.

9 My feelings of indignation against Angela here presented the second form of countertransference resistance. However, this time they may have been induced by the patient, as she herself may have been growing tired of her defense of superiority and indignation.

10 When a patient begins to feel towards the analyst the way they typically feel towards others, it is known as 'working with the transference.' At the foundation of twenty-first-century psychoanalysis is still the fundamental principle of working with transference and resistance.

11 Angela's fantasy that I was neglecting her and, instead, writing a shopping list during our session reflects the negative pictures she created about people in her own mind, which is known psychoanalytically as having a 'negative introject.'

12 Angela's transference to me at this point is known as the '*negative narcissistic transference*.' That is, she was creating an image of me as a negative person out of her own narcissism, projecting onto me her subjective belief that nobody cares about anybody in this world.

13 When we don't argue against our patient's projections, and explore them instead, we are helping them find words for unconscious, never-spoken ideas.

14 At this point, it is unclear whether my feelings of ineptness were subjective, which is to say coming from me, or objective, meaning they were induced by the patient. More important than analyzing the exact genesis of an impression, is registering it. Often its origin becomes clarified later in the treatment when the patient can corroborate having had the feeling or not.

15 Reconstructing for our patients a particular story or event about themselves that they seem to be missing is what we think of as 'interpretation.'

16 Freud put forth a fascinating idea called 'the pleasure principle,' which suggested that we are gratified by the expression of 'id' impulses, even when they don't help us to get what we want.

17 The negative picture Angela had of me in her mind is what is called the 'negative introject.' We can develop both negative and positive introjects, depending on how our own particular configuration of nature and nurture combined in our early experience of relationships.

5 Terrell and Rosalia in bed

Couples counseling

At her first session, Rosalia Cruz filled out the patient information sheet for me to bill her insurance company for sessions on her husband's plan and I noticed, reviewing the line items, that she had kept her maiden name. I said right out loud that I found that interesting. "Yeah, well," she said, "you got my number right. I'm not like most Latinas you have met. You'll see...I'm different. I'm very independent."[1]

I hardly thought that anyone with as much anxiety as Rosalia had could be truly "independent." She worked in the designer jeans section of a department store, but was having trouble dealing with the spoiled rich kids who shopped there. But what Rosalia meant by "independent" is that she had been forced to grow up fast. She had to leave home when she was just fourteen to go live with a friend because her father beat her so much when he got drunk. Unlike her siblings, she had unfortunately been born with the nerve to talk back to him.

After leaving home, Rosalia had joined a gang. But when they had almost raped her she had managed to jump out of a bathroom window and run. She was a fighter. She thought, maybe she was too much of a fighter—one time, she'd been incarcerated for assault.

Rosalia had tried therapy for anxiety before, but her previous therapist had seemed too interested in hearing about her rough life on the streets of Chicago. She told me that she wasn't there to amuse nobody. All of this anxiety wasn't fun. And besides, all that stuff had happened a long time ago. Now, she was married to a good man, trying to hold down her job and raise their daughter, who was nine.

I told Rosalia that I'd grown up as a teenager in New York City in the sixties and seventies, when it was still a dangerous place, to reassure her that there was little she could say to faze me. And then, I was careful to show no expression at all when she spoke of the atrocities of her life. I tried to mirror her own apparent lack of feeling; she didn't want to have any feeling about her past, which is probably why she had fired the previous therapist, for showing any feeling.

My faked nonchalant attitude seemed to make Rosalia comfortable enough to keep coming. It wasn't the atrocities of her external life that were troubling her: it was the feeling that whenever something happened that bothered her, she was going to jump out of her skin and punch somebody out. That would make anybody feel anxious.

About a month into her treatment, I began to see what Rosalia was doing with the feelings she wasn't letting herself have about her past. She was putting them on her daughter, Kiana, who, at nine, was becoming a little woman. Rosalia had started lecturing her on everything: how to be proud and how to be tough; how to be strong and how to talk back.

Here's how it went: every time little Kiana talked to Rosalia, either about the other kids in her class or about situations in the neighborhood, Rosalia would start freaking out and begin a diatribe on life, designed to make sure Kiana wouldn't make a wrong move and allow somebody evil to do something bad to her.

Denial about the past certainly helps us block pain in the day-to-day, but, ultimately, it also blocks having a good life. Denied feelings are like ghosts: they haunt us. That's Freud's basic theory of 'repression' from his Clark University Lectures back in 1909. Here's how the theory goes: let's say you have a stream and you put a rock in the middle of it. The water can't flow through the rock, so it will simply flow around it. Currents of energy just find another path.

So even though Rosalia had made herself numb to feelings about her childhood, the energy from those experiences still found expression through the feelings and anxiety she directed towards almost any event in her daughter Kiana's life. Energy has to flow to somewhere. And little Kiana was feeling all of that negative energy, and pulling away from her mother. The child was increasingly turning for closeness to her aunt on her father's side. This was upsetting Rosalia, who was competitive.

I told Rosalia point blank that she was being too intense with her daughter. "Why are you putting all your stuff on her?" I asked. This made Rosalia so mad that she started telling me about her life with true feeling. "If you had been through the shit that I'd been through, you'd talk that way too. How do you think I felt seeing my best friend gunned down, blood pouring out of his neck when there was nothin' I could do? Do you know how long it took for me to sleep again? I still can't sleep sometimes because of that. You think I shouldn't protect my daughter? That she should turn into a soft little spoiled brat or turn to the same shit that I turned to?" Rosalia's voice had gotten louder and louder as she spoke with feeling.

I listened as she then recounted another violent memory, this time between clenched teeth. I was glad she was finally letting me in, and revisiting something she hadn't come to terms with yet as an adult. Now that she was strong and settled, she could finally fall apart a little, which is why she was finally in therapy I imagined. I didn't want to make her too frustrated with me, but it would be better than her getting all indignant and ranting to poor Kiana. She didn't want to lose her daughter.

At the end of that difficult session, I said, "I feel like I'm finally getting to know you a little." Rosalia adjusted the little black conductor hat she liked to wear, and replied with a raspy laugh, "Yeah, well you pissed me off so much, it brought it all back."

Two years had passed since that session, and Rosalia had continued to come to therapy. She had gotten a lot better, finally coming to terms with her horrendous past and even crying about it once. Coming to terms with so much violence and abuse is arduous.

A technique called 'mental murder' had been working particularly well for Rosalia when her anxiety arose at work. With this technique, you create a mental murder when you are frustrated or angry with someone by killing them in your mind. You can use whatever creative visual method comes to you. You can create a stabbing, a gunning, a slow, secret poisoning, or just a gentle evaporation or disappearance—whatever works.

Although some people find this technique objectionable, it was working well for Rosalia who may have naturally been aggressive, because it allowed her to release the pent-up energies in her mind. When visualizing things in her mind, she punched people out, and sometimes her fantasies even became bloody. Rosalia was committing mental murders very successfully, smiling through many difficult situations, and becoming increasingly more able to deal with a wide set of challenges.

Loving-kindness meditations, perhaps counter-intuitively, do not always work in cases such as Rosalia's, where the mind is susceptible to violent images and impulses. I think it is because invoking those meditations inadvertently send a message to the brain that it is supposed to stop having violent images and impulses; to put a lid on them. A steaming kettle will, however, explode if you put a lid on it.

Accepting mental murders, on the other hand, relieves the mind, allowing aggressive energies to escape, and, ironically, creating calm. It's a way of learning to be present with destructive energies without acting on them. It is not always possible to change negative thoughts to positive ones, but that's OK; with mental murders you're simply dealing with them without fear. Eventually, the violent thoughts begin to change when, ironically, you get more comfortable with them.

Now that Rosalia had started to work through and deal more effectively with her past I was thinking that she would stop coming to treatment soon.[2] So I was quite surprised when Rosalia came in one day with a problem in her marriage. Rosalia's husband had been her ticket to a new and better life. She had managed, when she was eighteen, to get her mother to sign some papers for a program called CityYear, which was like a free boarding school/ internship program. It got her out of her neighborhood and that's where she had met Terrell, and, with him, moved to Boston.

Terrell was a nice, quiet man from a good family, and, dancing in the streets together and getting positive things done in the community, he fell in love with the charismatic Rosalia. They had gotten married shortly after finishing

CityYear, after he had finished college, and he had then gotten his master's in Library Science. He now worked as an administrator of a library consortium; he was a good, hard-working man. I hadn't heard any complaints before.

"I don't know how to say this exactly, but…he just ain't performing any more. Do you know what I mean?" I told Rosalia that I did.

"Yeah, I don't know what's going on, but he said he'd be willing to come in here with me. Seriously, I think we need sex therapy. Been wanting him to meet you anyways. We were watching Halle Berry last night—I told him, hey, Claudizzle look like her! Anybody ever tell you that? I call you Claudizzle at home. Yeah…I hope you like that name. I want him to meet you."

I laughed and told her it was all good.

I looked forward to meeting Terrell. Psychoanalysis is all about sex and aggression. We had worked on aggression a lot in this case, and now it was time for sex. It did not surprise me that Rosalia wanted to work on her marriage through physical means. I was interested to see where this would go.

Sex therapy

I was thinking about sex, wondering what would help this couple considering the wide range of sex therapy techniques available. The therapy can entail not working on 'the act' at all—no touching or even talking about sex per se, but simply talking about the relationship. You talk about what might be standing in the way of intimacy, like about what happened in the past or about current marital conflicts or future concerns. Often that kind of therapy naturally resolves barriers to having a fulfilling sex life. It's like stretching a fight out to get to make-up sex. It seemed unlikely though, knowing Rosalia, that there would be enough patience and enough self-reflection for that. There rarely is.

On the opposite side of the spectrum of sex therapies is the full-throttle, high-stimulation approach that involves building anticipation and feelings of lust by teasing each other all day long with phone calls, e-mails or foreplay, or watching sex-instruction videos or even porn together and generally creating a lot of arousal. It is like going on a sex diet with a full menu of titillating possibilities. This can certainly wake things up a little. The couple has to be in a playful, willing space for that adventure. Again, not likely here.

And finally, I could do something somewhere in between the two ends of those spectrums: suggesting building intimacy through some form of non-invasive touching, without genital stimulation, and processing what happens. I settled on that, knowing it would at the very least yield more information about their relationships, and figured we could tweak it as we went along.

Terrell came into the room looking glum and did not make eye contact with me. He was busy looking around for a place to sit, and settled on my office chair across from the couch where Rosalia had settled herself.

It is always interesting to see where couples sit in my office. Some couples sit right next to each other and want to hold hands or put their hands on each other's legs. Others sit across from each other, sometimes facing each other and sometimes facing me. When a couple sits on complete opposite sides of the room like this though, nobody really facing anybody, it says to me that they can't tolerate each other much.

"So, hello, this is my husband," Rosalia said, and we nodded to each other. "And, as you know, we are here because Terrell is…shall we say…not getting it up any more," Rosalia said, looking at Terrell who was managing to look completely disgusted.

He looked down at his feet as though he had done something wrong. "It's been comin' for a while now," Rosalia said, in a somewhat threatening tone, although I was not sure what, exactly, had been coming.

"I have tried," she continued, "to keep it to myself. But it ain't right. And I know it. And you know it too, Terrell. And I know that when I married a black, educated man, it wasn't only for the brains that I was going for it, if you catch my drift, Claudia."

"I hear you," I said.

"Yeah," Rosalia said, and then squared herself to stare at Terrell and see what he had to say. I turned to him myself.

"I don't know what to tell you," Terrell said. "I think this whole conversation is completely idiotic. Every man goes through periods when he can't perform. It's a known fact. I have a lot going on now, you know that Rosalia. In fact, I would say that when I have the most going on is when you become the most demanding." And with that, he crossed his arms defiantly and returned Rosalia's stare as if to indicate that he was not a man to stand down from his convictions. No pun intended.

"No, no, no, Mister," Rosalia said, and then turned to me again to explain.

"You see now Claudia, this is what he does. This is what he does every time. He upsets me, and then he's gotta be the one that's right. He can give you a scientific study for everything he say, but that do not mean that he is right."

"Anybody," Terrell said, with professorial solemnity, "can tell you that a man can't be expected to perform on demand. I'm sure you would agree with me, Claudia?"

"I'm not talkin' on demand, Terrell, I'm talkin' perform *period*. You know that you are drawing back. Because you don't give a shit about me anymore, Terrell. Long as you've got your plantains and your beef stew, you got all you need from me."

"That is absolutely ridiculous, Rosie. I can't even believe where you're going with this. Seriously, this is so idiotic I can't even believe I'm listening to this." Then, he turned to me and explained: "I work for a non-profit, essentially. To receive adequate funding we have to create a lot of reports every few years. I am in the middle of doing this now for a grant. The pressure is…unbelievable. Rosalia knows this—how idiotic this is."

Rosalia responded: "I can't even believe that you are sitting there calling me the idiot, because if you don't do something about your condition you ain't even gonna have a wife, Terrell, because I'm gonna go the fuck back to Chicago, and you can kiss my ass. And then where you gonna be?"

And then they turned to me, each with a look on their face that read, "Can you believe I have to deal with this?"

Rosalie continued to complain. "He won't even kiss me," she said. "Not that he ever kissed me right. He don't know how to kiss—I have tried and tried to work on this—he does this thing with his mouth, like he's some kind of fish. It ain't working for me—it is not working—none of this is working for me," with which she waved her arms to outline Terrell's form to make sure I understood that her statement included the entire package deal.

There was a time, years ago, when I would try to put a stop to couples fighting in my office; when I used to set out rules: no yelling, no mocking, no name-calling, no attacks. But I had given up on that long ago, because I could never make it work, and it isn't worth the expenditure of my meek energies to exert that level of control. I have decided to accept that this is how couples talk sometimes, and gotten used to the high tension states. When people are so enmeshed—so emotionally connected that their mutual happiness gets compromised because of what the other person says and does—I have to watch and ride things out. So I waited for them to be done.

"This is what she does," Terrell said. "She'll be releasing on me now for the next half hour."

"Well what would you like my help with?" I said quickly, sensing that this last comment from Terrell was apt to throw Rosalia into a worse tailspin.

Rosalia spoke first. "We need some sex therapy. Seriously. Because this marriage has taken a nose dive to nowhere."

"Are you amenable to sex therapy?" I asked Terrell.

He said: "I'm not into that. I don't need therapy. Of any kind. This is ridiculous. I have to tell you, I have a lot of stress in my life right now. Until this summer. And this is really not a priority for my life."

I could see Rosalia begin to shuffle in her seat. "What would be a priority for you?" I asked.

"My priority is to have Rosalia get off my back, to be honest," he replied.

I then turned to Rosalia and asked her: "Would you be willing to get off Terrell's back for a while until he feels less stressed?"

She said: "I gotta tell you this, Claudia, I've been off Terrell's back for way too long. You know if Terrell had his way, I'd be off his back permanently. Every time I tell him it's time to work on the relationship, it's always something. Always something. And I'm not going to stand for that. That'd be too damn easy for him. Everything is already too easy for him. He gets his food and his shirts done. Why should he have everything so easy? Marriage is *work*, Terrell. I'm not going to back down no more. You either make me a priority or I'm outta here, plain and simple." Silence reigned.

Finally, Terrell spoke.

"Ever since I was small," he explained to me, hoping, I am sure, that I might get him out of this predicament, "I was made to believe that lust was a sin. I have a bunch of half-sisters and brothers. My father had children by different women, and my mother hated that about him. She raised me to be a different kind of man. We went to church. She met another man, my stepfather, when I was twelve, who was much older. And I thought this is what Rosalia wanted. After everything she'd been through, with men who were raping women, abusing them, going around making all kinds of trouble, I thought that she would appreciate a good man. We have a child, I gave her that, and I am very happy serving my community and being what I think is a good husband. I don't see the need for this therapy, and I think Rosalia likes to create projects. I am her new project, and that's what makes her life interesting. I don't want to be used that way. She should go find another project and leave me be. We have a nice life, there's no problems. I don't beat her, I don't abuse her, I treat her well."

Rosalia looked at him in disbelief. "You treat me nice, Terrell, and you don't abuse me, but there's nothing between us no more. How am I supposed to feel, that you don't even so much as acknowledge me? I swear to God, if I left the house, you wouldn't even notice. Provided you had your dinner made. You off somewhere in your own world. Where are you, Terrell? Cuz you sure as hell ain't with me."

Terrell looked down at his feet again because he could see that he was not going to be able to get out of this. I asked him, "Well, are you willing to try to work with Rosalia, Terrell?" Terrell looked at me for a long moment and didn't say anything. And in that moment, an understanding developed between us that he was willing to go along because he had no choice.

"I am going to need a full medical evaluation and history if we want to go this route," I said to Rosalia, partly to stall for time since I could see that this poor man was hardly prepared to do much more than get in the car and walk up the path to my door. But Rosalia headed me off at the pass.

"Been there, done that," she said in clipped tones. "Last year. There's no low testosterone. There's no medical problem. There's no reason this is happening except for one thing. Terrell has decided and taken it upon his self to give me nothing. I get nothing, not a hello at the door. Not a thank you, that was a nice dinner. No sex, no nothing. So we do sex therapy, or I'm outta here."

"Would you like to try," I asked Rosalia and Terrell, "just to connect a little more, without worrying about intercourse or orgasm?" Rosalia shrugged. It seemed like she didn't even care, one way or the other, as long as her demands were being met in some form. Terrell looked uncomfortable.

"Would you like to learn more about it?" Neither of them said anything. "Yeah, I've read about that on the Internet," Rosalia finally said. "Sensation something something. You sit in bed naked, and you look into each other's eyes and you touch each other, but not your privates, right?" I nodded in assent.

"Terrell, you gonna have to put aside your work and give me that time. I'm not talking five minutes. I'm not talking taking fifteen minutes out of your night—you gotta give me time on this, you understand?" For someone who was demanding more intimacy and connectedness, Rosalia was completely unaware of the degree to which she was not inviting it. Making demands in angry tones is not that sexy.

But that's usually how it goes. We almost always blame our spouse for all the shortcomings in the marriage. As if, with someone else, we wouldn't be like this even though that's who we're being. Because someone else wouldn't lead us to be this demanding and angry and un-sexy. It is our spouse's deficiencies that turn us into this person. People often divorce because they can't change the person that they have become.

In fact, we are capable of continuing to be a person that we don't want to be year after year as we keep busy enumerating and analyzing our spouse's deficiencies—without any thought as to how we could change our own state of mind. We become convinced that we can't change our state of mind because our spouse frustrates us too much and turns us into the unhappy person we are.

Focusing on our spouse's failings gives us hope that we can change what's wrong so that we can become a better, less frustrated, less disappointed, less angry person. We don't usually focus on how difficult we are. If we did, we would not be able to forgive ourselves. We don't have the energy to know our own awfulness because we are too beaten down by the negative feelings that our spouse has for us.

Thinking your spouse, not yourself, is the problem is not in itself a bad thing, except when it leads to divorce. I once heard a famous psychoanalyst at a conference respond to the question, "Why do people even get married?" with the observation: "So that we can hate someone other than ourselves."

"Rosie," Terrell said in a pleading tone, "what is this about? We've been fine for eleven years. Where you taking me? What do you want from me? I've been good to you. Can't you leave me be?"

"You don't see me, Terrell. And you think being quiet gonna get you to avoid me. It don't work that way. You either gonna deal with me, or I told you, I'm not going to stay married to this. You gotta love yourself—sex and everything—if you want to love somebody else. You gotta learn to love yourself, Terrell. So you can love me."

I have often heard people say that you have to learn to love yourself before you can love somebody else. Or feel loved by someone else. But I do not agree with that. If that were true, who would ever get together? Who can completely love themselves? I don't believe I've ever seen a relationship that follows that linear pattern: "love yourself, then, get love." Instead, it's more like this: get someone to love you, and then find fault with them, and then get them to agree to become better, and reluctantly agree to become better yourself.

There's a back and forth motion that happens in a relationship. If there's been any unhappiness at all in childhood, you will re-experience the disappointment and rage in the marriage. You will be blamed for how bad your partner feels, and you will be accused of being crazy for how you feel. Heavy negotiations ensue as to who is more or less crazy, hopefully people evolve in the process, helping each other to feel better. I've seen it a thousand times, and

I'm convinced of it; this is how real love evolves: inch by inch, figuring out how to be more loving and be better loved. Together. If you can stay together through all that, you will definitely get better at giving and receiving love.

Relationships, good or bad, are a much more effective way to learn to love yourself than simply trying first to love yourself alone. And so it was with that the agreement was made that our course of sex therapy would begin, with this energetic woman, who had mental murder on the mind, and her gentle husband, who was impotent. I watched them walking down the path to their separate cars, and pity welled up in my heart for Terrell, watching Rosalia sauntering, her chest held high, as if she'd won the war.

The one-eyed monster

"I don't think this is going to work out," Rosalia said to me at the next couple's session, looking markedly angry. "I think me and my girl Kiana is gonna go back to Chicago where I came from. I miss my family anyways, and this ain't workin' out no more. This man don't want me. He ain't interested. The love is gone."

"What happened?" I asked.

Rosalie said: "I could see the disgust in his eyes. We got on the bed, and we was there, and doin' as you said, looking in each other's eyes. I said to Terrell, you are supposed to be touching me, but not the privates, and he started doing it, but honest to God, it was so fast like he was burping the baby. So I said to him to slow down. Then he was doin' it so slow over the same spot over and over, my skin was getting irritated. He wasn't there. It was like he was mocking me. Mocking me. I said, 'Enough of this shit.' I jumped off the bed, and I'm looking up divorce lawyers. This is hopeless. I've had enough of this shit."

"That is nothing at all like what happened," Terrell said pleadingly. "Why are you so dark?" Then he looked at me and explained, "I was trying to respond to her, to what she was asking. She is impossible to please. Her disappointment was so intense, I did all I could just to keep sitting there. I saw the same distaste for sex in her that I saw when my mother used to talk about my father. All women hate men. That's all there is to it. Women hate men. It doesn't matter what you do."

So the exercise had been very useful as a diagnostic tool to discern how far this couple actually was from being able to achieve intimacy. Apparently, intimacy was very far away. Rosalia had managed to prove to herself that she was, indeed, a physically and emotionally neglected woman. And Terrell had managed to prove to himself, most efficiently, that women fundamentally can't stand men. I understood a lot more about this family: the exercise had done its job.

Now, they could keep blaming each other for the bad feelings they each carried in their hearts. This is what marriage does: it arouses all of our worst inner demons, and then compounds them. Marriage is not for the faint of heart.

"I don't think this is going to work," Terrell said, and then added, "First of all, I am not that—and Rosalia should know this—that into sex. I never was. I think sex is over-rated and not something that should be discussed in public. Therapy for that is something that was developed by some white psychologists dealing with people that have nothing better to do than think about themselves and nobody else. In my culture, the line between what is personal and what is private is defined differently. And this is private."

Rosalia said, "Do you know what Terrell calls his penis, Claudia? The one-eyed monster. And it ain't no friendly nickname. Is that a good thing, now, a one-eyed *monster*? Do you consider that healthy?"

"Oh, Lord, here we go," Terrell said.

This, in fact, was not a good thing. It is never good when a man doesn't like his penis. No, this was not a friendly nickname.

"See, this is why he needs sex therapy, Claudia," Rosalia said, crossing her arms and sitting back on the couch.

Terrell started to shake his head. "I'm not going down this foolish road," he said. "This is private," he added, "and I'm not interested."

"He's not interested because he don't want to feel nothing," Rosalia said, and then she added, "You know what he did when our baby girl was born? He kept a pin in his pocket to poke his finger so not to cry. He feel himself crying, he put that pin to his finger."

One would think that this story about Terrell pricking his finger to keep himself from crying would arouse pity, or compassion. I certainly felt sorry for Terrell not being able to allow himself to shed even a single tear of joy at the birth of his first child. But Rosalia had become so impatient with Terrell's need to keep his feelings in check, that she had lost all pity or compassion for him. She just thought he was stupid.

Now, we had reached a magnificent standstill in this therapy. Rosalia wanted to try to establish some intimacy with her husband and get connected. But all Terrell wanted was for him and his poor one-eyed monster to be left alone.

The limits of reason

"Tell me I'm right, Claudia," Rosalia said, seeking commentary on the state of affairs in her marriage, to which she added, "Am I crazy?"

This was a very good question, I thought, that got right to the root of things. We can never be sure, when we are married, whether we should be having the feelings that we have or the feelings that our spouse is having. So even as Rosalia knew that her marriage needed work, she needed confirmation that she was right and Terrell was wrong.

Demonstrating just how much synchronicity there is between even the most estranged couples, Terrell then asked me the exact same question about himself. He said, "Don't you think it's reasonable to consider that during this intense period of grant writing, through which I am working at least seventy hour weeks, that Rosalia would think to give me a break?"

I looked at each of them and said, "Why do you think the other person is not able to help you?"

Terrell said, "It's a matter of timing. Rosalia's timing is unbelievable. All she thinks about is herself." Terrell then squared himself to face her, his hands together as if in prayer, imploring her, and then slowly spreading as if to make her fit into the shape of the box they were forming.

"You have to get more attuned to other people," he said.

"When you walk into a room, not everybody can turn around and start to pay you the attention that you insist on. You have to find out, as you walk into that room, where people are at. This goes for Kiana too. She can't always be at your beck and call—just because you want her to help you with the dishes or whatnot. Maybe she's doing homework, maybe she's on the phone with a friend, maybe she needs a minute. But you expect people to drop everything and come running to you because that is what you want in that moment. And Claudia, I can't talk about these things because whenever I do, she goes completely ballistic. She can't be reasonable."

Rosalia remained calm, but I could see that the calm was affected. It was the calm before the storm; the calm of mental murder. "Don't you bring my baby into this," she finally said, slowly, intoning the words between clenched teeth, with taut lips.

Then she continued: "I am raising that child to be obedient and not to be like you, sitting in a chair doing nothing for nobody else. You trying to hide. You hiding how little you're home even when you're home. You see, Terrell, I've been growing. I may not look like an educated woman, but I been educating myself about a lotta things. And Kiana been growing too. And you are staying the same. And there is nothing wrong with that, that's fine if you want to. Except that it's affecting the people around you. Because I'm the sorry wife that got no man, and Kiana got a mother who is unhappy. So, if you care so much about that child, then you will figure out how to make this marriage a priority. And you will figure out how to take care of things because I am not a dishrag. I am not some piece of shit you can walk all over with the same old story every time that someday, sometime you gonna change. You never change. You never, never change. Terrell, do you know what real love is? Real love isn't a nice quiet life like this. I been looking into what real love should be, and it isn't this. We supposed to be soul mates. But we're just roommates. I'm frustrated. And you know, I've been learning a lot. You not the only person with a brain, Terrell. Real love, Terrell, is that you can see the other person, see what they need. See what they looking for."

Now Rosalia and Terrell had both made their positions clear, and, it seemed to me, had done so very reasonably. There was absolutely no question in my mind that they were both right.

I have noticed that in every marriage problem that has ever crossed my path, there is a process of substantiation that each party puts himself through to add credence and respect to his defensive position. That substantiation usually comes in the form of a reference to an external standard like a research study, an ideal expressed by a guru, a statement about 'everybody,' or some conclusive research. I guess you could call it trying to sell the other person on objective 'reality,' if there is any such thing.

In this case, the substantiation was coming from Rosalia in the form of a concept of 'ideal love' and from Terrell in the form of the concept of 'reason.'

Unfortunately, both ideal love and reason, although we always long for more of them, are something that we never have enough of. I, at least, have never met a couple capable of creating perfect ideal love or being perfectly reasonable with each other all the time. And the reason for this is that it's pretty guaranteed that any union will have to sustain the burden of conflict.

Conflict always requires a negotiation as to whose needs will take precedence over the other's. There goes ideal love, in which the other person's needs always take precedence over yours or, even better, where there is no conflict.

And conflict will also obliterate any concept of reason, because it's perfectly reasonable that every couple, over the course of a long, productive union, will not be able to be on the same page all the time.

Conflict between your own needs and the needs of your partner create problems because they are confusing. The confusion is pretty much the same for all couples: whether to stand up for yourself or to accommodate the other person; whether to express your anger or give it up; whether to ask for something or sacrifice your needs. Even if we are perfectly able to be giving and loving in one area of a marriage—such as with money or with nursing our partner through illness—we may not be able to be as giving and loving in another area, such as where to go for vacation or how to discipline a child.

We all want our spouses to resolve our conflict for us—to tell us that we are right and they are wrong, and to spare us the guilt, frustration and disappointment that comes with being two different people with different needs, priorities and aspirations.

If only there were no conflict between wanting things to go our own way and wanting things to go our partner's way, it would be so easy to cope with the differences. We could be neutral and reasonable and calm about it. We would talk, we wouldn't raise our voices hoping to be heard. We wouldn't cry and make things harder for our partner, or get angry and add tension. We would be able to talk and negotiate, to compromise and understand.

But conflict makes our partner's position difficult to accept. We feel so betrayed and disappointed. We feel so frustrated by the lack of attunement. We feel so cheated out of the perfect spouse. We reel into despair about who we are, who our partner is, whether we should stay together, what went wrong. It is so painful sometimes. Why can't our partner be more of our ideal? And more reasonable?

But emotional conflicts are actually a testament to how connected we are to our spouse; how, in marriage, two lights become one. In fact, that's how the Jewish marriage prayer goes:

> From every human being there rises a light that reaches straight to heaven. And when two souls are destined for each other and find each other, their streams of light flow together and a single brighter light goes forth from their united being.
>
> (Baal Shem Tov)

The downside of our probably being hardwired to want to be "one light" is that in marriage there must always be conflict between our own needs and the differing needs of our partner. And therefore, we can't always see things clearly. Instead, we are in a constant state of discomfort knowing that we are disappointing and frustrating our spouse. We are annoyed at them because we annoy them, because we need them to love, respect, admire, cherish and nurture us.

Why can't we just accept that sometimes we have to disappoint each other? Accept that we can't always make each other happy? Why can't we love each other despite hurting each other?

Rosalia was certainly upset. Not so much because Terrell didn't want to grow their intimacy, but because his lack of support made her question needs: a double frustration. She kept trying to talk him out of his wish to be left alone in order to feel better about her own desires.

Similarly, Terrell wanted Rosalia to find another project so he wouldn't have to deal with her disappointment in him. It is so hard to accept our spouse's frustration and disappointment. That is the nature of the marital union: we long to be "one light" all the time, about everything.

Ideally, in a union, two lights do need to become one. How would Rosalia and Terrell achieve that oneness?

Irreconcilable differences

At the next session, because I didn't know how to help them, I decided to tell them what was going on. Sometimes, when you frame experience, it makes it easier to deal with it.

"What you two have here," I explained to them both, "is what's called an irreconcilable difference. When couples come to these places in their marriage, when they cannot agree on something because they are moving in different directions with different needs and priorities, it is very difficult. You two are in this difficult place."

"Well, what do we do about that?" Rosalia asked.

"Well, irreconcilable differences are irreconcilable," I said, and then added, "you can't reconcile them. Terrell probably married you, I am sure, because you are able to feel so much. And you probably married him because he's so nice and calm. But right now, it isn't working for you. The very reasons why we marry people are often the very reasons why we grow impatient with them. We seek out partners that will make us feel whole, but in the end it doesn't work to make us feel whole."

"Well, how do we become whole? We need to become whole," Rosalia said, as if she had suddenly realized that they were out of milk and was asking for directions to the grocery store.

"You have to understand the problem. So that you don't feel like it's your fault. Have you two ever been this disappointed in each other before? Ever had an irreconcilable difference before?"

Rosalia answered no immediately, but Terrell did not say anything—which spoke volumes.

"We've had a nice marriage," Terrell said, despondently. Rosalia added, "we have not been this frustrated before. But I've never been happy."

I said, "That's hard. Most couples do encounter irreconcilable differences way before ten years of marriage. But irreconcilable differences are unavoidable. I don't know anybody who has been married as long as you two have who has not encountered at least one. But usually more."

Rosalia said, "How do you survive this? Because marriage should not have so much frustration. I think we don't love each other anymore."

"Frustration is part of love," I said.

"So what is the opposite of love?" Terrell asked.

"Oh, the opposite of love would be indifference," I said. "And you two are not indifferent to each other, so that's good. We just have to figure out how to help you accept the disappointment and frustration."

"No, we're disappointed alright. Rosie is disappointed. I'm disappointed. I don't think I should have to fix this," Terrell said.

The time was up, but I was pleased to see that Terrell seemed interested in talking about disappointment. It is disappointing not to like your wife or your penis. This would be a good train of thought to follow.

Becoming Un-Reasonable

"I don't understand," Rosalia complained at their next session, "why Terrell can't see what's happening and want to get close. It makes no sense," Rosalia said.

"I mean, I was thinking," Rosalia continued, "about what Terrell was saying about women hating men. You know I'm not a hateful woman. People love me. I got more friends than I can count. I love people, I always have. You don't know me at all, Terrell."

Now that the conflict between their wants and needs was on the table and each party had created an effective argument substantiating their position, it was time for the defensiveness to set in. We always feel bad that we cause our spouse pain, and we feel bad when we are accused of being selfish, unfair, unreasonable, mean, you name it. We can't forgive ourselves for disappointing our spouse even if we don't personally believe we did.

"What about me?" Terrell asked, "You think I'm a horrible man just because I am not kissing and hugging you all the time and going crazy under the sheets. So I'm a bad husband."

Rosalia and Terrell had now moved on to tackling their mutual negative opinions of each other. This was a good idea. We should always try to get our spouse to change their negative opinion of us. We are not bad people.

"Neither of you is a bad person," I said, in fact.

"But I don't get it," Rosalia said. "What would it take? What would it take for Terrell to show me that he loves me? Am I asking for that much?"

Terrell replied, "I'm just afraid it's never going to be enough. If it isn't this problem it's just going to be something else. You will always find fault. You will always find something you want that I can't give. You will never be able to hear where I'm at."

And this is where I had my revelation. It came to me in a flash, why these two people had this problem that was so obviously irreconcilable, in which each person could and would not bend.

"Terrell," I said, "I think you're right. Rosalia has a lot of disappointment still to work through, which she brings to you. You have hit the nail on the head. And I hear you—you feel hopeless that you can fill that. I can understand why you have given up."

Terrell looked me square in the eye, and we engaged for a long moment in a wonderful mind-meld. I could see the wheels turning in his head as I relieved him of his title as 'bad husband' and blamed Rosalia's past for all the disappointment that she had in him.

"But now Rosalia, you've got a problem too," I said. "Because your husband had a mother who did not like men much, and didn't help him have his emotions. So he reads your needs that way. It's not your fault that Terrell reads you this way; he is just trying to be a good person. But he has to block all the ways that negativity comes his way. That's how he learned to protect himself. So he does that with you."

And then I turned to both of them and said, "You have to understand each other because the problems you have are very loaded. Your individual histories bring a lot of feeling to the marriage when the negativity comes up. It doesn't mean that you don't love each other. As far as I can tell, you love each other a lot."[3]

Rosalia and Terrell looked at me, and a strong silence descended upon the room. Terrell said, "I don't like to see Rosalia so disappointed."

"Well, you can't personalize it," I explained to him. "She has a lot to be disappointed about, and she brings that frustration to her life's challenges. But it's a vicious cycle. You don't want to disappoint each other. But you can't fix it for each other."

"I want to fix this," Rosalia said. "We need to fix how Terrell feels about his manhood."

"I know that. And that is a good idea. But I don't think you can fix how he has to shut you out when you get annoyed. Due to his own history."

"She gets annoyed a lot," Terrell said, and added, "Brushing her teeth annoys her. She's so high strung. I call her 'spin-dry' sometimes—she's like the washing machine the way she just spins around and around."

Rosalia's chest started heaving at that statement, and I said to her: "If you want your husband to be involved with you, you should be glad that he can say that. If you want him, you have to want all of him—you can't just want the part of him that loves you. The more he can express his frustrations, and the more I can help you with that, the closer he will be with you. Which is what you want."

"Yeah, no, I can't say anything," Terrell confirmed, "she goes ballistic. That's why I just sit in my chair and mind my business."

"I get it," I said, and added, "Rosalia doesn't do anger well. I know that. I'm glad this is all out on the table. Now you two don't have to be so afraid of each other."

I was managing the conversation very closely here, like a simultaneous interpreter helping each person understand the language of the other. It's a form of education, really, about how to form a union on the basis of your differences, and to negotiate the energies, however deluded the thinking behind them is perceived to be.

There is really no right or wrong person when it comes to how to stay together without too much suffering, because feelings aren't right or wrong. They are just loaded and exaggerated. So rather than looking to correct the perceptions, the couple has to come up with a unique, creative road to compromise and acceptance, made possible by whatever compassion and love can be eked out by understanding. It is an exercise in brokering energies, to see who can bend, who has the ability to give, what can be worked out given all of the distortions and illusions, the unmet needs, the longings and the broken dreams.

"If you want to fix the marriage," I explained to Rosalia, "you have to appreciate that Terrell's mother had trouble with men. And his feelings about that are very strong, so it is difficult for him to appreciate your disappointment in him outside of that painful reality."

"Terrell," Rosalia said, very gently, "you know I love you, Terrell. You know I love everything about you. Well, almost. I mean, I don't want you to feel this way about yourself—about me."

Terrell looked at her and said, "You know, this disappointment that you have in me, it just turns me off so much. And it's everything—if I sit in a chair sometimes, I feel like you're looking at me like I should be doing something. I can't even sit in a chair."

"That's just me being a woman, Terrell. All women gets irritated," Rosalia said.

I added to this: "Well, she's a very disappointed woman, Terrell. You don't have to fix it. You don't have to fix each other. You just have to know each other."

Rosalia started to cry at this point, relieved by my diagnosis of the condition of the marriage. She didn't want to go back to Chicago any more than she wanted to rot in hell.

"I know," I continued, "that you both have ideas in your head about what's 'right.' But you have to forget about all that. I have to help you heal each other—you know each other so well. I have to help you not take things personally. And not feel bad that you have to disappoint the other person. You both don't like to disappoint each other, to ask for things, to say no. We have to work on all that."

"Thank you," Terrell said, "thank you for explaining to Rosalia that I'm not such a bad man. I do love her." And then he said something I would never have expected from him: "You're right. I know I have a problem. I know that the way that I regard sexuality and my relationship to myself could be improved upon. But I have to do it on my own terms. This is something that I have to work on within myself. With myself. And I need that respected."

This was a big win for Rosalia, and she looked pleased. Women are often the ones, in a marriage, who move men along to a new place. Otherwise, if left to their own devices, a lot of men are perfectly happy to remain neglected emotionally, completely content to be left alone—not evolving or growing at all. Maybe this is why men die before women, from health issues: they keep too much in.

"I'll respect you," Rosalia said to Terrell, "as long as I know that you gonna do something about it."

"Yeah," Terrell said, swiping his nose, "I'll do it. I'll do it. But you gotta ease off, now, Rosie. You gotta ease off, and you can't be so disappointed all the time. I can't take it."

Rosalia didn't say anything at this. She was not very good at admitting she was wrong. I said, "I'll help her with that." Rosalia liked that. She said "Alright, Claudizzle."

Tantric sex

"We have some news for you," Rosalia announced at the next session. "We did something called tantric sex this weekend. Kinda like what you said, but different cause you don't gotta do nothing. You don't have to even look in each other's eyes if you don't want to. We sit there, and we close our eyes and feel each other breathing. That's all we do. And it worked. Like I calmed down, he stayed with me, you know."

Terrell was looking down at his feet, markedly uncomfortable. "Yeah, well," Rosalia added, "we did take it a step farther. Because despite what you said, I am going to fix this man, you know. I took his manhood, and I loved it, and I showed him how to love it—how to feel good about it, you know. And he responded."

"Why did you turn over though?" Terrell asked.

"I turned over," Rosalia explained, "because I thought if I gave you my ass, you wouldn't have to see no look on my face. You know, and I just wanted things to happen. And they did, you see." Rosalia looked very pleased with herself, and I was happy to see that she had gotten a good result from her creative form of Tantric sex. When couples start speaking the truth about everything they can't stand about each other, and they are helped to get over the conflict of having such mean and contradictory impressions, things start to pick up. No pun intended.

Grief

Couple's therapy had stopped for a few weeks to give Terrell a break through the pressures of his work situation since things seemed to be under control. But Rosalia was still coming in for sessions, so I was still getting updates on the state of the union. She had taken it upon herself to help him to open up and become more expressive and connected. But most importantly, she was becoming more able to tolerate his complaints about her without too much retaliation. She did this knowing that it would pay off for her in the bedroom.

More and more, Rosalia was able to understand Terrell and feel less disappointed and angry about his emotional reticence. She understood, thanks to her intelligence, that her anger was partly due to her own history of neglect and abuse, which got conjured up when she was frustrated. This helped her feel less unloved in the marriage.

In this particular session, Rosalia reported that Terrell's mother had died and that he had gone about his business, making all the funeral arrangements like a robot. But two days after the death, at 2 o'clock in the morning, she woke up only to find that Terrell wasn't in the bed beside her. She went into the living room and found him sitting in an armchair, staring into space.

"I went to him, and I kneeled by his side and looked at him. And then I just said it to him. I told him, 'Let it go, Terrell, let it go.' He started sobbing. I've never seen him cry. Now that his mother's gone, I think he can open up more, maybe," she said.

"You know," she continued, "I kissed him the way I want to be kissed that night. And he kissed me back. I don't know why I never kissed him that way. I thought he wasn't kissing me right. I wasn't kissing him right. I been waiting for him and it's no use waiting." Now, Rosalia was making her way towards being truly independent.[4]

I believe there may have been a time when it was assumed that complaining about your spouse, taking about what's not working, and pushing the other person to change would not be considered productive. And, I suppose, if that's all that ever happens, it might not be.

But if talking can open the door to understanding how the other person thinks and lives and breathes, and the couple can come to a good understanding, then all that opening up can be very powerful and good. What really counts, in the end, is being able to know and hear each other, and, finally, be willing to change for the other person—not necessarily because you agree you're wrong, but simply because you love the other person enough to agree to become what they need you to become, whether it's more loving, less disappointing, less hateful and angry and more.

Of course, it's always good to love the best in each other. But even better is when you can love each other despite the worst.

"You know, we got each other now," Rosalia said, "we got each other, in sickness and in health, for better or for worse, and that's what counts."

And when push comes to shove, marriage is certainly convenient when you need each other. It's nice to have someone to go out with, to stand by you, to bring you things when you are sick, to look at your baby's pictures with you when you're old.

So Rosalia and Terrell stayed married, and although Terrell was able to respond more to Rosalia's need to feel wanted and important, he never did become the ideal man of her dreams—the man who gave her what she wanted every day, who was able to be more attuned to her emotions, responsive and available to talk, and interested in lots of foreplay while they gazed into each other's eyes. But every now and then, he could become that man, when Rosalia needed him to, and it was enough.

And while I don't know if Terrell ever grew to completely love his one-eyed monster, over the years we learned to recognize that when his penis didn't work, it was because he had something disappointing to say, for example that he didn't want to pay for curtains or travel to visit extended family.

Terrell's penis seemed to have a mind of its own, to speak for him whenever he felt like a monster. The more he learned to say disappointing things though, the less his penis had to say them for him.

I'll never know for sure because he was so private, but I believe, from all his wife's accounts, that his was a penis that had learned to have some fun. Rosalia really loved that penis, no matter what. And as far as I know, she loves it still.

LISTENING TO THEORIES OF TECHNIQUE: EMOTIONAL COMMUNICATION

Emotional communication is, to me, the greatest thing to have happened to psychoanalysis since the birth of the term '*interpretation.*' I love it because of its focus on emotion over cognition, because of its potential to prepare the patient's mind for self-discovery, and because it is so much fun, creatively and intellectually, to design and implement emotional communications. Since our patients, given the multifarious vicissitudes of *regression* they present us with, don't always have much access to their cognition, emotional communications reach them where it counts.

We all know the power of an emotional communication in our own lives: how it feels when a child puts their arms around our neck and says, "I love you." Or how much it hurts when someone we care about, in an angry state, tells us we're horrible. Emotional communications, by and large, hit us where we feel them, at our emotional core.

The emotional communications psychoanalysts make similarly carry with them an emotional charge. This charge is designed, always, to prepare the patient's mind for self-discovery. To that end, emotional communications must address a metatheory of the mind that is appropriate to the particular patient. We may, for example, prepare a patient's mind by thinking about *structural theory*, saying things to strengthen our patient's ego, which may have been weakened by unbearable impulses or thoughts. A communication as simple as, "I can understand why you felt that way," would be an example.

Thinking from the standpoint of *object relations*, our emotional communications may be designed to help a patient develop more trust in others.[5] This would be achieved by helping them to have the experience of the analyst staying with them and not disappearing, despite their horrible, unwanted feelings.

In terms of *drive theory*, emotional communications that help the patient accept their unwanted aggressive or sexual impulses will serve to liberate some of the libidinal energy that is otherwise expended in the effort to block those impulses. If, on the other hand, we are working with a patient we believe has an intrapsychic conflict, our emotional communications could address the hidden side of that conflict. We might ask them, for example, what would happen if they thought or behaved in a different way.

Whenever we have the goal of preparing the patient's mind for self-discovery, our interventions become communications that have to carry an emotional charge. The emotional charge creates shifts in drives, highlights conflicts and increases trust. These emotional experiences make it possible for the patient to say new things and get closer to self-knowledge, all of which would not be possible without the mental preparation that emotional communications provide.

Many different kinds of interventions can serve as emotional communications. Commands, interpretations, questions and even instructions can be considered to be emotional communications, as long as they have in mind the patient's emotional dynamics.

These focused, emotional, goal-driven interventions are far more powerful than any purely rational therapeutic measure designed to promote insight could ever be. Those measures don't usually work when the patient is dominated by unconscious dynamics. We have all been witnesses, I am sure, to the problem of an unreasonable person refusing, at all costs, to come to reason.

I chose this story to discuss emotional communication with you for two reasons. The first is that you have to think outside the box when it comes to designing these interventions. Emotional communication goes way beyond coming up with questions or interpretations because the purpose of these interventions is greater than either investigation or revelation in preparing the patient's mind for self-discovery. So to encourage you to think outside the box, I am actually taking you outside the treatment room and into Terrell and Rosalia's bedroom.

Second, emotional communications are powerful tools that do not need to be relegated solely to the treatment setting. In fact, I like to make a joke about being married that I actually worked harder for my Mrs. than I did for my Ph.D. Marriage is not for the faint of heart, particularly if there were any impediments to happiness in childhood. These impediments are experienced anew, triggered by the inevitable frustrations of marriage. Which is also why there may be no better place to address unresolved disappointment and rage.

I love doing marriage and family therapy for this exact reason: it becomes much easier to understand the various forms of *projection*, distortion and unmet needs patients have when you can see them *in vivo*, as you see the various ways in which they show up in the family relationships. In other words, when each family member comes in, each with his or her own distorted version of reality, you can more easily begin to solve the mystery of what is happening as you explore each person's experience.

I realize that many therapists believe that working with families presents a conflict of interest and even ethical problems. I have never encountered any. People in families, in my experience, want and are able to understand each other, even as they remain, for however long is necessary, blind to themselves. When people feel safe in treatment, and trust the therapist on the basis of their individual treatment experience, they are amenable to working with me to prepare their family members' minds for self-discovery, becoming, in essence, psychoanalysts-in-training.

In this way, even as they cannot yet fully understand and see themselves, patients in family treatment are willing and able to work better with the distortions of their relatives. If I am ever accused of taking sides and perhaps agreeing too readily with a distorted impression (like when a wife tells me I am enabling her husband's negative impression of her), I simply explain that it is my job to be his ally, if I am to help him get better.

Family members, just like students, come to accept that before a person is able and ready to know themselves, there may be a long period of waiting—whatever period of time it will take to help them to develop stronger egos, more trusting relationships and greater acceptance of their difficult feelings. When family members start being able to join in the process of helping each other feel understood, respect defense structures and stop fighting against even the most unfairly distorted projections, it really speeds up the process of cure. In this case, for example, Rosalia had been in treatment with me for a few years. I knew, on the basis of her history and my experience with her, that she was easily frustrated and didn't have much tolerance for people when things didn't go her way. Worse, she used anger to mask a lot of longings because she could not imagine what it would be like to feel deeply loved. I could only imagine how difficult it must have been to live with her. Terrell, on the other hand, had adopted a very different set of defenses against unmanageable thoughts and feelings: he simply withdrew from them.

Their different styles are what originally attracted them to each other. For Terrell, it was Rosalia's vitality. And for Rosalia, it was Terrell's steadfastness. Gradually, these qualities morphed into what they most resented and despised in each other: Terrell, in the current rendition of their marriage, could no longer tolerate Rosalia's emotionality, while Rosalia could not stand Terrell's stoniness. Rather than measuring each other in a united whole, they now each felt unwanted and alone.

In marriage, one person looks to the other for completion, only to find the very thing they once desired or admired in the other becomes the object of disdain. The introverted partner with a desirably sociable mate may come later to resent the sociability. The sociable partner with a desirably calm mate may later come to feel depressed by the calm. Rather than complete each other, the couple comes to re-live in each other original deficits and re-experience, in the union, disappointment and rage.

If left unanalyzed, vicious cycles of negativity and anger between marriage partners can perpetuate for decades, culminating in what many psychoanalysts call 'the negative union.' Instead of the couple completing each other, the marriage simply becomes a powerful, painful arena for all the unresolved problems, each person trying to create in the other a new, better experience, which is the only gratification that can be derived from all the begging, pleading, fighting and acting resentful or withdrawn that is typical of these marriages. There is a strange form of intimacy that gets created in this otherwise bleak emotional terrain, an attachment born from the gratification of being unabashedly miserable and relentlessly unhappy. Those are the feelings that are familiar to each partner.

In the same way, Rosalia was discharging a lot of her fear and rage onto her daughter. My instructions to her to stop lecturing her daughter were therefore very frustrating for Rosalia because the lecturing did provide her with some relief from all the tension she carried as a result of the unconscious effort to ward off how scared and angry she was. In this frustrated state, she finally divulged the extreme conditions she had survived in, so the command to stop lecturing her daughter was effective in that way. Frustrating analytic patients in treatment often allows for the expression of strong feelings.

Loving-kindness meditation, designed to foster compassion, does not always work in cases such as Rosalia's unfortunately, when the mind is susceptible to violent images and impulses. Recommending the meditations when the patient's feelings have not yet had a chance to be expressed and come to terms with, can inadvertently send a message to the patient that they should stop having the images and impulses that they do, and that they are supposed to put a lid on them. A steaming kettle will, however, explode if you put a lid on it. Instead, my instruction to Rosalia to conduct mental murders communicated to her that I accepted the violent impulses that were coursing within her, and that I had a way to make them safe from causing any harm. Learning the difference between thought and action is very important in cases in which there is destructive impulsivity, and fantasy serves an important purpose for the patient to help them better manage those energies.

Mental murders provide relief to a mind plagued with aggressive impulses because it allows the aggressive energies to be admitted into consciousness. Perhaps ironically, this invitation to fantasy creates a calm for the patients as they learn how to be present with destructive energies without acting on them. It is not always possible to change negative thoughts to positive ones, but instructing patients to conduct mental murders helps them to surrender more easily to the unfortunate thoughts, and that helps loosen these thoughts' and impulses' grip on the mind. Mental murders can put an end to anxiety, and they are a beginning step toward mindfulness and eventually to loving-kindness meditations.

When sex and aggression figure as prominently in a case as they did in this treatment, it came as no surprise that the patient—as Rosalia did—would then want to know how to manage her sexual energies, which embodied her frustration over a lack of both intimacy and the feeling of being loved. My agreeing to sex therapy was in itself an emotional communication. I was communicating that I was willing to help her get the kind of sexual experience she needed and wanted.

Predictably, the sex therapy drifted by the wayside because Terrell and Rosalia were not really ready for intimacy. Instead, it provided more grist for the mill— more material for us to analyze. What emerged from the sessions is that Terrell did not want to engage, and Rosalia did not want to stop being angry.

Once I was able to tease apart each of their interpretations of the other's actions and to explain to each person what they were each experiencing, both Terrell and Rosalia could feel understood. Terrell felt that I understood how difficult and demanding Rosalia was, and Rosalia felt understood in my analysis of Terrell's way of withdrawing emotionally. After this period of analysis, discussion and reconnaissance, Rosalia took it upon herself to try sex therapy again.

Following Rosalia and Terrell into bed, we learned that Rosalia, to deal with Terrell's need for minimal emotional stimulation, turned her back to him, so to speak, or to use her language, "I gave you my ass." This was also a form of emotional communication to Terrell. Instead of conveying to him that he was inadequate to manage her emotions, she sheltered him from them, accepted his need to have some psychic space, and in that way they could achieve some intimacy and mutual satisfaction.

As both Rosalia and Terrell grew more able to understand, accept and talk to each other about their "irreconcilable differences," Rosalia became increasingly more able to leave Terrell alone, and Terrell became increasingly more able to express himself. In this way, the couple was learning to communicate emotionally to each other, that is, to hold the other person's consciousness in their mind with a new respect for the other's defenses, and to design things to say that would promote more talking, more understanding and more intimacy.

On the night that Terrell's mother died, when Rosalia found him frozen in an armchair, staring into space, she could gently encourage him to express his feelings, and they were finally able to meet each other on mutual ground, free of their habitual defensive patterns, in an arena replete with full emotion and loaded with the trust that had been borne of their growing ability to communicate emotionally. Emotional communication, when all is said and done, may simply be the best way to progress towards deep feelings of connectedness and love.

Notes

1 My intuitive sense that Rosalia would respond to my noticing that she had kept her maiden name is how we use our own personalities in treatment to form a positive relationship with the patient, rather than adopting a stance of neutrality that the patient might find distancing.
2 'Working through' is a term that defines the specific process of putting never-spoken, forbidden or otherwise horrifying thoughts and feelings into words. Only when the power of the challenging thoughts and feelings has been sufficiently diffused—so that the mind neither has to defend against them or be tormented by them—can we say that they have been worked through. As people evolve, old thoughts and feelings may have to get worked through repeatedly, because their power over the mind can get re-activated by new stressors.
3 In essence, I explained to Terrell and Rosalia each other's forms of 'projective identification.'
4 When we resolve early trauma that fixate us at certain levels of development, we become free to grow. In this case, Rosalia was becoming more able to see Terrell as a separate person, with his own thoughts, feelings and desires, and to own her own disappointment in favor of having a mature relationship.
5 The pictures our patients have in their minds about other people are known as their 'internal object representations.'

6 Mitzi's workshop

Loving words

I disliked Mitzi Rain from the moment she walked into my office. The reason for this—or so I believed at the time—was the way she had of killing words. She was an "expressive arts" therapist who drew her skills from an eclectic mix of Eastern religion, Jungian analysis, a master's degree in counseling and a few certificates in yoga and massage. Normally, I might have found her interesting.

Mitzi had come to me, ostensibly, to gain a new and fresh perspective on a workshop for pregnant women called 'Your Inner Sanctuary' that she was going to conduct at a local adult education center. The title rubbed me the wrong way, but I knew she had achieved a lot of success giving these types of workshops, out of which she'd developed a successful coaching practice.

However, she'd never worked with a psychoanalyst, she said, but I had come highly recommended by an old friend of hers who thought I was awesome. She thought working with me would make an interesting change since her mentor, a high-profile guru from California, had recently died.

As I studied her, I wondered how a person could become such a successful "healer" and yet dabble so lightly in so many different schools of thought—this didn't seem to me to be a very thorough approach. After all, I was the complete disciple of only one. I felt critical of her. Even the way that Mitzi dressed bothered me. She wore flowing, bright-colored clothes and turquoise jewelry, and her long hair was pushed back with elaborate enameled combs in a way that was designed to look unintentional. But to me, it felt clichéd.

We were working face-to-face, therapist-to-therapist, and almost as soon as she spoke it became clear to me that she was well versed in the language of psychology and that she would draw heavily from the lexicon that she assumed we shared.

Mostly, the words that Mitzi used are words that we all know. Words like: "OCD" or "co-dependent," "bipolar" or "abusive." But even when she used a word like "rebellious," to describe her teenage daughter, I felt she could kill the feeling of any word.

This is one of the first things she said to me: "You know, someday I'm going to have to get you to help me with a friend's recovery who's having a little PTSD. He is totally co-dependent with his wife. Actually, I'm wondering if maybe, the season of their love hasn't passed, you know? They both have no idea how to be in the present moment. I wish I could help move them into some more authentic intimacy together. They just project all their old stuff onto each other—those old tapes keep playing and playing." And then she laughed collegially, as if we had just shared some secret about the intricate workings of the mind.

I could hardly understand a word of what she was saying. There's no other way to say it—she just killed words for me. This was especially true when she used words that went even beyond labeling a behavior or a situation; words that sought to summarize an entire body of thought: like "enlightenment," "forgiveness" or "recovery." I knew they related to a whole belief system I was supposed to be connecting to, but yet, was unable to.

To me, it seemed like Mitzi used psychological terms to show off, in the way a kid shows off when they learn to ride a bike well—when they sit back on the seat and announce "no hands," their arms dangling by their sides, as if it's the most natural thing in the world to be performing this amazing act of acrobatics. Mitzi, to my mind, used words to present herself as someone whose facility with concepts and feelings was so incredibly expert she didn't have to have any emotion about anything any more. Everything had become categorized. It was all simple and uncomplicated.

I found myself entering into some kind of competition with Mitzi, over who deserved to own words more. I thought my relationship with words was much more expansive than hers, probably because my mother tongue was Italian. I had learned English later, and then French, in school. And later still, the best language of all came my way when I turned twelve and my Argentine grandmother came to live with us. I would walk into her room and she would say incredible things to me, like: "Mi alma! Mi sol! Mi vida!" ("My soul! My sun! My life!") Words spoken in Spanish, for me, are almost physical. Now that's how words should be spoken!

Even English, I had learned, could be spoken in many different ways. The English that I spoke as a child was British. Then, when I came to the United States, I started saying things like "right," instead of "correct." The American way of speaking English is so visual. In New York City, as a teen, I learned to pepper my language with good strong words like "bullshit." And now, living with my husband who is from Rhode Island, I drop my g's. I'll say, "I'm havin' dinner now." This is a private way, for me, of matching words with feelings. For me, it's a wonderfully relaxed way to speak—so intimate.

Words are the best way I have to enter into someone else's universe. Speaking several languages and having different ways of expressing myself have made it possible for me to be like a chameleon with words which, I think, has served me well for doing psychoanalysis with a diverse range of people. But this is also why it seemed so strange to me that I absolutely could not enter into Mitzi's lexicon, and that, in fact, I had contempt for it.

It was as though, with Mitzi, I was the lover of words—the one who liked to get inside them and let them take me places. Before I knew it, I was convincing myself that Mitzi's relationship to language was totally inferior to mine. Words, I told myself self-righteously, could lead me to pinnacles of joy, to places of belonging and oneness that could crash the gates of even the most intransigent aloneness with their potential to connect—and what was she doing with her neutral-spoken words?

No, Mitzi used words only to exhibit mastery and to dress up emotions; to cover up instead of to reveal their uglier underside—the things we really think and feel. And yet, I felt strangely jealous of Mitzi's utilitarian use of words, the way they made things simple for her.

But I could sense that something wasn't quite right here. There are times, when you are practicing psychoanalysis, when you recognize that you need supervision. Like when thoughts about a patient constantly seep into your personal life. Or when you have a dream about a patient, or when a feeling you have about a patient becomes really strong. That's when you know that, chances are, the feelings you are experiencing about that person may not simply be a part of getting to know them.[1]

Now, there's an ironic psychoanalytic law for you: if emotions about another person have an unusually strong intensity, duration or depth of feeling, they probably come more from you, not from the other person. You can't really use these more charged emotions to help the other person—either to get to know them better or to come to know what they can hear. When emotions come from you, they can, in fact, get in the way of being with the person. You have to separately analyze emotions that come from you. The message of my intense negative feelings toward Mitzi Rain was a no-brainer: I needed to talk about this case with a supervisor, fast.[2]

And there was another thing. Long ago I had learned that my impressions of people, when they are this intolerant, probably come from something that I still can't tolerate within myself.

I had never brought a case to my supervisor after only one session. But here it was. As I relay the story to you, from the vantage point of my supervisor's couch, you will see how sad it is when words cease to be gateways to new, wonderful places. When they become instead a means of staying enclosed within yourself in a sad state of stagnation and isolation and agitation that I would not wish on anyone.

Even seasoned psychoanalysts have to watch out for this; we too have to stay attuned to making sure that our own words will always serve as gateways to discovery. Because in the end, I was the one who had to learn to rediscover my relationship with words.

Supervision, Part I

"Geez, I think I've got my first intellectual airhead on my hands," I was saying to my supervisor, who I'd been talking to by then for over fifteen years. There's really nothing I couldn't say to this supervisor. I had prepared a little diatribe against Mitzi and was delivering it to her now, fully expecting, as was usually the case, that we would see things the same way, or that she would completely understand my new predicament.

"Her entire stream of thought is borrowed from someone else," I continued, "You know, people should not be allowed to use words once they become popularized. She's really into trying to find 'presence' with her pain body stuff she read in Eckhart Tolle."

"That doesn't sound bad," my supervisor said.

"No, in theory it doesn't, but you should hear this woman. There is nobody home! There's no substance to anything she says. She's like a new-age robot! No feeling!" I said.

My supervisor did not seem to be enjoying the diatribe as much as I was. "What are you thinking?" I asked her.

"I'm just trying to understand the case," my supervisor said quietly, her signature gentle voice alerting me to the fact that there was more to this than I was seeing perhaps.

"This woman," I explained patiently, "is one of those people who knows all the popular air-head theories, and she knows how to talk the talk. And she's incredibly successful! Words, when too many people start using them, should be outlawed. They just categorize and label experience. Objectify and dehumanize it. The essence of the person is lost with these words. This woman uses these words all the time. Words of the collective consciousness."

"What other words should she be using?" my supervisor asked.

"Really? You don't have a problem with those words? Do you like to use standardized words? Do you diagnose your patients according to the DSM IV and use words like OCD, and bipolar?" I asked.

"Well, I may use my emotions—just as you do—to assess the degree of tension in the room. That is how we diagnose, I know. But I do find it helpful, when I'm talking to others, to use those words. Yes."

"That's different," I said, folding my arms as if the case was closed.

"How is that different?" my supervisor asked.

"Because you don't understand this woman—she's a complete pseudo-personality," I explained.

"I know," my supervisor said, "but I'm trying to understand why you seem to be having so much feeling about it. What's wrong with her not having feelings with you yet? What if she's numb?"

"It pisses me off!"

"Why?" she asked.

"Because she's supposedly an expert! Doesn't it piss you off that these people are out there who have studied for like two years, and suddenly they are leading workshops on creating transformation? Calling themselves 'healers'? She has a very successful practice. She has the manner of someone who is at ease with herself. I'd love to have no brain cells and be confident. That would be great."

"Should you be leading the workshop?" my supervisor asked.

"That's what I'm saying," I said. "How come I don't get to do that stuff? Because I can't since I'm a psychoanalyst—I wouldn't even bother. We don't do that. I mean, her form of transformation is like, she takes people on guided tours of other people's revelations! Change is about discovering your own places. But this woman just packages transformation. I don't know how I'm supposed to help her deliver her workshop." I shook my head.

"What does she want to do with her workshop?" my supervisor asked calmly.

"She wants to help these pregnant women prepare for birth. She calls herself a healer, and she dresses totally flamboyantly—sheer long shirts in turquoise and green, big jewelry, long hair that she braids up—quite a character. No *tabula rasa* here," I added with a scoff.

By *tabula rasa*, I meant what Freud called a blank slate, although he originally used it to describe how we enter the world in infancy. Since then *tabula rasa* has become used to describe the neutral state that analysts should ideally present so that the patient can take center stage. If an analyst can be fairly neutral and non-revelatory, patients can project their own thoughts and feelings onto the analyst. For the patient to unfold in treatment, the analyst can't introduce her own character or personality into the treatment too much, ostensibly. Eventually, when you become seasoned as an analyst, you learn how to use your own personality and character as an instrument to relate to the patient. At the beginning of learning how to do treatment however, you are very afraid to reveal yourself, largely because doing so would be mostly about you. At this stage in my practice, I was somewhere in-between. I was good at helping my patients become center stage and be able to flower in the sessions, but I was still not as free as I could be yet to use my own personality creatively as a therapeutic tool. It takes a long time to learn how to become that free, and it has to happen in your own analysis.

"Is she having fun with her work?" my supervisor asked.

"Oh, my God yes," I exclaimed, "she physically touches her patients, which is part of her program of 'healing arts.' She hugs them when they cry, she has all the people in her workshop holding hands and singing. She draws from Buddhism, Jung, Unitarian Universalism...she's got a regular smorgasbord going on there," I said, trailing off, looking at the floor in front of me in an absent way. "Very dynamic," I added dejectedly.

"So what's the problem?" my supervisor said. "Sounds very good."

"Oh, come on," I said. I wanted my supervisor to tell me that the work that Mitzi Rain was doing wasn't real healing. That it was just play. Surface, bullshit healing that makes you feel better until, half an hour later, you're neurotic again, like when you eat junk food and feel hungry again almost immediately. Not as good as the nutritious psychoanalysis I do, which is like deep, lasting, soluble fiber: so good for you, expunging you of toxins and changing your brain waves, and therefore, the DNA of future generations. But not that tasty.

"You know," I continued, "I can't believe that people can get a two-year degree, and read a little bit of this and a little bit of that, and call themselves healers."

"Why not?" my supervisor asked me.

I blinked twice at her, thinking that if I adjusted my eyesight somehow, I wouldn't have to be hearing this. "Why have I been training here for so long?" I asked.

"I don't know," my supervisor said. "I thought you were getting cured."

"You don't believe that helping patients to say everything is what cures people?" I asked.

"I believe," my supervisor said, "that I haven't helped you to enjoy your work enough. It seems like this woman is enjoying what she does. And what she wears. And where she works. I'm not sure you are."

I thought about this for a minute and realized it was true. But I was mad at my supervisor.

"Why do I always take the hard road?" I asked her.

"What's wrong with taking the hard road?" she said.

"Doesn't it seem like it would be a lot more fun to be wearing flowing clothes in bright colors and hugging people?" I said.

"That does sound like fun," she agreed.

"Oh, Lord," I said. This was annoying. Why was Mitzi Rain allowed to have so much fun with patients, and be doing what felt good, and adopting the popular language of the collective consciousness, and having a workshop fill with eager participants, when I was sitting in a chair all day, in neutral clothes, riding beneath the radar of all humanity, listening?

"But you have to agree," I said to my supervisor, "that when you are as much of a personality as she is, it would make it difficult for the patient to project their feelings onto you. I can't imagine that dressing like that wouldn't be completely overstimulating to people. It's a manipulative way of getting people to listen to you."

"Well," my supervisor said, in the way she has of disagreeing with me, "I don't know. People have *transference* anyway. It's a matter of what kind of patients you attract. I know therapists who only work with depressed people because that's who they resonate with, and other therapists who only like to work with flamboyant billionaires."

"I can't believe you're saying this," I said. "I mean, I know what you're saying, but for me, the whole point is to try to resonate with as many people as possible. With as wide a range as possible. That's how I like to work. Like a chameleon."

"So why don't you dress up a little to work with this one?" my supervisor challenged. Again, I thought this was ridiculous. I wasn't about to become more like Mitzi Rain. She was the one who needed to become more like me: well-trained in the vicissitudes of transference and resistance and in the machinations of unconscious conflict; making use of sound clinical interventions that would be optimally designed to reverse the patterns of maladaptive behavior according to meta principles like *drive theory*. I frowned. I wasn't happy.

"Well," my supervisor said, "keep studying it."

"Keep studying it," means there's no clear answer yet as to what is really going on in the case. It was a good directive. My mission, should I choose to accept it, was to find out what, exactly, Mitzi Rain wanted, especially from a therapist like me, a psychoanalyst who used the couch—something that she had never done before.

The 'pain body'

Mitzi Rain had a great body because she did a lot of yoga. This was our second session, and she was wearing tight-fitting yoga pants and a loose blouse with an exquisite sheer scarf in a swirling pattern that looked like clouds, except that it had touches of red in it. My neutral colors looked even more neutral than ever by contrast.

She sat cross-legged on the couch across from me, and I instantly felt uncomfortable with how comfortable she seemed. It felt phony.

"So," she started, "we're going to talk about the workshop today, right?"

"Yes," I said.

"We'll workshop the workshop!" she punned.

"That's right!" I said, looking away.

"So…I've got fourteen pregnant women signed up already, and we met once. And…I don't know. Why don't I go ahead and show you what I did. Maybe you'll have a comment, maybe you won't. OK?"

She was open to whatever, and I said, "OK."

"So…" she started, taking out her glasses and studying some notes she had written in a leather-bound journal that was orange colored, with a long suede tie. I thought what an expensive book it was to put thoughts into. I was used to filling notepads that were sold on special for ninety-seven cents at Staples.

"I told them that this was a consciousness-raising class, and that we would be talking about being more at home in our bodies—some of the women are more 'preggers' than others. So I've got my list here of what I want to cover: first, enlightenment. Staying present in the 'now' and trying to breathe into birth and, hopefully, welcome the pain." Mitzi started to shuffle papers. She was very businesslike.

"You have read Eckhart Tolle, right?" she asked.

I nodded, but to myself I thought "not really."

"So…here is the page I read to them about the pain body, to make sure we were all on the same page—no pun intended! I printed this off a website. It's really good. OK. 'Pain body.'" She settled in more on her sitz bones, and read the following:

Pain Body. This accumulated pain is a negative energy field that occupies your body and mind. If you look on it as an invisible entity in its own right, you are getting quite close to the truth…

"Ain't that the truth?" Mitzi said, looking up at me over her glasses, and then she continued, "this is why I love, love, love, Eckhart Tolle. That's such a great way to see it—pain as an 'entity'. Sooooo…" Then, she continued reading:

The pain body wants to survive, just like every other entity in existence, and it can only survive if it gets you to unconsciously identify with it. It can then rise up, take you over, become you, and live through you.

"See, that's the main thing I want these women to understand," Mitzi said, taking off her glasses for a moment to make sure I got this. I don't want them to identify with their pain."

I didn't say anything, so she put her glasses back on and said, "Then I read them this last part, which is really good, I think. Really good."

The moment you observe, feel the 'pain body's' energy field within you, and take your attention into it, the identification is broken. A higher dimension of consciousness has come in. I call it 'presence.'

Then she looked at me. "Very good," I said.

"See, they're all so afraid about the births, you know." And then she continued, "They are so identified with their pain body. I want to try to help them break that identification, like he says." As she said the word "break," she swiped the air with her hand and then tapped the book affectionately.

"I want them," she continued, "to be able to feel that energy field in their bodies and not freak out so much. They're so freaked out, you know, so freaked out." She shook her head at this, since, obviously, she disapproved of emotion spent this way; she had come to be above all that.

"They started talking, you know," she said, "about all their fears. That something could go wrong, that something could be wrong with the baby, that their partners aren't going to come through, that the care is not going to be good…and the list goes on and on and on. You know, the pain body is so foolish—it is so ridiculous—clouds over everything. I have to help them stay in the moment. Have to."

"Right, huh," I said.

"But here's the thing," she said, taking off her glasses again, and putting them down somewhat impatiently. "It seems like they just want to keep talking about, you know, like, their fear of the births. Like…all the things that could go wrong. So…I don't know. You know, I want to try to move them—move them forward from that place." She started to make flowing motions with her arms as she said this.

"But they don't really want to move from it. So, now...you work with 'resistance' right? I was wondering what tools or techniques you might have as to how I could help them overcome their resistances to grabbing hold of these ideas? To ease into the ideas better? I'm just a little afraid, you know, of coming off like I won't do acceptance."

"Well," I said, marveling at how people believe they can shape ideas and character with "tools," "I like to *respect* the resistance. Try to understand it. We don't ever push through it."

"I thought Freud was all about overcoming resistance," Mitzi said.

"Yeah, but we've come a long way since Freud," I explained. "We've come to understand that there's usually a good reason why people resist. A mind without defenses, or a good means of blocking out unwanted sensation, can become disorganized or troubled, which is dangerous. So we don't 'overcome' it. We might 'explore' it."

"Oh. So Freud overcame, you explore. OK. So what does it mean to explore?" Mitzi said, patiently indulging my detour into what was clearly, to her, a linguistic technicality that only delayed her goal of getting to a "tool."

"By exploring, we 'resolve.'" I said, ignoring her question to continue my Psychoanalysis 101 lecture. She looked completely frustrated. I continued: "We 'resolve' resistances because that's what helps people get to where they want to be more naturally than by forcing anything. We don't force anything."

"So, how do you do that?" Mitzi asked.

"We just...support all the resistances and the defenses, and the illusions and the delusions. This support is strengthening. The patient does the rest."

She looked at me blankly. "But the pain body is foolish and unnecessary. Why would you support it? That feels like indulging it. I thought psychoanalysts used *interpretations* to clear that up," she said.

"Many of us don't use interpretation any more. And I'm not sure that we necessarily want to use the word 'foolish' to describe emotional pain. Pain body, is it?" I asked.

"Yes, no, that's what Tolle calls it though," Mitzi said insistently, and she started shuffling through papers with some degree of urgency.

"Yes, yes, here it is. Right here. I know he says the pain body is foolish. I figured a psychoanalyst would see all delusion in the same way," she said, looking up at me severely as she bent back the spine of Tolle's book, *The Power of Now*, really hard as if, by opening it as wide as possible, I would come to better understand what she was saying to me.

"Right here. Page 30. He says, 'Most people are still completely identified with the incessant stream of mind, of compulsive thinking, most of it *repetitive and pointless*.' OK, he says 'pointless,' not 'foolish,' but it's pretty close. That is what I want these women to understand—how pointless all their worries are. So they can awaken to the present moment and breathe into it."

"I know that," I said, "But Tolle is talking theory there. The theory is very different from the method."

"What do you mean, the 'method'?" she asked.

"Well, I certainly don't know Tolle," I said, "and it's been a while since I have looked at those pages." Actually, by "a while" I meant this lifetime. Sometimes, relating to a patient, I find it's good to stretch the truth of my words a little to minimize what was clearly becoming a great, gaping chasm between us.[3]

"I can't imagine," I continued, "since he is an 'enlightened' man, that Tolle would ever tell you, if you were in the throes of a pain body in his presence, that you were being 'foolish.'"

"Oh, I see what you're saying. No, I know what he would do. Wait a second, wait a minute. I do know what he would do...Hold it."

I waited, and I held my tongue.

"Oh!" she said, a huge smile crossing over her face.

"Here it is, yeah. Yeah." she continued. She read a passage silently to herself and put the book down. Then she said, "He would probably say to focus your attention on your body. You're right."

"OK, that makes sense," I said.

"Shoot. These ladies don't want to do that. They just want to chatter, chatter, chatter. This kind of pointless chatter. I have to find another way to break that moment. Without coming off as impatient?"

"So you're saying—Tolle is saying—that the chatter is illusory?" I said.

"Yeah, it's all illusion. Illusion. We don't need it. It's all ego. We want to awaken beyond it. We want to stop identifying with it. When we identify with the pain body we can't be present with it and awaken to the present moment."

"And what happens when you awaken?" I asked.

"Oh," she said, "you feel alive. Whole."

"I see," I said. She didn't have to consult the book on that part.

"Do you see that as a psychoanalyst?" she asked.

"Well, yes, of course, we see that our energies do need to land on illusory stories. Yes. That's 'transference.' Transference is everywhere. It's a way of projecting. It's projection."

"So how do you get past that?" she asked.

"We may not want to get past it right away. We may need to buy into our illusions," I said.

"Why? Why do we need them?" she asked.

"Because they protect us," I said.

"How do pointless, unnecessary stories protect us though?" Mitzi asked.

"Because sometimes, they keep us from knowing worse truths. Some stories are defenses against worse stories," I explained.

"Oh, defenses. Right. So things can stay unconscious," she said, surprising me by coming up with this.

"That's right," I said, "a painful story has to lead you, when you are in analysis, to another story—perhaps the 'mother lode' story about pain that resides in you, perhaps a worse story that you don't want to know, perhaps a truth about yourself or your past that you can't absorb until you've had enough analysis. But since you need defenses, you may not be able to 'awaken' to a place where you abandon them. Once you find the hidden, unconscious story— when you finally know it—then you can probably find presence with that story and awaken. And be at peace. Because that's the story you don't need to defend against any more."

"You know, that's interesting because you often read about people who are enlightened—that they have suffered a lot. Or gotten in touch with deep suffering." She reflected on this for a while, and then asked, "So the pain body is like...not always known to us?"

"I would imagine," I said, feeling a little condescending, "that it would be difficult to become aware and present with a pain body you don't really know yet. I would think you would only be able to have that space to be 'present' with suffering only once you had really gotten to know your unconscious motivation for staying in a state of suffering."

"Unconscious motivation. You mean...to keep suffering?" Mitzi asked.

"Right," I said. "That's the way the psyche works. We are motivated not only toward the good, but also, unconsciously, toward suffering. The brain does not differentiate between positive and negative, it only knows neural pathways that are familiar, either genetically or because of environmental patterning. That's the repetition compulsion—compulsion to repeat."

Mitzi said, "I don't get it."

I said, "If you feel inadequate, let's say, because you don't want to know that unconsciously you have a lot of anger, you will not be able to be present with the inadequacy. It won't resolve. It will keep being there. You won't get to feeling alive, or at peace, or happy or anything, until you get to the underlying unconscious anger." I felt like I was winning the debate on this point.

"I don't know," Mitzi said weakly, "I think if you keep trying, you can stop identifying with your 'pain body.' Awareness can create a shift."

"Have you found that to be true for yourself?" I challenged.

At this point she stared at me, somewhat defiantly I thought, as if to say that she was not going to give up on trying to achieve presence with a pain body, even though she hadn't been able to yet. I felt like I had got her on this one; made my point. On the scoreboard of life, this was one for the psychoanalyst, zero for enlightenment.

I shrugged as if to say, "You want to keep on trying to stop identifying with the 'pain body,' go ahead, good luck, be my guest."

She looked away and started to shut her book and put her papers in a pile. She looked dejected and said, "So I guess you guys believe in indulging the pain body and getting to repressed memories, right?"

"No," I said, correcting her on a technicality, "it's not about repressed memories any more. Now it's about repressed *emotions*. Or thoughts. I don't even know if we call them repressed any more. But not conscious, anyway. Hidden from our conscious emotional centers." I had a very strong need to set her right.

"But…" she said, and I could tell she was going to argue with me, "I still don't get how it wouldn't help to stop identifying with a pointless 'pain body.' Tolle doesn't differentiate between 'pain bodies'—repressed or otherwise. It's all about the identification. You stop the identification by being aware of the pain you feel. In your body. And then, the identification is broken."

"I know a lot of people who, if they stopped for a minute to listen to the pain they are actually in, might have a heart attack," I said.

"Wow, a heart attack," Mitzi said.

"Well, no," I corrected myself, "because they might not even be able to get to that suffering since our defenses usually stay pretty intact. You see, there is a very fine line between escapism—from trying to avoid pain by objectifying it or trying to alienate it with a theory about a 'pain body'—and being able to truly tolerate suffering, experience it and be at peace with it."

"How do you know the difference?" Mitzi asked.

"If you are trying to escape and latch onto a better energy, it won't work. Because you probably won't get present with a pain body when it serves to defend against another thought or feeling. I don't believe you can get present with defenses, at least not permanently."

"You mean you can't 'achieve presence,' not 'be present' with it," Mitzi corrected me.

"OK, whatever we call it—you can't create that space between yourself and your suffering if you are only trying to escape from deeper, or repressed or unconscious, suffering. And many of our stories are designed to defend against suffering. They aren't the real so-called pain body, to use your words, they are what you could call a pseudo-pain body. They are only a layer of pain body."

I really wanted to burst the little bubble of neutrality and feeling-less-ness that she was trying to create with this concept of achieving presence with the pain body. I felt like I had to break the news to her that oftentimes emotions have to take us to a few places before we can just put them up on a shelf and move on to feeling peaceful.

"I never heard Tolle talk about a pseudo-pain body," Mitzi said, looking confused.

"That's because I just made it up," I said.

"That's really interesting," Mitzi said, "because you're right, when I do what Tolle says, I don't really feel like I'm connecting to a feeling of aliveness in myself. Or around me. I thought I was doing it wrong. But maybe it's the wrong pain body. I mean I just feel worse sometimes when I feel my pain body in my body. Which doesn't seem right. Which feels like more 'ego.' Like, sometimes I feel a lot worse. It's like I awaken to more pain when I do what he says."

"Right," I said, looking pleased, which was crazy given what she was actually saying to me. But I couldn't hear what she was revealing to me about her state of mind because I was getting so caught up in the righteousness of my own words.[4]

"In my experience," I said, "people who can sit with their emotions sometimes open themselves up to more pain." I sounded very satisfied with this mortifying decree.

Mitzi looked at me blankly, and then, as if some mysterious force had broken her reverie, said, "So, getting back to business, what would you recommend then, just bringing this back home, about the workshop. So...I should explore the pain bodies more?"

This just made me want to scream. If this healer thought she was going to get to unconscious material in a workshop by singing *Kumbaya* and all swaying together to the collective sound of a wailing 'pain body,' she would have to run that workshop forever because it takes years of analysis to get strong enough to bear what you don't want to know. This is what a dabbler in knowledge, like herself, could not realize since it had taken me so many, many years of study thus far to understand it well myself.

"Yeah, I think you're probably going to have to let these women talk a little more. Because there's probably a lot more going on, with each of them, than meets the eye."

"OK," Mitzi said, looking disappointed. "So you're saying I should probably just sit and let them chatter then. Create a holding environment for that experience. Like Tolle might."

"Try it," I said. And with that, she packed up and left.

Later that week, I got a call from her. She had forgotten that she had a doctor's appointment. She had to cancel the session. In fact, she had something else on the following week too. So she said she'd see me again not in the next two weeks, but three.

Supervision, Part II

"Something's not right," I said to my supervisor, looking down sheepishly, "She didn't show. I mean, she called, but..." This was like a badge of honor thing for me, having people keep their appointments. Mitzi's having skipped two of hers meant that I wasn't doing something right for her.

"How did you get rid of this patient?" my supervisor asked.

"She's coming back in a few weeks. And she's not a patient," I said to her sharply. I didn't want my supervisor to think I was returning to a time when I couldn't keep any of my patients.

"She is a patient," she replied.

"I don't know," I said. And then I added, "Yeah, no, she doesn't want to be taught."

"Of course not," my supervisor said.

"I don't know what she's doing in my office."

"What's getting in the way of finding out?" my supervisor asked.

"No, there's no way to find out," I said defensively. "All she wants to talk about is this enlightenment bullshit and the workshop."

"She wants help with something," my supervisor said.

"What?" I said.

"Well, do you have any notes?"

I started shuffling through my notes. "Yeah, listen to this. I wrote it down almost verbatim after the session because I couldn't believe it. This is what she said. Almost exactly." I chuckled a little before continuing, looking up at my supervisor knowingly after every word I've put in bold: "She said, 'I have a friend with **PTSD**. He and his wife are **co-dependent**. The **season of their love** has passed. They can't be in the **present moment**. They don't have **authentic intimacy.** Their **tapes** play over and over.' The jargon!" I looked at my supervisor to see if she would find that as funny as I did.

"So she has PTSD, and she can't break out of something," my supervisor said.

I looked down at my notes to see if there was something there that I had missed.

"You think she's the one with the PTSD?" I asked.

"I don't know if she is or not. All I can know is what was in her consciousness when she first spoke to you. It must have been on her mind for a reason," she said.

"You know, she had absolutely no feeling about it. It was like she wanted to talk about it, but we had the business of the workshop to talk about so she shelved it. But she was shaking her head because of how co-dependent this couple was, how they couldn't get to some more authentic place."

"Right," my supervisor said.

"Oh, my gosh—do you think that's why she came to me?"

"I don't know. I'm just going by what you're presenting to me."

"Oh, for goodness' sake. I really messed this one up," I said, running my hand through my shaggy hair.

"How badly did you mess it up?"

"Well, she was talking about this thing—the pain body? Have you heard of it—Eckhart Tolle?" I asked.

"Yes, sure," my supervisor said.

"And she was saying that she wanted to help her class not identify with their suffering. To create the space between their bad feeling and themselves, and not have to buy into it. So she thinks she can be aware of her negativity and get at peace with it."

"That sounds like a very good idea," my supervisor said.

"But it's ridiculous," I said.

"I know, but why wouldn't you join her? Sounds like she wants to feel hopeful about what to do with what she's feeling."

"Because number one, she's there for supervision. She just wants to understand how psychoanalysis works," I said.

"But you just said that you realized she's not really there to be taught," my supervisor pointed out.

"Something is getting in my way of treating her," I finally said.

"I know," my supervisor said. And then she added, "I have the idea that you resent her."

"I do!" I groaned, covering my face with my hands. "She's having so much goddamned fun."

"Well, how can I help you to have more fun, so you can treat her?"

"How can I feel good about what I'm doing when I'm with this woman? She's made a career of dabbling in this and that and spewing and calling herself a 'healer.' Reading easy-to-read books, trying to move people into a better place. She hugs people, touches them, cries, laughs with them... Shit."

"Why aren't you having more fun?" my supervisor asked.

"How can I have more fun?" I said, almost yelling. "Psychoanalysis is so hard. We sit there; we have to tolerate all this emotion; we barely say anything. We have to wait for the patient to contact us, to wait for the patient to bring feelings into the room so we can make an intervention. This woman is doing dance. She's making at least as much money as I do, maybe even more...How does this happen?" My voice trailed off at this point.

My supervisor said, "Why can't you do all that?"

"We don't do that!" I said. I felt like my grandmother when you told her you wanted to try tofu in one of her empanadas.

"Sounds to me like you aren't doing what you want to be doing."

"I just don't get it," I said, "Why these gurus are out there, and we have to be so invisible. Unseen. Transparent. Waiting to become mirrors for people, so that they can speak to their own reflections and cure themselves."

"Why can't you become a guru?" she asked.

"Come on," I said.

"What's stopping you?"

"You are!" I said.

"How am I stopping you?" my supervisor said gently.

"We don't do that stuff. We're analysts," I insisted.

"Listen," my supervisor said, and I could tell she was going to break some kind of bad news to me, "why do you have to do what I want you to do?"

I realized, as soon as she said this, how ridiculous this was. Nobody was stopping me from doing anything. I had chosen to live in the cocoon of psychoanalysis since finding refuge there in my teens. And despite laying claim to four languages, and despite my intimate exposure to three corners of the world, it had done nothing to prevent how provincial I had become in my thinking, so afraid to venture out into a broader world of thought.

"I have seen," I said to my supervisor, "that there are other people here at the school who are religious. Who read Jung. Who meditate."

"That's right," my supervisor said. "Sometimes all psychoanalysis does is open you up to other things. It may remove barriers to learning—to living. Once you have been analyzed, you might get interested in any number of things. And become more free to enjoy being yourself in the session as a greater way to resonate with the patient."

I looked at my shoes. "I don't have anything but this kind of psychoanalysis," I said.

"I know," my supervisor said. "Maybe you need to do more than just have a practice. A lot of us teach, we write…"

"Write?" I said, perking my ears up.

"Sure!" my supervisor said.

"That's my secret fantasy," I said. "I have never told anyone. I have secret conversations with Oprah on her shows, where I tell her our ways for getting to know the unconscious. Or sometimes I pretend I'm on Charlie Rose, talking about emotional experiences, the new frontier of psychoanalysis, because of the book I've written about it."

"That sounds wonderful. So what's stopping you? That sounds very good," my supervisor said.

"It's not wonderful," I explained. "It's painful. I get all tied up in knots thinking about it."

"Why?" my supervisor asked.

"It's not good to fantasize about acclaim. My parents were performers, remember? And when I'd see them on stage I'd feel so proud and scared with them because every concert mattered. Their bread was buttered by acclaim. If they didn't get it, it was crushing. So much depended on each concert. My father would lock himself in the living room all day to practice. We weren't allowed to go in there. We couldn't see him."

"He worked hard," my supervisor said.

"Yes, and it's in my blood, I'm sure of it. But I don't want to be hardwired for performance. It isn't real. Your life is always on edge, worrying. Sometimes I think of performing, but you know I can't. I'm a psychoanalyst; I can't talk about myself. It's not what we do."

"Why not?" my supervisor asked.

"We're there for others. It's not about us. If I did it, I'd be leaving the field—the culture of who we are. It's like I want to be on stage with my parents in that sad, hard life, but I don't. I don't want to live for that. It only brings people pain. That's why I don't make art. You get lost when you make art. I don't want to leave you—leave everybody."

"What's wrong with leaving everybody?" my supervisor asked.

"I feel the pull to it, but I don't want to. Then I would be so unhappy. Alone."

"Sounds like you are determined to be unhappy and alone no matter what. To belong here, you have to squelch yourself and how you may be wired for performance. But if you leave, you'll be very unhappy and alone." She looked at me hard at this point, and then added, "It's perfectly OK with me if you want to be unhappy. Why not keep suffering if you still need to?" she asked gently.

"Oh my God, is that what I'm doing?" I asked. And then it hit me: "Oh Lord, do you know what this is?" I asked, leaning forward from the sheer energy of revelation.

"What is it?" my supervisor asked.

"This is my 'pain body,'" I explained, completely taken aback by how much the concept suddenly became alive for me. I realized that I was identifying with stories that I had made up in my head that justified and fed my suffering. That performing would kill me. That I would betray psychoanalysis if I chose to write or speak. It was all made up, designed to maintain my suffering. Why hadn't I seen this before? It would be good to get away from those stories. To awaken to the present moment; to experience and tap into all that was alive in me. Maybe Eckhart Tolle could help me break out of all this.

"The pain body," I explained to her, "is the story you make up—that you identify with—that brings you pain. That keeps you from feeling whole—fully alive. The fucked-up stories feed the *ego* that defines us rather than letting us live fully. It's not "ego" as we analysts use the word, which is as a sense of self that is strong and can manage and create the spaces between everything we think and feel and how we go forward in life. The concept of ego, to them, is something that is contrived. If I wrote my book I could do it without "ego" as they think of it. I would write it with *our* concept of ego—without all this delusion and bullshit around fame and my parents and my insecurities and delusions of grandeur. I just have something I want to say. That I need to say. That is the moment I have to be in."

"Why don't you do it? That really is all you have to do. Write what you want to say," my supervisor said.

"Yeah, write because I have something I want to say. See, when I think about what I want to say, and about saying it, all this other stupid stuff falls away and I feel alive. It would be so fun to write a book. So fun."

"Yes, just write what you want to say for the people who will enjoy it and who need it," my supervisor corroborated affably. She knew I was a good writer because I had already won an award for a clinical paper. She knew how much I had enjoyed writing it. It made me want to write for her.

"Yes, I have to write because I have something I want to say. Then I can enjoy it. Yes. That's what I have to do," I said, pulling my hair back neatly. And then, for good measure, I repeated it. "That's what I have to do." And then I said it again. And each time I said it, I felt that I had rediscovered my direction, and my purpose blossomed.

Then I asked my supervisor, "Do you believe that getting cured is like becoming enlightened?"

"I really don't know," she said. But then she added, "I guess it would depend on whether or not you believe that there is more than one road to salvation."

The man rant

Mitzi's face was strained when she came in, which I felt certain was due to the fact that she was planning to fire me. The energies hadn't been right in this case, and I had not followed her feelings, tried to understand her or figured out why she was there. All I had done was lecture her, correct her, and act otherwise condescending and superior. Why would she stay?

"So," she said, pursing her lips as if not wanting to say what she had to say next, "I'm not sure psychoanalytic supervision is for me." Well, that was no surprise.

"What happened?"

"Um," she said, looking down, "let's just say the director got a complaint—I don't know from who—that the workshop was just meandering. No structure. It was just a man rant. All they did was complain about their partners. I let it go on, and I just listened, and it was all about disappointment, frustration— like if they didn't have these partners they might feel better. It was pretty bad, but I thought that's what they wanted."

"The supervision wasn't helpful?" I said.

"I don't know if it wasn't helpful," Mitzi said because she was nice. "But for me, it's not something I can integrate into my workshop format. People aren't there just to talk. They want to learn something. To have an experience that will be uplifting. So just listening to them, like you said— it's not something I can use yet. I should have told them to listen to their bodies."

"I understand," I said, waiting for the next sentence to be "thanks, but we need to break up now."

"But I did find what you said about the pain body very interesting. I realize," she continued, "that I've been trying to get rid of feelings rather than accepting them—or even feeling them."

"Oh," I said, feeling impressed.

"Yeah, you helped me to see that's why I've had trouble letting go of it. I can't become present with my pain body. I…I can't. I was thinking…did you read *Eat, Pray, Love*?"

"I've heard of it," I said.

"Well, there's this one part where Elizabeth Gilbert, the author, is working with her guru in Bali. Hold on…"

She took her book out at this point, along with a few others. Mitzi Rain was a scholar. She opened *Eat, Pray, Love*, and said, "On page 261 here, she's with her guru Ketut in Bali, and he says to her that there are meditations that go down seven levels below the world. It's a dangerous meditation, only for masters. You reach enlightenment by going through hell. Some Christian mystics say that 'as above, so below.'" She put the book down.

"Elizabeth Gilbert," she continued, "said she didn't really understand it. She just mentioned it in passing, but I underlined it, and I wanted to know what you thought of it."

"I hear you," I said. Mitzi Rain was not just borrowing words or platitudes; she was synthesizing ideas, and trying them on for size. I was fascinated.

"Elizabeth Lesser," she continued, opening another book, "wrote this book here, *Breaking Open*." Mitzi opened that one slowly, almost lovingly.

"She kind of says something like that. I have it here, page 71, to be 'at home with the night.'" And then she looked up at me and said, "That's what scares me."

"It's scary," I agreed, impressed. Mitzi Rain wasn't borrowing words, just trying to find them now.

"I wonder," she said, "if I don't need to do some work of my own."

"What kind of work?"

"Well," she said, "just on a trauma that I thought I had put behind me long ago."

"That's a good idea," I said gently.

"I may need to return to that. But I'm not sure you're the right practitioner for me."

"Why not?" I asked, knowing full well what the reason for her feeling might be.

"I just have the feeling that, I don't know—that the chemistry is not right between us." At this point, my admiration for Mitzi Rain peaked. Not only was she smart, but she knew what she was feeling, and she could use it. This woman had a lot of wisdom. Maybe, having educated herself in all these different disciplines and schools of thought had served her well.

"My friend Annabelle said that you've helped her family a lot. She speaks so highly of you." She looked downcast at this point, as if it didn't make sense that the person she was experiencing in me, could have been so therapeutic to someone else.

"You know," I said, "I would like to work with you. I confess, I'm much more comfortable doing analysis than I am coaching. I am not sure that I supervised you well because, perhaps, it wasn't what we were supposed to be doing together."

At this, she nodded her head in agreement. I thought that maybe the way that our intelligences were matching in this moment could make up for the loss we had experienced in positive chemistry. I was beginning to see that all her reading, all her "dabbling" in different kinds of thought, and all her open-mindedness were what had led to her being a success, and not some superficial flamboyancy. There was a reason why she had done as well as she had. I could finally see it now.

She said, "What would you recommend?"

"Would you like to try my couch? See how it goes?" I asked.

"You mean—lie down?"

"Why not?" I said.

"OK," she said, looking at me hard. I was happy that she was able to be open to the person who I was now, in that moment, rather than the person I had been before my last supervision. I made a promise to myself to practice being in the moment more.

So Mitzi Rain took off her shoes as I placed my rug at the end of my couch, placed the pillows on the other end, and got out one of my folded dental bib napkins, laying it, as I always do, on the pillow where her head would be. She took the couch, and I didn't say anything.

After some silence, I asked her the question it would have made most sense to ask her back in the first session, but which we had both managed to avoid, "What made you decide to work with pregnant women?"

"Funny you should ask that," she said. "It has to do with some PTSD I've been trying to achieve more presence with. Part of a meditation practice to help you tolerate your suffering, to expose yourself to situations that arouse suffering. But I haven't been able to get comfortable there."

I said nothing, and some time passed, and I could tell she was reviewing something in her head. Then she said, "I had a miscarriage about five years ago."

After more silence, I said softly, "I'm sorry."

"Yes. Well, no, that's not...that's not..." and her voice trailed off.

Then she said, "My husband...the bad part..."

Then there was a lot of silence. After a few minutes, I asked, "Is the silence comfortable for you?"

She said, "Not really. The bad part was that my husband at the time, he...I found him. In the garage. I came home a few days after the miscarriage, and he...he had hung himself."

I thought, "Oh my God," and suddenly Mitzi started to stretch. I thought this was some form of grief yoga, but then, I realized that she was reaching her hands back toward me so that I would hold them. Ideally, psychoanalysts say no to touch, in preference to using words. As a student, you may get very rigid about technique. But I'd been doing this for some time, and knew that sometimes you have to break the rules. So I took her hands.

We didn't speak. She squeezed my hands more tightly, and I felt a powerful wave of comfort and strength wash over me from the synergy of our touch.

Then she started to rub my hands with her thumbs. This was not like anything I had ever experienced before—not the touch of my husband with the intent to arouse, or the caresses of my children conveying their love, or the soothing holding of my mother's or my grandmother's hands. This touch conducted the implicit business of touch, as she had been trained to put faith in, designed to heal—to strengthen and to bond.

And so it was that Mitzi Rain's analysis began. Our hands conjoined, anchoring us against her deep despair.

Discovery

One day, in a session weeks later, Mitzi Rain spoke the unthinkable: on the day she miscarried her baby, she had wished it was her husband who had died. After he had killed himself, she had wondered: What if she hadn't had that thought? Would he have lived? Did she have the power to destroy life growing both inside and outside herself? What if she did have this kind of power? Could she live, having encountered these destructive energies coursing through her?

The more she learned to bear the things that she sometimes thought and felt, the more dynamic Mitzi's workshops became. She became more and more adept at turning the things that her participants experienced in the workshops into lessons everybody could learn from, lessons that were reassuring, calming, growth-promoting and powerful. She got rave reviews. When you can know and tolerate what you feel, you come into your power.

As Mitzi Rain went down "several levels below the world" to find herself, I rose up to become more of what I wanted to be. I gave a talk in my town that many people came to. People laughed a lot at what I said; the truth is funny. A stylish friend dressed me for the occasion in a wonderful outfit that, years later, I still kept in my closet where it made me happy when my eyes landed on it. I keep notes on the other talks that I will give someday—maybe when my children are older, when I have more time. I've been having fun. And I've been writing this book.

How had it come to pass that Mitzi Rain and I had gotten so lost in the words from our respective trains of thought: she in the new-age parlance of the day; me, in a century-old practice? How does it happen that even though we flow alongside nature's inevitable transmutations, that yet, we cannot always find new words to help us move in tandem with this flow of change?

We all get lost sometimes within the comfort and security of what we know. So that is why I say to you: invite curiosity. Do what Mitzi Rain and I did: keep searching for new words, and to discover what it is that you may need to keep growing, learning and stretching even beyond what you dreamed possible.

LISTENING TO COUNTERTRANSFERENCE

I want to talk to you, in this commentary, about *countertransference*. Because it is truly a tricky thing. On the one hand, it may be the most significant diagnostic and clinical instrument of twenty-first-century psychoanalysis. Without using our emotions, we can neither gauge the severity of the patient's condition, or know how best to intervene emotionally. But on the other hand, as I tried to convey in this story, a *countertransference resistance* can trip you up terribly, making it not only impossible to reach a patient, but also painful.

The beauty of psychoanalysis, however, and perhaps its greatest challenge, is that in doing this work we never arrive; we are always evolving. Mitzi, who seemed to me to be leading a very creative, artistic life, ignited in me a terrible resentment. Given that my own parents were artists and had spent weeks away from me when I was a child, I had to give up my contempt for art to treat her. Trading up my enjoyable, stabilizing anger for painful longings and self-doubt was painful but ultimately liberating.

In turn Mitzi, to do her workshop, had to resolve what it meant to her to have miscarried her child and then lost her husband. We had both gotten stuck, our creativity extinguished by implicit narratives that we didn't even realize we were upholding, until they could be spoken and thus, overcome.[5]

The best way to manage the potentially debilitating event of a countertransference resistance is through supervision. When you enter into training, your supervisor becomes like another analyst to you. They need to work just as your analyst would, using their sensitivity to follow your contact and make the right *emotional communications* to prepare your mind for self-discovery.

By the time I had started treating Mitzi, I had enough emotional experience under my belt to recognize almost immediately that I did not have the right therapeutic attitude towards her—that I was "off." I knew that I had to go to my supervisor immediately to talk about what I was feeling.

Still, I had initially hoped my supervisor would help me maintain my superior attitude, which had been enjoyable. I was actually quite surprised to learn that she didn't share my contempt for Mitzi. Instead, she worked to help me look further into myself.

Now, in this story, I had been in supervision for a long time. My relationship with my supervisor was very solid, and I had developed some ego strength by then. This is why she was able to interpret my difficulty to me. She could tell me that my envy was interfering with the treatment and explore with me why I had not yet fully succeeded in designing the kind of life for myself that was of my choosing. The process of realizing I was defending against separation anxiety and existential loneliness was not long.

At another epoch in my psychoanalytic training however, I might not have gotten this response from my supervisor. In fact, in Chapter 3, 'Searching for Anita,' the supervisor never interpreted to me that I was defending against feeling like a freak. I had to fail the academic internship before I could learn that I was defended at all, and only then was I sufficiently motivated and prepared to explore my own mind—which, way back then, meant learning how afraid I was of mental illness.

The difficulty posed by these subjective countertransference resistances, particularly before the student analyst is sufficiently analyzed, is significant. It is why many psychoanalytic institutes require years of study and analysis (including group analysis) before the student can graduate to higher levels of clinical work in an outpatient setting.

When I was a student, the pre-requisite for observing psychosis at a state mental hospital was one full year of training analysis along with classroom work. This ground level of training could be in and of itself a multi-year experience. Often, students who applied for the field practicum, as it was called then, were told they were not yet ready. Once accepted into fieldwork, it could then take an additional few years for a student to graduate to the second level of clinical work, particularly if they were held back as I was, to practice in the out-patient treatment service at the school.

In fact, I have heard many, many supervisors suggest to students struggling with patients because of their own unresolved feelings,[6] "Why do you want to treat this awful patient? Just transfer them to someone else!" This is a wonderful emotional communication to make to a student who is not yet ready for self-discovery, blaming the patient for the difficulty and helping the student to move forward without the patient until they are ready to know their own resistances. Because therapists were not always supervised to keep a patient, patients entering through the treatment service might travel through three of four student therapists before making a contract for treatment with any one.

I distinctly remember one student who was completely unable to keep any patient for more than one session. The school decided to assign every single new patient who came through the treatment service to this student first. This was tremendously strengthening for the student. Sure enough, she soon became able to keep one or two, and the normal rotating scheduling of new intakes to all students could resume. (Most patients are happy to know that they don't have to contract with a therapist they can't connect to; it gives them a feeling of control, and didn't seem to pose a problem.)

Finally, after many years of your own analysis, including group analysis, intensive clinical studies in classrooms and a lot of supervision, you do become more readily able to discern which feelings come from you and which ones are induced by the patient. For example, if you are feeling frustrated, sleepy or tense in the room with a patient, and those sensations leave the moment the patient exits the office, chances are the feelings were induced by the patient. Somehow, your own subjective feelings, when they are either not shared by the patient or perhaps when they just compound an appropriate *induction*, are more intense, physical and enduring.

Subjective feelings also generally have a certain measure of dread attached to them. They may feel familiar, or so confusing you can't even make out the nature of the confusion in a session. These feelings will usually stay with you beyond a session, perhaps entering into your dreams or waking fantasies. And if, on top of all that, you find that you're thinking about the dynamics or the patient a great deal, that's a sure sign that something has hooked you that is subjective, and which needs exploring within yourself.

Over time, it becomes progressively more possible to know when, exactly, you need to get yourself over to supervision—to make sure that you are not contaminating a treatment with your own narrative, or resisting the patient's story because it is too occluded by your own feelings. Once you are in supervision, your supervisor helps you tease through the morass of emotion, until you unpack and resolve the stories and achieve some clarity. It can take time.

The need for supervision, however, becomes no less critical or urgent even as you develop a relative ease in the playground of emotion. Even senior training analysts at most psychoanalytic institutes who are approved to analyze students are typically required to be in supervision. The supervision requirement for training analysts when I was a student was that they had to talk about each student analyst at least once for every four private supervision sessions. Supervision is unquestionably the best control psychoanalysts have against contaminating the treatment with their own potentially unresolved issues.

In effect, the process of treatment is like a protracted theatrical production in which you may have to tolerate being in suspended animation when it comes to fully understanding what is happening. You become involved in a real-life drama that gradually unfolds and have to stay tuned in long enough to see what happens. As long as you are aware of the emotional dynamics, and can tolerate them in a relaxed way, the treatment is safe from the risks of either contaminating the treatment with your own *projections*, or resisting against the patient with your own *subjective countertransference*.

Unquestionably, when you become a psychoanalyst, some of the feelings you encounter, either in a patient or in yourself, can bring you to your knees. And you really have to let go of trying to change things or want them to be different. You have to be willing to be completely vulnerable, and totally curious about this other person you are getting to know so deeply, as well as about your own reactions, sensations, thoughts and feelings. Eventually, you learn to trust that in time, if you can just keep talking and stick it out long enough through the confusing, disturbing, tight and downright awful emotional spaces you may find yourself in, something new will open up. That is where we see discovery, and *therapeutic action*.

For the past decade or so, since treating Mitzi, I've had a recurring dream. In this dream, I discover new space in my house that I didn't know I had. Once, I found a hidden door to a narrow attic closet, full of clothes. In another dream, I discovered a back door to a large empty apartment that I hadn't realized was attached to mine. In another dream, I found myself living in a mansion that looked like a modern art museum full of people having a good time. Perhaps my favorite of these dreams was when I discovered an entire ancient city that was mine, replete with graded cobblestone and white statues that made it look a little like Piazza Navona, in Rome, where I grew up. Always, in each of these dreams, I felt a measure of relief, delight and amazement that I didn't know all this was mine.

Recently, in real life, my husband and I moved to a big house. Off the master bedroom is a high balcony, with views of the Hudson River. Standing on the balcony, I get the same feeling that I've had in my recurring dream. I think, "How could I not have imagined that someday I'd have all this?" There is no question in my mind that when we can amplify our emotions, and find the courage to realize things we didn't even know we think and feel, then somehow the outside world too becomes a place that offers more than we could ever dream possible.

Notes

1   The technical term for what was happening inside me is 'subjective countertransference resistance.' That is, my own subjective feelings were getting in the way of my getting to know this patient.
2   Continuous supervision is psychoanalysis' best control over potential contamination of the treatment due to the psychoanalyst's subjective elements.
3   The technical term for how we diminish the chasm of consciousness between ourselves and our patients is called to 'foster the narcissistic transference.'
4   This is the subjective countertransference resistance in action.
5   Twenty-first-century psychoanalysis works with resistance not by barreling through it with interpretation, but by helping the patient to say everything. When we see patients overcome their resistance this way, it is also known as 'working through.' Working through feelings requires that we locate thoughts and feelings through realizations, memories, revelations or epiphanies, and then talk about them sufficiently so that they no longer have to unwittingly dominate our behavior and hijack our life.
6   This is what is known as 'subjective countertransference resistance.'

Part III
Putting it all together

7 Mercy gets a tattoo

Mismatch

I almost chuckled aloud watching this couple come up the path. Mercy, who was sixteen, had her hair in a shaggy bun that couldn't contain unruly pink bangs and that defied the concept of neon. Her mother Diana, by contrast, wore a blow-dried shoulder-length hairdo that bespoke complete order.

And while Mercy's jeans were torn in all the right places, Diana's suit looked newly pressed. Mercy ambled, the way many teens do, in ankle-high converse sneakers while Diana's gait, as she walked in her conservative beige pumps, was crisp and purposeful. Everything about them screamed radical mismatch.

Diana was a professional organizer. And she looked organized. But Mercy was a failing student at a private high school. Her pronouncement, a week or so ago, that she was going to get a full-arm tattoo of a pink and turquoise mermaid, had precipitated their call. This, in itself, seemed strange to me. Why would a conflict over a tattoo lead them to seek treatment, and not the fact that Mercy was failing school?

The two did not speak a word as they came up the path. Entering my office, Diana extended her hand boldly with a broad smile. I shook her hand and ignored Mercy who hung back, avoiding me. They sat down, Diana leaning toward me on the edge of the couch right by my chair, and Mercy on my extra chair across the room, where she turned to stare out of the window absently, prepared to zone out until her mother had her say.

"Oh, my goodness," Diana said smiling, exhaling deeply, "we probably should have come here long ago. This is my daughter Mercy. Mercy, say hi to Dr. Luiz." Mercy and I made eye contact, and she said, "Hi," obediently. I nodded.

"We have had a little problem, as I mentioned to you over the phone," Diana began, "in that my daughter Mercy has decided to lead her own life." She said this in a disparaging tone, lips pursed, stern and disapproving.

"This started early, if I were to think about it, two years ago. Her room is always a pigsty. I know she's been smoking marijuana, and she is doing very poorly in school. I think she's with a boy—I don't know. Now she went to her father and told him she's getting this tattoo."

At that, Diana reached into her bag and pulled out a wrinkled little magazine cutout that looked like it had been thrown in the trash and then retrieved. It was a very sweet drawing in pink and aquamarine of a mermaid undulating in a back flip.

I looked over at Mercy who was studying me. I felt as though she wanted to talk. But she didn't. I looked at the picture of the mermaid again and smiled at her to let her know I liked the feeling of the image.

Diana continued, "She was always absent-minded and disorganized, but I have tried to help instill good qualities in her. But it seems that no matter what I say or do, she is intent on defying me. She has never wanted to listen. I don't have this problem with her sister Hope, who is a year and a half younger. I know we're not supposed to compare, but Hope does try, and I wish that Mercy could see what good results you get from that. Mercy is not interested in her schoolwork. We just learned that she is failing math, and her whole life is just falling apart. She doesn't care about her room; she doesn't care what she eats. I don't know what she cares about. A tattoo I suppose."

The tension in Diana's voice was concentrated. She was totally fed up with this kid.

"Another thing you have to understand," Diana explained, "is that I have a certain image in the community, and I have asked Mercy to respect that. I am a professional organizer, as I also mentioned to you over the phone, and I am expected to go into people's homes. They have to see me as a respectable member of the community. How can she go around looking like this? She doesn't realize how all this affects the family—even giving the wrong impression to Hope's future teachers. I understand if Mercy wants to fail school; she would not be the first person in the family who didn't choose the academic path. Fine, we can afford to support a business venture or whatever she decides to do with herself. But getting a tattoo is too much. She wants one on her arm—her whole arm! And that will hurt us—hurt the family. We live in a conservative town. People seeing her, who know she's mine, are not going to want to hire me. That's hurtful. This has gone too far." I nodded. Now I got why they were here.

"So I want you to see her, to see what you can do to help her—to make something of herself. Clearly, she doesn't care any more. Clearly, she has decided to go down the wrong path, and that is her choice. But she is not going to bring us down with her, no sir." At this point, Diana paused.

And then she continued, as if to conclude her summary of the problem: "We don't know what happened, what went wrong."

Evidently Diana was not only a good professional organizer but also a very good professional criticizer. I don't know that I had ever heard a mother speak of her own child with so much vitriol.

In Diana's defense, people sometimes do step into my office and pour their hearts out; maybe she'd been keeping her feelings to herself for a while. But the contempt she showed for Mercy now was no-holds-barred.

"Wow, Mom," Mercy said in a calm but clearly mocking voice. Then she added, more to herself than anybody else, "Why don't you, like, throw me away and get a new model so I'll look more like Hope if I'm 'just throwing my life away.'"

"You keep Hope out of this," Diana said sharply. "I don't want to hear anything negative about Hope, do you understand?"

Then Diana turned to me and said, "She hates Hope. Always trying to put her down. That's another problem. Hope likes to do things properly so Mercy hates her. I don't think it's healthy to allow these kinds of put-downs in my family."

By now, I had a lot of vital information about this family. Diana was completely fed up to the point where she couldn't even be polite to Mercy. Mercy was expected to behave nicely and be cooperative—to greet me properly and act polite. Which I could see, she did. Although wanting a tattoo probably wasn't very cooperative. Maybe, Mercy was penny-wise and pound-foolish when it came to cooperating, saving being uncooperative only for the really big things.

And then, I could also see that negativity was not allowed in this family; Mercy should like and act nice towards her sister, which clearly, she couldn't do.

Mercy turned to me and said, in a smooth and even tone, "I don't, like, *hate* Hope. She's not who I want to be. I'm not Hope. I'm never going to be Hope. I never want to be Hope." She was very composed. I could tell that her mother no longer got to her.[1]

"Is this the problem?" Diana asked me. "Is she trying to form her own identity?" I looked at Mercy who, at being analyzed this way, started looking out of the window again. These two were very deeply disconnected.

I said, "Well, we are going to have to find out what's going on." Diana uttered "tsk" at this and sat back, which I translated to mean that it was plain to see what was going on: this was a rotten, lazy, horrible kid.

"I think," Diana reflected, "that Mercy needs to think about what she's doing with her life because she's being hurtful to herself. Mercy, is this really the identity you want?"

At this point, Diana turned her attention to Mercy and added, "Mercy, you have so many great things going for you. You are talented, beautiful. You don't need to hide behind this mask—all this pink hair or tattoos. The teachers used to tell us you were among the brightest of the kids in the class. There's no reason for you to squelch yourself like this, and not let your true qualities show, sweetheart. Your wonderful, beautiful qualities."

Mercy looked Diana in the eye and said, "Thanks for your opinion of me, Mom. Means a lot." And then she looked out of the window again.

Diana threw up her hands and said, "I just can't reach her. She won't let me in. I don't know what to do. I don't know what to do." Diana was becoming more agitated, which was only making Mercy even more cool and distant.

I asked Mercy, "Would you like me to help your mother understand you?"

Mercy scoffed at that and said, "Be my guest. But I don't think my parents...I don't know," she added. She was suddenly inarticulate.

I said, "Are you willing to come see me next Tuesday to explain the situation to me?" She shrugged her shoulders and said, "Sure."

"Great," I said, and then turned to Diana and asked, "Will it be possible for you and your husband to come see me so I can get a full history and help you work with your daughter?"

Diana looked a little surprised. She said, "Of course, we'll do whatever you recommend." I took that to mean that she had not expected to have to come in. After all, she was not the one throwing her life away. She had probably been hoping I would find that special something that would help Mercy finally understand herself—some big "aha" moment that would get her to stop all this destructive ugly neon mermaid nonsense.

"But in the meantime," Diana added, "We would like your recommendation about what to do about the marijuana. We think she is doing a lot of it. Mercy, do you want to say something to Dr. Luiz about this problem?"

Mercy breathed in deeply and turned to me and said, "I smoke weed to survive my family." Diana became extremely agitated at this and opened up her pocketbook to look for something. She then closed it, looked up, and said, "Are we really that bad, Mercy? Have you been abused?" And then she added, each word rolled out disgustedly in an exasperated staccato, "What are you surviving, for goodness, Pete's, sake?"

At this point, Mercy looked at her hands in a thoughtful way. She was more composed than I have ever seen any teen be in light of the accusations being leveled against her. Then she took another deep breath and looked at me resignedly.

I said, "We have a lot of work to do here." At this, Diana started shaking her head because she felt so hopeless. I said to her, "we will work on all the things that you would like to see addressed. Everything in good time. For now, coming here is all that really needs to happen."

People come to therapy to precipitate and to ignite positive change. What they usually fail to realize is that just by walking through my door they have already made that change.

"All you have to do is come here and talk," I said, and if I've said that once, by the way, I've said it a thousand times. With that, we scheduled some sessions for the coming months.

Marijuana

"I am not going to stop smoking weed," Mercy explained to me at her session. "I think weed is a really good thing. I know I probably smoke more than I should. I don't know...and I'm not going to stop smoking if that's what my mother wants. It helps me relax. Seriously. Like, sometimes I just take a hit to settle down. I hope you are not like...I'm not going to stop getting high."

"Why would I want you to stop?" I asked.[2]

"Because it's illegal. That's all adults care about. I don't care. I seriously can't be around my mother unless I'm high. I'm not talking about, like I can't remember who or where I am. I don't get like that high. I get a little buzzed." I nodded.

She said, "OK, I'm glad you're cool with it. Do you get high?"

People often assume that I get high or that I'm cool with it. I'm not sure why. Is it my wiry hair? My focused introspection? I was dressing more colorfully these days. And I suppose to some degree I am cool about drug and alcohol use because I believe they are a crutch. And of course, people do need crutches before they can learn to walk on their own, or else, obviously, they will fall. I really don't like to see people fall. So I don't mind crutches. As long as you are working on getting strong enough to move ahead without drugs and alcohol eventually, I can tolerate them for as long as needed. And as long as you're not driving.

"Would you rather believe I get high or that I don't? Sometimes people would rather believe a therapist does not get high," I asked Mercy.

"I don't care," she said, and shrugged. She didn't care about what I thought or did yet.

Truth is, I love getting people to stop using drugs—street drugs, prescription drugs, you name it. In fact, I see my job as a healer to help people get to a place where they no longer depend on them. There's nothing like the triumph of that moment when the pleasure of getting high finally takes second place to feeling inconvenienced by it. And no matter what the drug, substance abuse always requires some sacrifice.

For people to stand without crutches—for the sacrifices they make to take substances to start to become burdensome—the substance abuse has to get replaced with something that feels even better. There are a lot of better feelings that top the feeling of getting high. But it takes a lot of faith to know that without actually having had those feelings.

Marijuana users, like all drug users, certainly want to avoid feelings. But even more so, they want to fill an emptiness they do not even know is there. I feel this emptiness, and I know it well. The emptiness is deeply buried underneath all the frustrations of being alive—it takes a while to find it. In fact, the feeling of emptiness is only felt once you have finally slogged through a lot of layers of negativity that provide the illusion of fullness. People think it's emotional chaos and disturbance that cause drug relapses. But actually, it's dangerous whiffs of emptiness.

But when that emptiness is felt and can be spoken to someone else who also knows it, so that you are no longer alone with the experience, it can dissolve. Then the desire to feel high—to be filled with pleasant sensation, floating in the moment, not worrying about the future—starts to feel old, and a new anxiety and distaste for being high takes over.

Mercy was floating now, trying to make her own life. "Everything feels better when I'm high," she explained to me, "going to the movies, eating a slice of pizza, even sitting down to read something."

"Yeah," I said, nodding in agreement with how important it is to feel better.

"I don't know—it's like I feel safe when I'm high," Mercy added. Marijuana makes people paranoid, yet people feel better, and safer, when they're high on it. This is because paranoia doesn't always take the form of "they are out to get me." It can also take the form of "no one's here for me." Since feeling empty and alone is familiar to the marijuana user, they don't notice or mind the side effect of that particular brand of paranoia—in fact, it resonates. That's the hard part about treating marijuana users: they can love and be loved but they can't bear disappointment, because it smacks of emptiness.

So I knew that Mercy knew no deep emotional comfort. That she was alone, disappointed and agitated.

"I have no problem with your getting high. In fact, I'm surprised you don't do more than smoke weed," I said to Mercy, reflecting on how much contempt her mother had for her. "How have you managed not to become a heroin addict?"

"I don't know," she said. "Sometimes I wonder. I'm strong I guess." Then she looked at me and asked, "Why do you say that?"

I said, "I don't think your family understands you at all."

"I know," Mercy said, looking at me intently. And then she looked down and said, "But I don't care, I'm used to it. I manage. I can't wait to leave home. I think about going to my cousin's house. They live in Virginia."

Then Mercy started opening up to me. About her hopes and dreams; who she was and what she wanted. She was very bitter about her home life.

I understood how painful things were for Mercy at home. I got that she was strong. I got that she needed a place that wasn't going to try to move her to a "better" place—that could meet her where she was, appreciating that it wasn't easy for a child to be so alone. I got that she needed to keep filling up her empty spaces by getting high, as much as my heart bled for how alone she was.

Ted and Diana

Mercy's father Ted was short, about fifty pounds overweight, and had a beady-eyed expression that bespoke a calculating nature. He did not look to me like a man it would be easy to love. The discomfort aroused by his look was much relieved by the way he dressed: a silky grey suit and dark blue shirt. If nothing else, you might be seduced by his air of power and money.

Ted had driven up in a Mercedes convertible that looked small alongside Diana's Cadillac Escalade, similar to how they looked in person since she was taller than him. Just like his daughter, Ted did not make eye contact with me. When he sat down across from me on the couch, the way he released his breath let me know that this visit was requiring some patience and that he was experiencing some exasperation.

"You gonna fix my kid?" he then bellowed, and I smiled at his playfulness.

"I don't know," I said, "she's pretty stubborn!"

"You got that right," he said as he undid the button on his jacket. "She gets that from her mother."

"Very funny, Ted," Diana said. "Come on."

"I know Mercy is stubborn," she continued, "but we have to do something. We can protect her up to a point. Other family members have not done well in school, but we have the means to fund projects. Maybe Mercy will marry; she is certainly a beautiful girl. But if she gets a tattoo, you see, it will make it impossible for her to move ahead with any of that. She is basically shooting herself in the foot. So we really need some direction here for how to help her come to her senses. She is threatening that if we don't sign the papers for this tattoo, since she's a minor, she's just going to forge them and get it done herself with a friend who drives."

Ted started to breathe hard at this point and shuffle in his seat.

"Do you feel the same way, Ted?" I asked.

"Oh, jeez. You know, I don't even know why we're here. She's fine. A tattoo isn't going to make or break her. So she'll open a shop that sells leather, I don't know. My wife has a tendency to get a little dramatic. I told her I don't think she should get in such a heap about it, but she's insisting this is serious. I don't believe it."

Diana said, "Ted wants to tell Mercy she can get the tattoo. I am forbidding it. Forbidding it."

"OK, OK, I hear you—I'm not doing anything," Ted said, hurriedly, placating her.

"Did your wife tell you why I wanted to see you?" I asked.

"Tell me yourself," he said, "I don't always trust my wife." Ted's eyes got even narrower at this, and I could see that he was scrutinizing me.

"Oh, I like to get a history," I explained.

"For what?" Ted asked confrontationally. "What's the plan here?"

My plan is always the same: to get people to talk until they say everything. "I like to get a history, and to understand what our goals should be," I explained, starting to feel cornered by this small corpulent man.

"Yeah, I get that. I will do my best," he said, but the feeling I had was that his cooperation was not heartfelt. In all likelihood, he didn't feel that he had much to offer in these emotional affairs.

"Ted is very busy running his financial company and hasn't been that involved with raising the kids," Diana explained. And then she added, "We have an arrangement that he manages the financial affairs, and I manage the house and the kids."

A good arrangement, I thought. Very sensible. Maybe it hadn't been such a good idea to invite Ted to the session, despite my protocol.

"Ted was not raised by his parents," Diana explained to me. "His mother was a teenager when he was born, and his grandparents raised him. They pretty much let him do whatever he wanted, so he didn't learn to respect his parents the way I was raised. I never spoke against my mother or did anything that she didn't approve of. So we raise the children more in keeping with how I was raised, which we both agree is probably the better way."

Diana sat back at this, as if waiting for something. Ted wiped his brow and said, "Oh, give me a break." His entire face scrunched up at this, and then his hand left his brow, and he dismissed her with it.

"I wasn't raised right, I know it, but what my wife always ceases to remember," he explained with feigned decorum, "is that she and her mother, God rest her soul, fought like cats."

"That's different," Diana said, totally incensed by this. "My mother was a wonderful woman."

"Oh, for crying out loud," Ted said with a look of disbelief. "If your mother was such a saint, Di, why'd you cry almost every week after we'd see her on Sunday when we got married?"

Diana turned to me and explained, "I didn't understand my mother back then, and I'm sure it wasn't easy for her. She was very exacting about what I should be, and I'm happy for it now. I'm grateful, and you should be too, Ted, for how she raised me. I only wish that she was alive today to see what I've been able to accomplish—that's my one regret."

"When did she pass?" I asked.

"About three years ago."

I started doing calculations in my head. Mercy was sixteen. That meant she would have been thirteen when her grandmother died—about the same time she had started getting "bad," as Diana put it. Was there a relationship between these parallel trajectories of change?

Ted said, "Personally, I think Mercy needs a little tough love. I told her, she gets that tattoo, her mother is going to have a heart attack. I won't keep giving her the allowance I'm giving; I won't buy her a car, nothing. It's that simple. You don't earn it; you don't get paid for it. But my wife says I'm off base."

The look on Diana's face was markedly anxious. This was totally different from the expression of disgust she'd worn throughout the session with her daughter.

"I don't know if tough love is the answer," she explained. "It seems we've been trying that and she's getting worse. I feel like we're losing her. I want Ted to be easier on her. He's so gruff with her."

"I'm not gruff," Ted huffed, "I'm honest. I don't want to see you like this. I try to be nice, your way, what's the point? How come you're allowed to tell her what you think, but I'm supposed to walk around the house like I'm not there?"

Diana looked at me imploringly, then said to him, "Ted, you don't get it. It's different. I'm her mother. I have to help her. But you're just mean. I'm not mean."

Diana didn't think she was being mean, and Ted didn't think he was being mean either. This is because when you speak your mind, you feel so much better that you can't connect to how mean you're being. It just feels so good to let off steam; it feels honest. Parents do what feels right for years, even when it completely fails, because it feels so good to say what feels right.

Of course, the truth is they were both mean. I'd witnessed it.

"So what is your position, Doctor, on parenting? Do you believe in tough love or do you believe in spare the rod?"

Actually, I have a very concrete parenting method, and I believe it takes into account all our sociological, psychological and even evolutionary diversities. As far as I can tell, my method has so far been proven to work with any and all children, to transcend generational lines, cultural evolution and any potential genetic predispositions to mental illness. It also crosses international boundaries, religious inclinations, socio-economic status and personal style. And yet I can outline it so simply in two words: act friendly.

That's it; that's all there is to it. If you can act friendly to your child, you have got it made as a parent—that's really all you have to do. Any and everything else is simply frosting on the cake.

Of course, there is one major problem with this method. And that is that, actually, there are zillions of things that interfere with acting friendly toward your child. Because children frustrate us, behave badly, require limits and lessons, and, for reasons of our own, we don't always feel friendly.

It's hard to act friendly through disappointment, worry, anxiety and frustration. Some parents can't hold on to positive feelings for their child through conflict and they withdraw emotionally. Other parents don't take the time to scratch beneath the surface of "bad" behavior, becoming punitive because they can't bear the thought of their child behaving so badly, and they are impelled to correct the behavior right away, without regard for the underlying feelings. It certainly can be difficult to be friendly towards children in the midst of problems, when children do not arouse loving or relaxed feelings. And to make matters worse, children can interpret mere stress as plain unfriendliness.

So acting friendly is the work of a lifetime, and it is not quite as easy as it sounds. I could see that Ted and Diana had stopped acting friendly with their Mercy and that they felt justified in acting unfriendly, perhaps towards each other, too. And in that justification, they had become blind to what they were doing in deed and attitude.

Now, some unfriendliness is natural in a family. That's what apologies are for, and it is how children learn that no one is perfect and that people have moods and idiosyncrasies. When there's conflict, unfriendliness is natural and required to push an agenda along and drive negotiations. Thank god there is no perfect, friendly parent, or a child would never make it in the real world. But chronic, deep unfriendliness creates pathology and has to be analyzed, prevented and cured.

"My parenting strategy," I said, not wishing to speak my two-word method and thus be taken for a fool, "is to see what works to get the child to do better. That's why we have to start here and understand what hasn't worked. That's why I wanted to talk to you today," I explained.

Diana said, "Well we've tried everything. I swear. I have tried talking to her, tried to reach her. I believe in trying to have a good, positive influence on your child. I have tried and tried to show her that the direction she is going in is self-destructive. Not healthy."

I would have liked to tell Diana right away that for a child such as Mercy, this was not a friendly thing to do.

Ted said: "You just have to put a stop to what you don't like, plain and simple." He paused here, for emphasis.

"I don't know," Diana said, looking worried. "I don't know why I can't take a stand with her," she added, looking at me anxiously.

"Maybe," I suggested, "she is too stubborn to respond to it."

"That's it, that's it," Diana said, pointing at me with a look of relief on her face, and then looking at Ted in a satisfied way. Diana was one of those people who wasn't sure exactly what she thought or felt until it could become reflected in another person's mind.

"See, Mercy's an Accumulator, Ted," Diana said.

"Oh, here we go," Ted said, and then explained to me, "Welcome to the philosophy of clutter."

"Ted thinks it's silly," Diana explained, "But I learn a lot about psychology in my work. See, Mercy's an Accumulator, meaning that she accumulates a lot of stuff. She still has stuffed animals and all the little plaques and figurines that she painted at Plaster Fun Time when she was little. And she has to have everything out in the open—it's all on shelves with knickknacks, clutter, stuff. Now, I'm a Tosser. Tossers get rid of everything. And Tossers and Accumulators have the hardest time getting along."

"Wait a minute, wait a minute," Ted said, with that scrunched up look again, "there's nothing wrong with having stuff, Diana."

"No, Ted," Diana argued, "because you're a Collector. That's different. You like to accumulate stuff, but it has a purpose. That can be organized. The Accumulator is a mess. It's different."

Ted looked at his phone.

Diana continued, "I have worked to get Mercy to be more of a Concealer so that we can put some of the stuff away. It makes me crazy. Tossers and Accumulators really can't get along—they are too different as people."

"So it feels hopeless," I said.

Diana looked thoughtful and corroborated, "Yes. It is pretty hopeless to have an Accumulator and a Tosser under the same roof. Clutter gurus recommend that if you're dating an Accumulator romantically and you're a Tosser, you should break up with that person because you are going to be very unhappy living together otherwise. You'll be too different and drive each other crazy."

Ted's phone started vibrating, and he put it to his ear faster than you can say Jack Rabbit. I thought he was going to get up and step out of the office to take the call since it was a nice day outside, but he didn't bother.

"Yeah," he said into the phone. Diana started looking at her shoes. Then he said, "Give it to Joe, give it to Joe. I don't care. Not your problem." He listened a little longer to the other voice on the line, and Diana looked up at me apologetically. People deferred to Ted in this family.

Ted said into the phone, "I'll be there when I get there." Then he removed it from his ear ending the call expertly with his thumb as he lowered it.

"So you still need me?" he said to Diana, as if his job had been done.

"I don't know. Dr. Luiz, do you think you need Ted?"

"May I please be excused?" Ted said to me, a smile playing on his thin lips.

"Thanks for coming, Ted," I said.

"No problem at all," Ted said, and as he got up, he said, "Doctor, I don't mean to speak disrespectfully to you in any way—I am sure you know what you are doing. But I don't really believe in therapy. Mercy is not going to listen to anybody. I was fully grown by the time I was eleven. She is not going to listen to any one of us."

"I think you have hit the nail on the head," I said.

"So you agree? So…why are we here?"

"Because there is still something that you haven't tried," I said. "Somewhere between trying to control her with limits and trying to change her mind with conversation is something you can do to save her," I explained. And Ted sat down.

"There is no bridge between you all," I explained.

"Well, we've been trying very hard to build one," Diana said.

"It hasn't worked," I said, "because no one has shown you how as yet."

"What kind of bridge are you talking about?" Ted asked.

"The way to build a bridge with a child who, as you say, is fully grown, is not by trying to sell her on the advantages of being in your world, as fine as we all know that it is," I said.

"But she's only sixteen!" Diana said.

"Fully grown, honey," Ted said.

"She's like me," he explained. "I had a mind of my own. My wife Diana is different. She didn't grow up until her mother died."

"Ted!" Diana said, "How can you say that? I was married; I had two children; I was completely an adult before my mother died."

Ted dismissed her with that scrunched up face again and said, "That woman had all her children under her thumb and none of them made a move without her. And nothing you could ever do was right."

Diana was shuffling uncomfortably, and I could see that this perception of her role as daughter was unsettling for her. "My mother was a wonderful woman," she said to me in a prim way. No negativity allowed.

"Let's stick with the problem, Ted, the problem is Mercy," she added.

"Well you're going to have to stop babying her," Ted said.

"I agree," I said. Experts today all say we spoil and baby our children, but that's not it. What we're trying to do with all our accolades and money, anxiety and attention, is spare them our corresponding chronic negativity. We don't want to reveal any of our intense disapproval, even as it throbs within us. We're trying to be better than our insensitive parents. Problem is, we have all those negative feelings. It's not the accolades and gifts that are the problem; it's that our negativity is still showing through, more unwanted and forbidden than ever, and therefore perhaps even more toxic than ever. In this case, there was so much negativity it had become the new normal; Mercy's parents weren't even aware of it any more. They were just exasperated.

I said, "Mercy is smart, Diana—she can feel your disapproval. No matter how much you sugarcoat it by telling her how wonderful she is and giving her pep talks about what she could do with herself."

"Well, I do disapprove," Diana said, who, like all people who had parents who were critical or disapproving, end up feeling disappointed in and critical of their own children. This is how we all build a bridge back to our own parents to feel complete: by siding with them in our minds and wanting our children to be better. It's a form of internalizing the aggressor.

"The bridge you have to build is not from her world back to yours. It has to be built from your side to hers. You have to hide your disappointment, even though it's justified, because that keeps the bridge from being built."

"I'm sorry, I don't fully understand. What does this bridge do exactly, if she's not going to listen to us?" Diana asked.

"Well, when you build a bridge to her world, instead of trying to talk her into coming into your world, you have to make your way to hers—so she will get connected to you. That connection is what will ultimately help her to thrive."

"But if you say she's fully grown, what is the point? What if she's made up her mind to be like this for the rest of her life?"

"It doesn't matter how old your child is when you learn how to build a bridge to them. You can do this even if they're forty-five. It's good for the whole family."

Diana looked disappointed. It's so enticing to become your mother—in this case, a critical, disappointed woman. It connects all the dots. To change and leave home, explore new horizons and get to know your children in a new way, is unsettling. I knew this, and I knew it would be hard for Diana to try something different. It would almost mean she would have to return to feeling oppressed, this time by her daughter.

Ted said, "Diana, you can talk to Mercy till you're blue in the face, and I'm done getting into these screaming matches with her. I don't have time for it. I say, let's do this thing. Let's go over to her world or what have you, and try it. What have we got to lose, a few months of our lives?"

Building bridges takes many years, so I didn't say anything here, just nodded. We'd take it one step at a time. Starting with lesson one.

Lesson 1: How to help parents stop preaching and teaching

"Unfortunately," I explained to Diana at our next session, "when you try to coach, guide and teach Mercy all these good things—how to organize her time or her closet, how to dress or appear—she takes it as a criticism. We are hardwired to teach our children, but with kids like Mercy it just doesn't work."

"But it isn't criticism," Diana insisted, a slight smile playing on her face that revealed the enjoyment she got from giving her coaching lectures.

"I know," I said, "and you're a parent. That's what parents do. We are hardwired to create children in our image to be the best that they can be, I know."

"That's right," Diana practically wailed, looking incensed that anyone would take it any other way.

"That's what we're supposed to do, and it generally works with children to be guided and taught. But some children don't take it that way, unfortunately, because they're negative people."

"There's no such thing—all children are God's angels. Mercy's just a little stubborn," Diana said.

"That's right," I said. I stood corrected. Diana didn't like negative statements.

"I swear she was born stubborn. Do you know, even when I changed her diaper or tried to nurse her, sometimes she would arch her back. You know, like she wouldn't go with it."

My mind instantly flashed to the mermaid doing a backflip. Babies arch their backs sometimes to try to get away from what is happening because they're stressed or overstimulated. The arched mermaid, I realized, was a metaphor for freedom—for a way to stretch the body out of a state of tension.

"So we have to find a positive way to deal with this 'stubbornness.' And talking sense to her hasn't worked yet," I explained.

"I swear, I'm destined to be surrounded by stubborn people," Diana said.

"Say more," I said.

"My mother was stubborn, my husband is stubborn, and now my daughter. Nobody ever wants to listen to me. I'm nothing. I'm nobody."

Now I could understand why Diana could not be friendly to Mercy. She felt overlooked.

"Well, I'm very glad you're saying that here," I said. I was damned if I wasn't going to hear this poor woman out. "It is very hard living with bull-headed people."

"It is, it is, it is," Diana said.

"Can you stand it a little longer to build a bridge to Mercy? Or do you want me to help you not be overlooked by your husband and daughter instead?" I asked.

Diana threw up her arms at that. "I give up," she said, and added, "at least *you'll* listen to me."

"I certainly will," I agreed, "you can always come and talk to me."[3]

Lesson 2: How to pretend to be friendly

We were six months into the treatment, and Diana had been coming in once a month and talking about what Mercy was doing and how to stay clear of "teaching" her.

Mercy, in the meantime, had been coming in weekly, having figured out that I was on her side since her parents had almost completely stopped hounding her since she'd been coming.

I also knew that Mercy had struck up a sexual relationship with another girl in her class, and that her parents didn't know a thing about it. Or so I thought. Which is why I was surprised to see Ted walking purposely up the path with Diana at her next scheduled appointment, until I realized: they knew.

As they came in, Diana's lips were pursed, and she avoided eye contact with me. I felt like Ted was her bodyguard. He greeted me.

"To what do I owe the pleasure of your company here today, Ted?" I asked.

"Well," Ted exhaled, "I think we've got ourselves a little problem."

"I can't do this," Diana said, her eyes welling up with tears. "I can't believe what's happened; I can't believe it. It was on Tuesday, and I went in to Mercy's room to get her laundry, and she was there with her little friend Jana. I walk in and I swear to God…" at this, she lowered her head and shielded her eyes as if to shield the truth, "they were making out."

Ted looked out the window and silence descended upon the room. Then he said, "Diana's a devout Christian, Claudia."

"I know," I said.

"That's not all of it," Diana said.

"They had their shirts off. And my baby has a full body tattoo—the mermaid—across her whole side. The head is coming down over her belly, the tail going to her back."

Mercy had done it.

"It looked red in some places," Diana was crying hard at this point, "my baby… That must have hurt so much."

"This…" Diana said, "this is beyond stubborn, Ted," as if he was to blame for having underestimated the degree of Mercy's independence.

"This is beyond anything," she continued. "This is a direct slap in my face. This is like saying to me, 'I hate you, I don't like you, I don't care about you or anything you stand for.' I think she has to leave. I think we have to find her someplace else to live."

"What do you think, Ted?" I asked.

"Well, I think she's clearly gone too far," he said, "don't you?"

"I think that it's to be expected," I said. "As you yourself analyzed, Ted, she's got her own life. She's been living it for a long time, and kids today do have more open fields to experiment."

Diana said, "I thought if we built a bridge and stopped telling her what we thought, it was going to help. But it's only getting worse."

"It's not getting worse," I explained, "it's only showing more."

"Well, how are we supposed to deal with this?" Diana wailed.

I said, "Can you stand to keep building the bridge? Can you stand to live with her as she starts to reveal her own world and act out her independence?"

Diana and Ted thought about this. Then Ted shrugged his shoulders and said, "I would like to, but my wife wants me to find a home for her. But I would like her to stay." Then he quickly added, to appease his wife, "I know it's not appropriate."

I said, "It may not be appropriate, but she is living her own life, as you know. And if you can stand it, things will get better. The bridge will get built."

"How can I build a bridge to this?" Diana said softly, as if to herself, tears pouring out of her eyes.

"By acting," I explained. "You bring your feelings here and find something in what she's done to feel positive about."

Diana liked positivity, but this was a stretch. "Tell me one positive thing about this," she cried.

"Well, what's positive about it is that it gives you a chance not to judge her, and to show that you are not going to do what you have always done— try to get her to be a part of your world—and that you will try to be open to being a part of hers."

"God help me," Diana said, "I don't know if I can do this."

"Sure you can," Ted said. "It's not so bad."

Diana looked at him as if he was crazy. He was actually much more open-minded than she was, but had been afraid to say so.

"My Aunt Ella was a dyke," he said. "I loved her."

Diana scoffed at this, and looked betrayed and terrified.

"I don't want to kick her out," Ted said, "I had no mother. What the hell. So what. Who gives a shit."

Diana's eyes widened at that, and she looked long and hard at Ted. She had not realized how little he cared about Mercy walking the straight and narrow path.

"I don't know," she said, dismissing him. "What do I do if she says something? I'll have to pretend she's not my child. I'll have to pretend she's someone else's. I don't know how I'm going to do this."

Diana's creative imagination was at work, and despite the desperation behind how she was going to pull off connecting to her daughter, she was really trying to stretch her mind to being different.

"Building a bridge is quite an acting job," I said, knowing that for Diana to exercise restraint in trying to build a bridge would be a serious stretch.

It would be easier for Ted because he was more removed. He was in his own thoughts a lot and had grown up as independent as Mercy. His family, which he had always believed was beneath Diana's, was full of quirky people. Now, his way was helping them to build a bridge to his daughter. This was good for him.

But for Diana to act as if everything was normal and these atrocities weren't going on under her own roof—things that felt so totally unacceptable and foreign—was going to be the hardest thing she'd ever do.

"Di, I feel like we're reaching her. She talks to me more. She feels more relaxed. Claudia, she even came out to dinner a few nights ago and sat with us. Didn't talk much, but hey, it was a start."

"I feel like I'm living with a monster—this isn't my child," Diana said.

"She's not the devil, Di," Ted said. "She's just a little confused. She's all right. You haven't done anything bad or wrong—it's a different time." Ted really understood Mercy much better than Diana could. Thank goodness for him.

Lesson 3: How to invite negativity

Diana had learned to have what paralleled, in some ways, an out-of-body experience with Mercy. When she was around her, her attitude was something in between hopelessness and passivity. It was hard for her to give up teaching Mercy how to look and how to act, but she was doing it, coming to see me every other week to process things and get support. She was really in analysis herself at this point, realizing some things about her own brand of emptiness.

In fact, she was doing a good job of being friendly towards Mercy. When Mercy came into a room, Diana would say "hello," politely, holding in her mind the image of Mercy as a toddler, when she was delightful.

While Mercy had not come any closer to being connected to her parents than she ever had, she wasn't doing badly. She had gained an interest in selling handmade jewelry on the Etsy website, and she spent a lot of time making things and selling them.

Actually, things had come to a bit of a standstill. I don't push things because I do not exactly welcome crisis—it comes when it comes. Still, crisis is probably the best instigator to move something along, so I suppose it was a good thing that it was about to happen.

The weather had fittingly just turned cold when Diana arrived for her session, almost a year after Mercy had gotten her mermaid tattoo, and she was angry. This time, she arrived without Ted to act as her bodyguard. I guess that was progress.

"Something happened yesterday, I'm sure you'll hear about it. I don't know what to do. I think things are getting worse. Mercy showed up at the door; she was with her friend Wendy, and Wendy was holding her up. I mean, literally, holding her up. And she looked green. I said 'What's the matter, Honey? You look like you're not feeling well.' She didn't answer me. So I followed them—I was worried sick. Then Wendy comes out and tells me that apparently they smoked marijuana with some boys outside of a movie theater, and Mercy must have had some kind of bad reaction. It must have been laced with something. Wendy told me that Mercy was screaming and screaming, and she thought she was going to die. She's getting worse.

It's getting worse. I'm really scared. We have to talk about this together as a family—something's gotta give."

I agreed to Diana's asking Mercy to join her at her next session. I had no idea how it would go, but I was worried about how desperate Diana seemed about the self-destructiveness she'd witnessed in her child, and the degree to which she could not accept it any more. This could result in going backwards if it was not managed properly, by talking.

Mercy came in with her mother two days later looking tired; dark circles lined her eyes, and the heavy black liner that she winged over her lids was smudged. Diana, on the other hand, looked as crisp as ever.

"Mercy," she said, "I don't know what to do."

Mercy looked up at her. "'Do,' Mom?" she said.

"Yes, Mercy. I don't know what to do. I'm concerned about you."

"You're concerned about me. Wow. Really?"

"Yes, Honey, that's right, I'm downright worried. The condition I saw you in the other night was atrocious. You looked green. What happened?" Diana asked.

"Nothing 'happened,' Mom. It's none of your business," Mercy answered, looking at me conspiratorially, since I had heard about it and knew Mercy was thinking of stopping getting high altogether after a bad drug experience.

"None of my business? I'm your mother. If something ever happened to you, I don't know what I'd do."

Mercy looked out of the window.

I told her, "Say it."

Mercy did not say anything.

"Say it," I repeated.

Mercy slowly turned her head toward her mother, her eyes filled with poison.

"What the fuck, Mom," she said, and turned away again.

"What the fff...?" Diana repeated. "What does that mean?"

"What does THAT mean?" Mercy said. "It means what the FUCK do you give a shit? When the FUCK is it ever about anybody but yourself, your ideas, your values, your teachings, YOU, YOU, YOU. That's what 'what the fuck' means, Mom. OK?"

Diana grew pale. She looked shell-shocked. She said, "This is bad," into the atmosphere.

"No it isn't," I said gently, and her gaze turned to me although it still was blank.

"Your daughter's giving you the gift of her thoughts," I said.

"She hates me," Diana said, crying.

"Hate is not the opposite of love. Indifference is. These are strong feelings. Hear them. You should be honored that you're finally getting them. Here is the bridge."

"Oh," Diana said, and then added, "Mercy, Mercy my baby," and she started crying more.

She said, "You know I love you so much. You know…when you were born, I felt my life had truly started. You and I, holding you…"

"That's not who I am, Mom," Mercy interrupted sharply. "I'm not a baby anymore that you can carry around and dress up and hold against you like I'm some kind of appendage. I'm not an appendage. I am a PERSON. I am DIFFERENT from you. Can you see that? You've never SEEN me, Mom. You can't even see me right now," and then Mercy started crying.

"How can I see you, Sweetheart? Tell me how to see you," Diana pleaded.

"Just *listen* to me, Mom. Listen to what I'm saying. Stop judging me. Stop thinking that you know what I am—some kind of failure. I'm not. I'm a person. I feel things. I hate myself. You just make me feel like shit, Mom. I come within a foot of you and I want to fucking kick something."

"Oh, Mercy, Mercy, I'm so sorry," Diana said. "Tell me, show me how to love you."

"It's too late, Mom," Mercy said, drawing herself up. "It's way too late for that."

Diana looked at me, as if to ask me what she should do with that pronouncement. I closed both my eyes to tell her to have patience.

Then I said, "It may be too late for you to be friends. But I think it's a good idea for you to understand each other. And keep talking."

"My own mother could never give me feelings that I needed," Diana said to me and to Mercy. "I don't know how to do this."

"Mercy will help you," I said. "She knows what she needs, and she did a wonderful job of telling you today. She needs for you to hear her, and today you heard her."

Diana nodded her head, accepting that perhaps, she had done a good job being a mother today. It was different from the feeling she had always had growing up, of not doing anything right. Still, I could see her descend into a dark place, but there was nothing I could do about it because I knew the best thing for the family now was for Mercy to be heard. I would help Diana later to deal with her feelings after being so brutally accused of being so inadequate as a mother.

Diana was sacrificing feeling righteous and proper to learn how to build a bridge to Mercy. She deserved a medal. But motherhood is all about sacrifice, even if what you must sacrifice is your own idea about what's right. That's probably the greatest lesson having children gives: how to become selfless in doing what you have to do for your child.

Lesson 4: How to listen and hear

"Once upon a time," I said, beginning my story for Diana at her next session, to help her deal with the depression she was experiencing thanks to the enormousness of Mercy's anger and disappointment, "there were two mothers."

"These mothers," I continued, "were in a pregnancy group at a nursery school run by some psychoanalysts in New York City where I worked.

"Now, one of the mothers was an older woman. She had waited for a long time to have a baby, and she loved being pregnant. Loved it. She had quit work and couldn't wait to hold her baby—to cuddle it and bond with it, to carry it around and introduce it to the world. In fact, she was in the therapy group precisely because she wanted to process her childhood to make sure not to repeat her own mother's mistakes."

"The other woman was a young career woman. She had wanted to have a family but her pregnancy felt like the invasion of the body-snatchers. She had joined the group to get support because she was feeling so stressed out by the pregnancy. To prepare for her baby's birth, she had already lined up nannies and a daycare, and couldn't wait to get her body and her life back."

"The day arrived when both these women gave birth; the woman who couldn't wait to meet her baby had a son, and the career woman had a daughter."

"The son, unfortunately, did not turn out to be a baby who wanted to be held and cuddled. He fussed loudly whenever his poor mother tried to hold him. She always ended up having to put him down. He needed lots of space. He didn't even like to be swaddled, preferring to kick his legs and punch his arms out. He pulled on her nipple fiercely when he fed, then spat her out when he was done. I remember how she cried and cried at the hands of that little tyrant."

"The daughter, on the other hand, could not be put down. The career woman looked enviously at the boy baby, happy in his bassinette while she felt stressed and exhausted from having to continually hold her infant girl. She had to wear the baby all the time, a new form of invasion she hadn't counted on, which often lasted throughout the night. The little whiner had made her a wreck."

"What a cruel twist of fate that these two mothers would have children so intrinsically ill-suited to them. If only they could have had each other's babies! The career woman would have loved the independent baby boy and would have reveled in his spirit and his strength rather than have seen him as a tyrant. The older woman would have loved that baby girl, and would have held and swaddled her all day and night without a pause instead of seeing her as needy."

"So that is how it goes sometimes," I pointed out to Diana. "We get a child we are less suited to."

"What did those mothers do?" Diana asked.

"They did what you are doing now. They had to get to know their children and learn how not to feel tormented, and how not to feel badly toward the child and understand it instead. They had to learn to gird their loins to give the child what that child needed, and to act friendly toward the child."

"What does my child need?" Diana asked.

"I think, right now, your child needs you to know that she has felt alone for a long time. And also, that she can't imagine ever feeling close to you. If you can understand that, and hear it, you are building the bridge because she will no longer be alone in speaking her truth. In fact, she is already not alone—you have succeeded in that. You're doing a good job. You should be proud of yourself."

Diana looked at me meekly. "If you say so," she said.

"I'm saying so," I told her. "I am definitely saying so."[4]

Lesson 5: How to re-interpret things

Ted had asked to come in to the next session, and he arrived with a book in his hands called *Brand New Mind*, by Daniel Pink, that he had been offered at an organizational management conference.

"Have you seen this?"

"Sure," I lied.[5]

"Brilliant, brilliant," he said. "Explains everything. I want you to explain this to Di."

Diana rolled her eyes.

"See we're not in the information age any more," he explained to me.

"We're in what he calls the communication age. Do you see where I'm going?"

"OK," Diana said, in a patronizing tone.

"So that means our kid is going to be OK."

"How is that, dear?" she asked.

"Because, lookit, these kids need a brand new set of competencies—storytelling, design. This is not about being a lawyer or a doctor anymore—because of the Internet, because of the demand for stories to give meaning to products in a competitive market. See? There isn't just one phone any more, there's ten. So design becomes imperative, get it?" Ted was really excited about this.

"That's who Mercy is—she's so into design. She's an innovator, this is good," he explained.

"She's a 'SHE' is what she is, Ted," Diana said.

"Oh, please," Ted sighed, exasperated.

"Sidetracked Home Executive—this is from Flylady," Diana explained.

"A 'SHE' is someone who is sidetracked and disorganized, and a 'BO'—Born Organized—is someone who remembers to look at their calendar, cleans up after themselves and can stay organized. I'm starting to understand a SHE," Diana added.

I could see that the psychological model Diana borrowed from the world of organizing had shifted away from one of hopelessness about ever being compatible with Mercy, to one of greater understanding about the different way they operated.

"I get it now," Diana explained. "I didn't help Mercy because I did not understand her. Her style. She's a SHE, and I'm a BO."

"You didn't get her style," Ted said, hope lifting. "She is a child of the future, and this is what we've got to foster because that's what she's come into. You know Hope is more old-fashioned like us. But to be honest, I think that Mercy is the real powerhouse here. You know, the one who is gonna make millions. So I was thinking, Dr.—tell me what you think of this 'cause Di is fighting me. There's an internship—a design internship—at one of the big financial companies we work with. Those guys have kids go in, and the kids make their way around. Di says Mercy's not up to it. I need to fight her on this."

"She's not up to it," Diana said. "She sleeps until noon when she can; her hair is blue, with the eyeliner. She's not going to fit in there. Don't you think, Claudia? A SHE is not a corporation person."

"Ask her," I counseled. "Consult with her on it."

So Ted invited his daughter to apply for the internship at the financial company in their design department. And guess what? Mercy liked the idea. She applied, and got in. And she got up every morning and went to work.

One evening Mercy approached Diana. She told her mother about one of the people in the department who had dismissed her and been a little hostile. Diana listened quietly and did not try to get her to have a better, more positive attitude. She really wanted to say, "Maybe you should dye your hair brown; some people are intimidated by that neon color." Instead, she said, "That guy sounds like a jerk."[6] She was becoming so very good at being friendly. A friendly relationship was starting to bud.

The key to patience

Mercy decided to definitively stop smoking marijuana regularly exactly three years after her first session, before going to college. She went through the usual months-long withdrawal symptoms: insomnia, horrible dreams, anxiety and intense cravings to get high. But she got over it, and enjoyed the feeling of being clear-headed and strong. She said she felt like she was waking up.

Diana continued to work with me for many years, and occasionally brought Ted in when they could not see eye-to-eye. I met Hope, too, who was not as perfect as she had seemed. She carried a lot of tension in her body. Diana was able to help her start to talk as well.

Many years later, the family came to visit me as a whole, on a whim before a family event they were all attending. "Remember when you told me we would never be friends?" Diana reminisced, looking at Mercy. Mercy laughed. "Sorry, Mom!" she said. Diana's eyes welled up with tears. This was the moment when I could see that the sacrifices she'd made had paid off.

"Took a lot of patience," Ted said, in a somewhat disapproving tone.

"No it didn't," Mercy said. "You guys needed me to rescue you from suburban mediocrity."

"You must be a very patient person," Diana said to me. "It's quite an art."

I almost laughed out loud when I heard that; I am not a patient person. My mind, as I work, is always churning. Even when I appear to be saying nothing, I'm very busy, thinking about theories of the mind and clinical metatheory.

I'm assessing my feelings and where they're coming from, considering what is needed from me in both quantity and quality of words, determining how to match myself to the tenor and the manners in the room, gauging whether there is enough tension to keep someone engaged or if there's not enough, and whether it is time or not to intervene.

I have the voices of all my supervisors inside my head, a magic hat filled with interventions I can pick and choose from that can range from sweet to cold, and a way of understanding what it takes to keep a person's thoughts still flowing and not cut them off with a hasty conclusion. I think about whether the person's energy is turned inward against themselves or outward in some form of hostility against the world. I think about whether, once I feel that hostility, I should take it by the horns or, like a troubadour, deflect it so that it keeps moving past me to a safer place.

There is a lot of knowledge, gleaned from a lot of training, that helps me build what looks like patience and that keeps me occupied as I am designing what I will do. I know that preparing a mind for self-discovery requires time and the right emotional experiences, but I don't always know what those emotional experiences will be, when they will happen and whether they will work, leaving me in a perennial place of uncertainty; a constant state of suspended animation.

It's all a big experiment. Each patient a new subject for research about how the doors inside a person's mind open up to new parts of themselves. And because each person is as unique as their own thumbprint, there is no map. Sometimes I know that I must talk and guide and solve, and other times, just understand and say nothing at all.

So it may look like I am patient, but I really like to think of what I do as being in the name of science: applying a research method through which I dispense dosages of emotion that keep energies flowing in a better direction, build bridges of connectedness and create strength of mind so that continued talking will lead to greater discoveries.

I smiled at Diana, realizing how much patience she had exercised without much more than a little faith and maybe some steadfast, good encouragement from Ted and me. But she had learned a lot along the way: about how to be friendly, how to hear and how to follow Mercy's feelings. About how to listen beyond mere awareness to what was being said; and about how to stand against incredibly negative forces and stay the course, steady and upright. She had herself become an excellent analyst.

Ultimately it was Diana, far more than me, who had helped Mercy to grow and to love and to accept herself, because a good mother is the most powerful change agent there can be. And here they all were now, thanking me. It was a wonderful moment for me, and rare. A moment in which I could deeply enjoy the virtuosity I had achieved being an analyst. "Congratulations to all of you," I said. "You are all doing a wonderful job of helping each other to feel understood, and grow." And I meant every word.

LAYERS OF LISTENING

The word 'virtuosity' brings to my mind the image of a great violinist or pianist who not only has impeccable mastery over their instrument, but who also brings their own unique brand of creative genius to a piece of music. One day, about fifteen years into my training, I had the wonderful feeling that I too had achieved a measure of virtuosity practicing psychoanalysis.

It was in a signature session with a very angry man who told me he wanted to leave treatment. Of course, I've never liked being left—it's one of those emotional experiences that I perhaps most dislike. But while my *subjective countertransference* throbbed dully in the background, I was practiced enough in dealing with the dynamic by then that I could sufficiently ignore it.

I understood too, what was happening inside him: he was angry because he had learned that I was giving a talk at a school. It made him realize that I had an exciting life. Apparently, that made him feel like, by comparison, he had no life. What was the point of staying in treatment? Why should he pay me so I could keep having a good life, while he continued to suffer? I felt that by trying to leave treatment, he was not only punishing me by depriving me of his money, but also trying to transfer over to me some of the feelings of failure that he lived with chronically, by proving that I had failed to help him.

I certainly wanted him to transfer feelings of failure to me—that would be good for him, and I was willing to shoulder the feelings. If he could direct some of his aggression outwards towards me, instead of back onto himself, that would constitute progress.

I had actually been feeling like a failure with this case for some time, and had talked frequently with my supervisor, who had helped me with my *countertransference resistance* to accepting the feelings since this man truly refused to get better, and would not stop complaining about his lot in life. So I was prepared to help him talk about my being a failure out loud. The question was: could I become the inadequate person in the room without his having to leave treatment to prove it to me?

As the session unfolded, I said, "I know I have not been able to figure out how to help you yet. But why can't you stay with me anyway, and give me another chance?" Here, I was able to design an *emotional communication* that carried enough of a mix of frustration and gratification, by agreeing with him and yet asking him to do something he didn't want to do, to help him find words for his frustration and rage.

As we struggled to find a narrative for how I had managed to fail him, this patient could finally see it and say it: I was the failure—not him. This, I knew, would create a seismic change in how he typically organized his rage, as it may very possibly have been the first time he had ever told anyone how frustrated and disappointed he was. It may have also been the first time anybody had withstood his rage and willingly shared in its burden.

At the next juncture in the session, as his unspoken feelings of profound frustration and loneliness found expression, I began to feel deeply exhilarated by the power of psychoanalysis. In the silence that followed the expression of his feelings, the room felt deeply charged with emotion, both solemn and profound. The exhilaration was combined with a sense of relief and unburdening, as we had arrived at a place where he and I could finally connect about the bitter truth of his inner life. Needless to say, he stayed in treatment.

My feeling of virtuosity came in realizing how much had gone into helping this patient talk about such heavily-charged, never-spoken feelings. So much had gone into being able to work with him—I had been able to juggle so many things: my knowledge of him with a theory of the mind, an understanding of clinical theory, my own induced feelings and the internalized voice of my supervisor telling me what to say. In the process, I had also enjoyed my creativity, being able to come up with a way to intervene with this patient in a way that felt authentic and therapeutic.

If you are in training you too will have to juggle all of the components I have tried to bring to you in this book about the making of a psychoanalyst. You too will learn new ways to listen to your feelings, to theories of the mind, to clinical theory, to supervisors and mentors and, most importantly, to the patient.

And you too will have that gleaming day when you would first enjoy experiencing real psychoanalytic virtuosity, juggling all of the impressions and knowledge, and then coming up with an emotional communication that could lead your patient to say something they have never been able to say before.

Perhaps the hardest part is mastering yourself, the juggler. It's really difficult to get to know yourself. Most people don't want to know bad things about themselves. And often, when they do, it makes them feel worse. Eventually, with enough treatment, you can not only stand knowing horrible truths about yourself, but also increase your compassion for your own condition. This is what can build your resolve to create a better life.

The virtuosity, then, begins to extend outside the treatment setting where you are doing meaningful work with well-intentioned people. Your entire life in fact becomes infused with meaning and purpose, even and perhaps especially in your darkest hours.

The road is long. There were many times when I truly thought I wouldn't make it, either in the room with a particular analyst, in my school or in life. I have discovered that at each new rung on the ladder of getting better, I have to revisit old dynamics in the new context, and get to know myself better from a different light. Fortunately, all you have to do to keep progressing is stay with your own analysts, supervisors and teachers, who are there to help you.

Through this hard, hard work though, come the shining, gleaming moments of recognition that the life of a psychoanalyst is a very emotionally rich one indeed. You become very central to a lot of people's lives. You learn to invite yourself in and stop leaving yourself out in the cold. You develop relationships around you that are loving, through even the most enormous and challenging feelings of rage, hurt or pure exasperation.

Of course, becoming a psychoanalyst is different for each student. Learning how to use your own personality as an instrument for creating psychological change in others requires you to learn to navigate the terrain of your own interior life, which no one else has charted before you. But if there was one thing I would want every student reading this book to come away with, it would be this: psychoanalytic work is incredibly rich and rewarding. For me, there has been nothing more rewarding than the feeling of finally being able to put all the pieces together as you are treating a patient, not only by understanding what is happening in the room, but also by being able to bring my own brand of creative genius to the design of an intervention that stands the chance of changing someone else's life, so deeply, for the good.

Notes

1 Sibling rivalry takes many forms. Defying parental expectations by differentiating oneself against a preferred offspring is one way to compete against that sibling. Each sibling is filled with resentment in this case.

2 As a psychoanalyst confronted with an addiction problem, my primary interest is in knowing what the addiction serves to defend against. Then, I proceed with the usual process of preparing the patient's mind for self-discovery, with the idea in mind that being able to tolerate thoughts and feelings consciously will resolve the addiction. In this sense, addictions are conceptualized psychoanalytically as symptoms, and we don't work to resolve the symptom but rather to cure the underlying pathology.

3 By *joining* Diana in her feeling that she was overlooked by bull-headed people, I was supporting and therefore strengthening her in her version of reality. Her *transference* to Mercy, once verbalized, would be neutralized somewhat, which would help her with her goal to learn what Mercy needed.

4 In essence, I was teaching Diana how to 'join' which is a primary technique the twenty-first-century psychoanalyst uses to enter into the consciousness of another person. This is what best prepares the mind for self-discovery.

5 I may pretend to know the references my patients make to external materials because I believe it helps to foster the narcissistic transference, and they don't then have to worry about cluing me in to what they're talking about at the expense of continuing to talk about their own ideas.

6 This emotional communication had the effect of protecting and supporting Mercy's ego, which is strengthening. She was able to join Mercy's perception that someone had been hostile towards her, rather than correct the perception and try to change the problem.

8   Sylvie Spider

Swivel chair

Within moments of coming through my door, little Sylvie, who was only seven, made a beeline for my swivel chair. This chair, which I did my writing in, was a very fancy one. I could adjust the seat height, the angle of the tilt, the degree of back support and the exact position of the neck pillow. And it had been set to absolute perfection.

Adjusting the settings on this chair had been no small matter for me, requiring a very deep attunement to my body that I don't usually exercise. I had made a supreme effort to tune my body to this chair in order to avoid the violent revolution my body had staged against the prior one. And I had spent a lot of money on this chair; after all, one of Freud's first rules was: be comfortable.

After achieving that perfect synchronicity between my body and each aspect of this costly chair, waves of relief and thankfulness to all of the Gods of Supreme Comfort had washed over me as I sat in it. I actually whispered hallelujah out loud to myself; that's how comfortable this chair felt. Sylvie managed to destroy all that within a nanosecond.

Spinning around and around, she stopped for a moment to play with the up and down positions. This she did in little jolts, as if in synchronization with some rhythm in her head. She stopped again, this time to say, "I like your chair," and then she went back to the busy and important tasks of swiveling, tilting, raising and lowering.

When I had first seen Sylvie pop out of her mother's car and walk up my brick path, I was surprised that her mother drove away so quickly, and then that Sylvie had such a pleasant countenance. I had expected someone more glum, given how stressed and unhappy her mother seemed to be. But here she was having a fun time, playing with my chair. Children don't always like therapy—especially if they think they're there because somebody else is saying there's something wrong with them. I can't even count the number of times I've had to sit with a disgruntled child, having to welcome their negativity and offer to play cards or do something more fun than do this foolish, unnecessary therapy, hoping and praying that we would become friendly enough to start talking about a few things until "bingo!" we could have something that might be construed as therapy.

But hating therapy was not the problem here. Sylvie seemed perfectly happy to be with me. Not that she saw me as her pathway to salvation, but at least she was having an excellent amusement-park-like experience with the chair. She started to roll around the room.

I was wondering if I should set some limits on the use of the chair. You have to set limits on some behavior so that the child will feel safe and your office will be safe. But I was not sure, technically speaking, whether swiveling and rolling around in my personal, private chair constituted out-of-control behavior. Probably not. I hate setting limits. I was going to have to let this one go.

Sylvie was no longer spinning, but I realized that I was feeling kind of dizzy myself. Not the kind of dizzy where the world is actually spinning. Or the kind where you feel riveted by anxiety. It was more of a calm, hazy feeling of not being quite sure of where you are situated in space and time.

The types of emotions and sensations that people expose you to are never quite the same with every patient, but with children they are much easier to discern. Treating children is different from treating adults because children don't have a lot of theories about themselves yet. They usually do not yet have a story for what is happening inside themselves.

Children speak to you instead in a kind of code. This code is filled with sensations you have to listen to and behaviors that betray and reveal their true emotions. Maybe it's a sad sensation, like one that you might see in a child who talks particularly slowly and whose eyes seem a little hollow, who draws the same picture over and over again, trying to recreate something.

Maybe it's a code that expresses itself in the way a child moves around the room, constricting their limbs, which makes you think they have become inhibited, or flailing their arms as if electrified by an emotion they cannot yet contain.

Becoming attuned to the code that gets expressed when there is as yet no apparent story is vital to deciphering a hidden story. For example, a patient will tell me that she love-love-loves me, but then tell her mother that she doesn't want to come. What does that say about her feelings? It says that she doesn't enjoy loving me so much. Another child keeps forgetting to bring me the necklace she promised me, betraying not really wanting to give me anything, but yet calls to see if she can come and see me a day earlier.[1] Nothing can be relied upon for a single truth. All behaviors can be viewed as a code that may express some things that can't be said in words yet.

And sometimes it isn't a behavior that you must decode. Sometimes it is a feeling that is induced in you, an emotion that early in treatment you may not yet fully understand or even recognize. Some children, for example, terrify me. Others depress me. Some can really annoy me, and still others arouse in me the desire to take them into my arms and initiate adoption procedures. But this one was definitely making me feel dizzy.[2]

And even though Sylvie had finally moved over to a table where paper and pencils were set, I still felt dizzy. Was this how she felt? Doing therapy with children is no different from working with adults in this regard. Eventually you must decode sensation to figure out exactly what your mind and body is telling you about the case.

Sylvie took a pencil and started scribbling furiously. "You probably want me to draw something nice, but this is what I'm drawing," she said, looking over her shoulder at me, her pencil still wildly in motion. I looked over at the paper, at the hard, bold lines she was drawing. There was no form or story to what she drew, just endless obtuse spirals. I didn't know why she thought I wouldn't like that. Had someone told her that she had to draw between the lines? Conform to something that she did not want to acquiesce to?

She continued scribbling defiantly until she had filled a few pages, and maybe because I didn't seem to care one way or the other, she lost interest in it. She seemed to relax a little. Maybe this wasn't going to be a place that would control her.

Needless to say, the drawing added to my feeling dizzy. Usually, by this time in a treatment, I begin to formulate a diagnosis by making an assessment of how organized or disorganized I think a psyche finds itself. It was getting progressively easier to reach a firm diagnosis for this child; my thoughts—or maybe hers—were swirling. No wonder she couldn't pay attention.[3]

Less than a minute later, Sylvie walked over to my desk and began to study what was hanging on the wall over it. Her glance moved to a small picture of a green watermelon with a head of broccoli growing out of its side. One of my childhood friends who knew me well had made it for me. It was called *Melon-Ccoly*.

"What is *THAT*?" Sylvie demanded after staring at it for some time.

"Oh, that's a crazy vegetable that reminds me that sadness is a funny thing sometimes," I said.

"That's *weird*," said Sylvie, shaking her head. She was creating her own diagnosis.

She then started swinging her arms around herself nonchalantly, which I took as an invitation to initiate a little conversation. "Do you know why your mama brought you here, Sylvie?" I asked.

"Oh, yes, I know," she said. "It's because she wants me to be more like my brothers and my sister. And I don't eat her cooking. But I'm not hungry. I can't help it." With this, she plopped down on my couch.

"She gets so mad when I don't eat her dinner. But when I eat it I feel sick. I'm not lying—I get a stomach ache. I don't want to eat it. I told her it makes me sick and my Dad told her, but she thinks if I eat it, my homework will be better. Because it's good food, and the teachers say that my work is sloppy. It's not my fault. My hand is messy. I try to think about what I'm doing, but my mind goes to other places. It just goes to different places. I can't help it. My grandma says I'm a daydreamer."

"What do you daydream about?" I asked.

"Oh, you know, like…wherever my mind goes. Sometimes I think about a show I watched on TV or about riding my bike later. I don't know. It just goes where it goes," Sylvie said, shrugging her shoulders. She was resigned to her lot in life; it didn't seem to make her either sad or mad. She started telling me about a show she'd watched and then a friend and then her new piano.

I was feeling less dizzy hearing about Sylvie's wandering mind. I could see how nice it was for her mind to be able to go places in the midst of all that dizziness. It seemed to settle upon different things, like a butterfly gently fluttering and landing here and there. Her wandering mind was calming.

Sometimes, it's easy to tell why a person settles on a way to organize their thoughts, even if they're doing strange things like having to check the stove ten times before leaving the house. It's easy to see the relief that it provides and to find the logic in a way of thinking, however skewed and ineffectual it is in practical life.

"Would you like me to help your mother and your teachers understand how nice it is to let your mind wander?" I asked Sylvie.

"Oh, forget about it," Sylvie said, and looked at me as if I was crazy. "Well," she continued, "if you want, you could tell my mother to buy me that bear I want. Even though I didn't get the questions right on my worksheets yesterday. Because I knew the answers. I just got them wrong that day. That bear is sooo cute."

Sylvie had been indoctrinated to think in terms of being rewarded. The idea that anyone could ever understand her wandering mind was completely ludicrous to her. Most parents haven't learned how to read the code of strange behavior, so when their child can't operate within the lines, they find it hard to understand—and sometimes horrifying to even consider understanding, given the implication that something could be going wrong.

"What does the bear look like?" I asked.

"Well," Sylvie explained, "first of all it is very soft and big and cuddly. It has these cute little brown eyes. I wish I could hug that bear when I'm sleeping—my old bear is no good any more. He's too old. I want to throw him out. I throw him down off my bed every single day, but my mother keeps putting him up there even though I tell her—*I hate that bear*. The new bear I want is soooo much better."

Now, this was an interesting thought I could take a crack at decoding. We all know that hope about a bigger, better bear is beautiful. But it's unusual for a child to want to be rid of a stuffed animal she has slept with for some time. For children, most old stuffed bears represent the comforts of childhood. But Sylvie had no nostalgia whatsoever about that childhood bear. You might deduce: maybe her childhood didn't have those childhood comforts. This was a possibility I'd have to collect more evidence for; a hypothesis I would have to test with more evidence.

Sometimes, of course, the code you must decipher cannot provide you with a steadfast truth. You may develop a hypothesis, and only later gather all the evidence you need to confirm if it is right or wrong. Deciphering code is not like magic. Hypotheses or hunches are only there to test reality, not write it. You have to try to find a story first, and then to test, through continued observation, if it is true.

Japanese families

Six weeks of scribbling and swiveling and hearing Sylvie's daydreams passed by. She had mastered the chair. Her favorite thing was to set it to full tilt so it was almost horizontal, which put her in a semi-reclined position. Then she'd lower herself down until her feet touched the floor, so she could roll around slowly, staring at the ceiling. She looked like a giant spider.

I was able to confirm my diagnosis fairly comprehensively by now: the dizzy feeling was pretty chronic, and it matched the reports of possible Attention Deficit Disorder (ADD) that were coming in from the school counselor. Sylvie was less a hyperactive kid than she was a kid whose mind would simply flit too quickly from one thing to the next, making her unable to start learning to play an instrument, to read or to play nicely with her siblings, none of whom had these problems.

A ruthless disdain that Sylvie had about her life persisted: she didn't like her bedroom and dreamed about belonging to a family in Japan she had read about that she considered really cool because they couldn't wear shoes in their house, and they had to sleep on the floor, which was not very nice…but nobody complained!

I believe these "Japanese" families represented for Sylvie something that was not yet attainable for her emotionally: peace and calm. She herself was not OK with the discomforts in her life. Her parents were not OK with her wandering mind. Her teachers were not OK with it either.

Japan, in code, was a really calm place that wasn't anything like the place that Sylvie lived in now. I asked her if Japan was far away. "Oh, Japan is very far away," she said, looking surprised that I would even venture the question. "Don't you *know* that? It's *sooo* far."

Isabella

On the eighth week of Sylvie's treatment, it was time for the scheduled parent meeting. Seymour, Sylvie's father, couldn't make it. Isabella, Sylvie's mother, missed the appointment and had to reschedule. Not everybody is counting the seconds before they can get to see me again.

Isabella finally made it in, sat across from me at the farthest corner of my couch close to the exit and perched her handbag on her lap the way you do at a doctor's office when you are about to have a very short consultation. I could see she was uncomfortable.

She wanted the lowdown. "So, how do you think things are going?" she asked. "Well," I said, "your daughter is a lovely child."

"Oh," Isabella said, looking distracted, "yes, she is better. She does what I say more lately. Do you think we can do more about the lack of focus?"

"Well," I replied, "I think she might be a little overstimulated."

"Overstimulated?" Isabella said, and added, "What do you mean by that?"

"Oh," I explained, "it's like her head is spinning. It's hard for her to think straight."

Isabella looked at me blankly for a while, and I waited for her to challenge or question my diagnosis. She asked, "Is that something you can help her with?"

The correct answer to this question should have been yes, with more treatment, but since I wanted to explore whether she might be willing to participate in the treatment, I was trying to think up something else to say that could possibly lead us in that direction.

Isabella interrupted my thoughts and said, "You know, I have an appointment for her to see her pediatrician next week to see if she has ADD or ADHD, or whatever you call it. Maybe she should be on some medication." Here now was a possibility: Isabella could replace our treatment with a double-daily pill.

I was trying to gather my thoughts for a fresh idea on what to say that would help her get involved with the case, when Isabella unexpectedly started to cry.

"What's making you cry?" I asked.

"Oh, just that I guess I know people whose kids are on medication," Isabella explained. "I didn't think one of my own would have to go that route. I don't know about the side effects. I hate putting foreign chemicals in her body—what if it destroys her liver? I just want to feed her my good food and watch her grow well and do well. We keep Kosher. You are Jewish, no?[4] You must know. I just don't know what to do any more. She just can't go along with the family like the others. She is so difficult. She doesn't come when I call, forgets to do what I say, can't get to school on time. It's impossible."

Even though there were not one, but two boxes of tissues right by her side, Isabella snapped open her pocketbook and took out her own tissues. What I deciphered here was that she wasn't sure yet that she wanted any part of me. This business with her daughter was taxing enough.

"Well," I said, wanting to comfort her, "it certainly is a good idea to talk to your primary care physician and to have a consultation with a specialist. In the meantime, we can also work on Sylvie's problem, you know. This is not a hard problem to work on. It's common to many, many children."

"Really?" Isabella said, "You think she can get better?"

"When a child is a little dizzy," I explained, "it can take a little while to figure what would help her be able to be more focused."

"Oh," Isabella said, sniffling, "but you know—we have tried *everything*."

I have to admit I was impressed hearing Isabella recount everything they'd tried with Sylvie. She and Seymour had implemented four of the current parenting strategies. Usually people try one or two things—a reward system or a motivation system maybe—but not three or four different things.

But Sylvie's parents had bought two off-the-shelf behavioral programs, each including stickers, charts and an elaborate system of rewards based on either performance or lack thereof. Then they had tried to make the family function more effectively, staging family meetings with agendas to explain and discuss priorities and expectations. And most recently, they had started giving consequences for bad behavior.

Unfortunately, giving consequences for bad behaviors requires two very difficult procedures that most parents cannot fully execute. The first is to find age-appropriate consequences, like no TV, no treats, no something. The second is to follow through on the consequences consistently, which can feel sadistic to the offending child, as it does not allow for any checking-in as to what the child might be feeling in any given moment.

But the real problem that Sylvie's parents had encountered when giving Sylvie consequences—a circumstance that had put them over the edge and led to their calling me—was that Sylvie was one of those children, and there are quite a lot of them, who simply doesn't respond to consequences. You can punitively take everything away from children like this—every piece of candy, TV show, playdate and privilege, leave them with absolutely nothing all alone in their rooms—and it simply won't make one hoot of a difference. In Sylvie's case, the consequences only seemed to make her worse. I have seen the most unbelievable power struggles ensue from each generation upping the ante on punishment and defiance, each trying to exert the most power and control.

Now, Isabella wanted to know if I had a strategy they had not tried yet. I made an effort to quickly come up with something that wouldn't sound like "we have to keep talking," which was the real answer, but always a disappointing one for those desperate for a quicker fix to their problems.

I explained, "We have to start figuring out what makes her dizzy. And then, on the other side of the equation, what makes it possible for her to focus more. We have to study her. Some kids can be directed and coached. Those are the kids that the behavioral programs work for. Other kids—like Sylvie—can't be directed. They have to be followed. They can't 'listen.' You have to learn how to listen to them."

Isabella shifted uncomfortably in her seat, and I realized this was a lot of information. I wondered if she had any clue at all what Sylvie was feeling, and asked her, "Have you noticed if sometimes Sylvie is better than at other times?"

"It's funny you should say that," Isabella said, "because I have noticed that sometimes she decides to be good and other times she just won't. It's so frustrating. I don't get it."

"I know," I added, "these things are confusing."

Isabella asked, "Is this something you can figure out?"

"Sure, I'm working on it." I answered, "But in a way, it would be better, since you are with her all the time, if you could study her in the day-to-day. If we could work together on what to notice. Then you could let me know what you are seeing. We could process it together."

"But," Isabella wondered, "what if we see what makes her act more difficult and what makes her better? Like that she had a hard day or something? I can't do anything about that. I've got three other kids to worry about. What good would that do?"

"Well, believe me, if we can figure out what may be going on, we will know better what to do," I said.

I really could not explain to Isabella that figuring out what Sylvie was experiencing was not about assessing whether she had had a good day or a bad day. It was about what emotions were in the air, and how Sylvie was responding to and processing them. Parents always want to change the conditions of their children's lives—to take away their troubles and help them to be happy. But working with kids who are struggling requires only that you help them get more comfortable with what they feel.

Figuring out why Sylvie was scattering her thoughts would involve learning what she was responding to in her environment, and why. It would require helping her find language for what she was feeling so that she would be able to develop a narrative she could then attach herself to, which would anchor her psyche and focus her thoughts. We would have to help her feel more at peace with herself and with her family.

But mostly, helping Sylvie was about doing what I'd been doing with her in the comfort of my own office—trying to get into her world and decipher her code. For me, this work, though frustrating and confusing, was also inspiring—I wanted to write about the case. But while I was filled with purpose, Isabella was strung out. I couldn't expect her to join my bandwagon of enthusiasm and focused observation. I had to be careful.

In fact, I could see that Isabella looked agitated, so I said, "When we find out more about what is going on, it will guide us." This was true. Isabella started to avert her eyes, though. I knew exactly what she was feeling: she wanted to do the best for her child, but this was not very straightforward.

"What are your thoughts?" I asked.

"Just that…I don't really get it. I don't really know if I can observe her. I mean, to be honest, things are a little crazy at home with four kids. By four o'clock in the afternoon, I'm focused on getting the kids fed, cleaning up the kitchen, getting them into their baths, getting their lunches packed…and keeping things moving." Isabella did, indeed, have her hands full.

Even with just one or two children, this would have been the case for Isabella. There are so many, many things that get in the way of studying children and learning how they think and what they need.

First, there is the problem of our own parents' lack of emotional involvement with us. Most of us didn't learn how to tune into emotions. Then, there is our lack of time; it takes being somewhat relaxed to get curious and study things. And finally, our instincts are to guide our children, not observe them. We are hardwired to create children in our image, not learn from them. It's just ridiculously hard to get curious about our children.

I tried to help her. "You really don't have to do anything. This is the easiest parenting strategy there is. You just have to leave her alone, and watch her a little. And think about it here with me."

Isabella looked me in the eye for a long time. I could tell she wasn't really seeing me, but trying to see how this would work, exactly.

"And remind me again, this is going to do what, exactly?" Isabella asked.

Isabella, at this juncture in the session, was trying to settle in to this new parenting strategy. And the strategy I was proposing had at its core something that none of her previous strategies did: it was confusing. It lacked certainty. While all the contemporary solutions she had tried provided certainty and direction, all I was offering was a searchlight and a prayer.

I explained the problem to Isabella. "It is very confusing," I said, "when you have children who don't respond to anything. These children try our patience like no others. And here you are now, with three other children. Very hard. But Sylvie is a very special child. There is something so magical about Sylvie. If you can stand the confusion, we will figure out how to help her. We will come up with the perfect customized solution to her problem."

Isabella's eyes welled up. Maybe she was relieved or maybe she was frustrated—I don't know. Maybe she could see that I, at least, had fallen in love with Sylvie, the sweet little swivel spider. Or maybe she knew it was time to look at things more closely. People don't usually relish the idea of studying emotional dynamics when they are doing everything in their power to manage them.

But Isabella was a good mother, and she did sincerely want to improve things, and I was, after all, offering something she had not tried before. So she said, "OK. I guess I'll try it. I could come on Wednesdays, I guess. But I can't come every week. Every other week. And I think you should also keep seeing Sylvie," she quickly added. "I think she's better after she sees you."

"She does like my swivel chair," I said, and Isabella looked at me strangely. I realized in that moment that I was severely underestimating what had being happening in the sessions. Sylvie, in fact, was doing much better because she had found, in me, someone who'd join her, who didn't have any complaints about her wandering mind, who wasn't trying to change her and direct her all the time. In fact, I liked just watching her. For many children, this is so rare.

Deciphering code

Two weeks later, Isabella arrived with a determined look, lips pursed resolutely in an unsmiling face. As she settled on the couch, I felt as though I had hired her to do a job and she had come prepared. I love working with mothers intent on helping their children. No matter how much they themselves have suffered, how stressed their own personal life is or how supremely difficult the child is, the selflessness and strength of every parent's determination and commitment to help their child is one of the most powerful, amazing and beautiful forces in nature that I am privileged to witness in my practice.

In fact, I am very dismayed by the current accusations that are being leveled against parents today: that we spoil our kids and hover over them too much. It shows such a tremendous lack of understanding for how each parent strives today to do better than previous generations, to be present and to provide the best. Providing amply for and being deeply involved with our kids comes from a deep place of love and connectedness. "Spoiling" and "hovering" are not the problem. The problem is underneath those behaviors, which comes from not knowing how to manage difficult emotions.

Isabella's emotional challenges would have to be dealt with, and she was ready. "OK, let's talk about a real problem we have here at dinnertime," Isabella said. "This is one of the worst times."

"What happens?" I asked.

"Well, you know Sylvie's the eldest," Isabella started.

"Yes," I said.

"So she's supposed to set the example for the younger children."

"Right," I agreed, because I could see that Isabella was setting up an argument that would lead to justifying something.

"And you know that dinnertime is supposed to be sacred, in the sense that families that eat together are the most successful families. All the statistics show this; all the data point to the importance of family dinners."

"Right," I agreed. Actually, I hate this particular statistic because when family dinners create too much stress for a family, for whatever reason, families should not be advised to plan them. Parents get very worried and anxious that their kids are going to become drug addicts, and that the whole family will fall apart if they don't sit together for dinner. This is ridiculous. The important thing is how to generate good feeling. Not adhere to a behavior that should generate it, but in fact doesn't. But I'll leave that alone for now.

"So when I call the whole family for dinner, I expect everybody to come. I read that in *Mean Moms*," Isabella added to further substantiate the absolute correctness of her strategy by referencing a book she'd read. This wasn't just her need that was conveying her; it was a real live expert's solution to a common parenting dilemma.

"So Sylvie, who is the oldest, doesn't come. Oy. And then, when I call her, she doesn't come again. So I go up there—and I tell you, I'm pretty mad because this is the one thing that I am not going to stand for. I'm not going to stand for, number one, waiting. Number two, having the other kids see this kind of defiance, and then, God forbid, copying her. And finally, number three, I don't have the time or the energy to have to chase kids all over creation. When I do that, it really ruins dinner. We're there, the other kids are there, and Sylvie just creates so much chaos. I don't know why it seems like it's getting worse. Literally, before I start calling the family to dinner, I get tense. Now it's at the point where I actually dread the family dinners, and I'm sure the other kids can see what a bad mood I'm in because she ruins it almost every time. I'm either screaming for her to come down for the fourth time, or else I actually have to go up there."

I could see that Isabella was exasperated. She not only had an important goal for the health and well-being of the family, but she also needed Sylvie to set the tone for the other children coming up the pike. This, in combination with the frustration she was having to endure with Sylvie, was leading her to pull away from Sylvie emotionally. Parents want their children to make things better emotionally, and, in this case, Sylvie had been slotted to support the child-rearing of all her younger siblings. Unfortunately, children aren't up to the task they're slotted for.

"Does Sylvie help you in other ways with the other children?" I asked.

"No, actually, I'm glad you said that," Isabella started to explain. "You would think, as the eldest, that she would be a little bit more mindful of the others. I ask her to bring me a diaper, or even to change the youngest sometimes, and she just takes such a long time with it that I get so frustrated with her that sometimes I just end up getting it myself. I don't know what's wrong with this child. Seymour says she's like his Aunt Hesbia. She was a strange one, too. Head in the clouds. Never married. Never had kids. Lived with her mother her whole life. God forbid."

I could see now that the feelings about Sylvie's dizziness had evolved into a whole picture of the family dynasty and her place in it. This is dangerous. As soon as a child starts to fit into a larger story, it is hard for a parent to begin to see that child in any other way, and then the child picks up how she fits in and often becomes that character.[5] Children pick up that they are supposed to be strange and unmarried and an outcast.

"So you see," Isabella continued, "that meal times are a nightmare with Sylvie. Aside from the fact that, also, she won't eat. The other kids have no problem with eating, with my cooking. I have cooked the same foods that my mother cooked and that her mother cooked and her mother before that. There is nothing wrong with my cooking." Isabella had become indignant. Sylvie's lack of appetite was an affront to her dignity as a mother. The level of frustration and pain that Sylvie was bringing to Isabella was becoming very apparent.

"So how should I handle that?" Isabella asked. And then she added, "What can I do with this girl who is so badly behaved and so defiant with me?"

"Well," I said, "you don't have to worry about any of that for now. You can take a rest from teaching her and guiding her and trying to move her in a better direction because while we 'observe' her, we pretty much have to leave her alone."

"I can't do that," Isabella said.

"Oh," I said, a little surprised by the definitiveness of her inability to follow my prescription. This woman was very clear about what she thought.

"Because if I leave her alone, it's going to set a bad example for the little ones. What if they start thinking that they don't have to come to dinner when I call, or that they can refuse to do what I ask? That's going to turn my whole house upside down."

"I see what you're saying, and that is very important," I said. "So you have to address that. You have to tell the other children that Sylvie, for a few weeks, is going to come to dinner when she gets to it, but that is not the rule for them in the house. You have to explain, if they say that's not fair, that life isn't always fair and, sometimes, things are not clear-cut. As long as they know what is expected of them from you, her behavior should not be a negative influence. You need a break from trying to teach Sylvie, and while we observe her, the pressure must be off."

"OK," Isabella said, "I think I can do that. But you know, I always thought that it was important to be consistent. You know, all the books talk about that. That if you're not consistent following through on what you believe, the kids will take advantage of you and do whatever they want and think they can get away with everything."

"Consistency is something that you have to carry in your heart in response to your different children," I explained to Isabella. "You water an orchid differently than you water a daffodil. You have to be consistent emotionally with each child so that you can respond to what will work with that child. If you just follow these rules, and not the child, you miss something. While you are on vacation from getting Sylvie to behave, take notes. How late she is going to be to dinner? How much does she dillydally in the morning? How bad is her concentration? How much does she want to be with the family—or to be alone? Just take a mental note—you don't have to write it down. And then next time I see you, tell me what happens."

Isabella liked this plan because at least it had a direction, and she needed the certainty with which I delivered my injunction and explicit assignment. The word "vacation" didn't hurt.

Observation

Isabella was fabulous at taking direction. "I have to admit to you," she revealed "that this observation is like having a vacation. I am so happy not to have to worry about that dinner bell. I feel a little guilty that I am leaving Sylvie alone. I feel like I am neglecting her."

It is always interesting for me to hear, when parents are able to back down from power struggles, that they feel guilty. Why would they feel guilty if they feel better toward the child, especially given that I know how much better children always do when their parents can back down from their punitive and rigid, ineffective stubbornness? But in the life of the mind, a negative connection is nonetheless a powerful connection. Isabella felt guilty letting go of that negative connection, perhaps because she didn't want to know how much she really didn't want to parent Sylvie in the least.

"Your mother gave you a lot of attention?" I asked.

"Oh, God, no," Isabella said, "I wish she had!" This was interesting too. Was Sylvie the recipient of Isabella's frustration as a result of Isabella not having gotten enough attention from her own mother? I would have to learn more about Isabella and her mother.

"A very interesting thing is happening, too," Isabella said, looking at her shoes. She laughed a little. "You're not going to believe it," she continued, looking decidedly sheepish. "I haven't been 'observing' her that much—I'm sorry, I'm so busy! But I can tell you this. The first few days, she didn't come to dinner until pretty late. I could feel my feathers getting ruffled but...you know...I did as you said, I watched it, and I figured I'd tell you about it. But the third day, she came down! Go figure! What is that about?"

"That's fascinating. What do you make of that?"

"I don't know." Isabella said, "Maybe she does better if I leave her alone! My mother left me alone and I hated it. I was one of seven children. I wished I had had more attention!

I did not believe we had come to really understand much more about Sylvie and what she was feeling, but the pressure being taken off of Sylvie to "do" better had in itself led to an amazing result. The child magically started doing better. Isabella could not help but notice this.

So she started to back down even more from pushing Sylvie. If Sylvie came late to dinner, that was fine. If she couldn't get herself ready for school in time, she took her in without her hair being perfectly brushed. If Sylvie didn't finish her homework, she let the teacher deal with it.

Isabella also got Sylvie's father Seymour on board: to just leave her alone in the name of studying her. Ironically, with this total "non-plan" Sylvie's parents were observing a discovery: it worked to take the pressure off.

We all started to realize that the way this family had worked to keep things in control and regimented with their brood of children had been causing Sylvie some anxiety. Of course, she had never said to them, "I'm anxious." Nor was she one to wet the bed or develop a fear of things.

Instead, Sylvie had decided not to let her mind rest on anything for too long. In that way she could shut things out. Sylvie was a sensitive child. Being in a house with a whole group of kids, in a somewhat regimented environment, was not very suitable for her.

Children get dizzy sometimes when their feelings are too negative or too intense. In fact, this is probably why none of the behavioral tactics—the rewards and consequences—that work for so many children worked at all for Sylvie. The one common denominator they all had was in the delivery: their implementation had always been made in an atmosphere of tension and frustration. And since Sylvie was sensitive to feelings, the tension and frustration had caused her to shut down.

Before long, however, Sylvie's parents did come up with the perfect customized plan to help Sylvie be more focused and cooperative: 1) take the pressure off and 2) when that wasn't possible, deliver a command in a very, very soft voice.

Of course, it wasn't always possible to follow the plan—life is never perfect. Sylvie's parents did still shout at her sometimes, and patience was not always at the ready. A third aspect to the plan was added: Sylvie's parents would apologize to her if they shouted. This helped Sylvie to shut them out less and to remain more focused, and find a narrative for her own anger and frustration.

It's amazing, when you can start to read the code of emotion, what you learn about how people actually react to things.

How to read code

I was extremely pleased that Isabella had agreed to tolerate her confusion and start working with me on how to help Sylvie be less dizzy. This, by the way, is pretty much the first requirement for learning to decipher the code of emotion: to admit and allow confusion. Confusion means your mind is open, and new things can come into it. Then, horizons broaden and a bigger world, replete with endless possibilities, unfurls. After a decade or so of psychoanalytic training, the uncertainty became second nature to me; I lost most of the insecurity that can unfortunately couple with uncertainty in the early years of learning how to do this work.

In the luxury of my private office now, and if I have the added luxury of time when my patients are willing to commit to at least a year or two of initial treatment, it is not that hard to tolerate the uncertainty. But to ask Isabella— to ask most parents—to become curious and therefore tolerate confusion, watching, seeing what emotions are being expressed, interpreting behavior, entering into the world of emotion long enough to understand it—is really hard. I know that. The hardest part is tolerating the insecurity that comes with allowing all of the confusion and worry.

But Isabella continued to study Sylvie and to wonder about her, and I hoped her curiosity and my reassurance would quell her confusion and frustration. We would start by just talking about Sylvie and what was working and not working. But soon, I would learn about Isabella's own tension and frustration. We put onto our kids whatever remains unspoken about our own history; the tensions and frustrations we experienced in our original families simply get repeated in our new families. That is why we get more upset with our children than we can understand or than they sometimes deserve.

Parents have difficulty seeing this at first, but whenever they become free of their own tensions and frustrations, they can begin to see their children. Then, they can learn how to be more consistently there for them emotionally: flexible and responsive, understanding and gentle. And when we need to be firm with them, to do it with bodies that are relaxed and with minds that are at ease.

If I could help Isabella to get more at peace with her emotions around Sylvie, settle into them a little better and stop reeling into fantasies of all the bad things that were going to happen to Sylvie—ADD and failing school and becoming a withering spinster aunt—it would eventually become easier for her to follow my recommendation to continue to observe and analyze her child.

In the meantime, I decided to buy a special fancy swivel chair for kids, make my own special chair off limits and, in this way, preserve my settings. Sylvie, predictably, started becoming more centered, doing better in school and finding her appetite. My hope was that the feelings in "Japan" would never be too far away.

THE FUTURE OF PSYCHOANALYSIS

The future of psychoanalysis looks good to me. It's bedrock in curiosity could very well be what guarantees its future. Consider all the things that people in our society were never very curious about in past generations—gender identity, spousal abuse, post-traumatic stress disorder (PTSD), alcoholism and so much more—subjects that were often thought of as "nonsense," "foolish" or even worse. The "problems" we once talked about privately, if at all, and in hushed tones when we did, are now the subject of everyday conversation, mainstream media and even public policy.

Currently, our world is still really big on manufactured change, though. Despite the ever-apparent failure of many of our current therapeutic modalities to alter deep-set patterns of self-sabotage, we still approach our mental health in the same spirit as we pioneered America. That is, with brute strength, believing that we'll conquer natural forces through the power of our own intentionality; by the sheer force of our conviction in a pre-set, delineated timeframe. And that just doesn't work with our unconscious. You can no more command yourself to stop being negative in light of unresolved, repressed feelings than you can tell yourself to turn blue.

In thinking about the future, Sylvie's case illustrates both the greatest challenges to psychoanalysis as well as its deepest promise. The biggest challenge, of course, is the degree to which, as a culture, we mostly still operate from a standpoint of cognition. Sylvie, for example, had passed unsuccessfully through several off-the-shelf child development programs that offered her both rewards and consequences to help her adapt more productively to the demands of her environment. But none of them had worked to shed any light on the underlying problem.

The second greatest challenge facing psychoanalysis is fear, which usually stunts curiosity in favor of the illusory calm gained from certainty, however misguided it may be. Sylvie's parents personified this challenge because they were afraid of bending to Sylvie's "bad behavior" so as not to further indulge it. They chose to operate instead from an erroneous belief that if they gave her an inch they would not only further enable her dysfunction, but also condone more bad behavior. Their anxieties, which led to rigidity in their dealings with her, are typical of most obstacles to curiosity, and are wholly representative of how our current society usually manages most problems: by trying to correct and redirect them, barely scratching the surface of the problem to find out what, inside a person's head, is really going on.

Despite these challenges, Sylvie's mother, thanks to her inherent mistrust of psychotropic medications, found her way to me. I will now dissect and analyze what happened in the treatment, to illustrate what I believe to be the great promise of psychoanalysis to the future of our collective mental health: to help generate more hope and purpose about the value of curiosity.

From the moment that I laid eyes on Sylvie as she came up my walk, my curiosity was piqued. I observed how happy-go-lucky she seemed to be for a kid who had been reported to be anxious. But she made me feel topsy-turvy in no time, especially when she wheeled herself around on my chair, upside down and acted unruly—behavior that bespoke of an emotional tumultuousness. Then, I began to gather many more observations. She wanted to be defiant, scribbling things madly in her own way while convinced I wanted her to draw between the lines. At other times, she seemed defeated, wishing she would live in Japan where things, she imagined, could be more peaceful. She showed little attachment to what most happy children would ordinarily cherish, like a favorite stuffed animal.

As I tried to piece together who Sylvie was, observing my emotions in the room with her as well as her behaviors, while bringing in my understanding of her external environment, a new and different narrative began to take shape from the one her parents had developed, which maintained that Sylvie was distracted and unreachable. Instead, I realized that she was a basically sweet and cooperative child, but due to her circumstances, she felt angry, frustrated and dejected. In treatment, the more she could talk about what she'd rather be doing or where she would rather be, and the more her parents could subsequently respond to her need for flexibility and space, the better she did. As soon as she could construct a narrative that adequately acknowledged her frustration at having to conform when she didn't want to, she could focus more, concentrate on her schoolwork and appear to be more responsive and present.

When it comes to unresolved unconscious conflicts and repressed thoughts and feelings, we are all like Sylvie: helpless children with a limited capacity for insight, and without a fully functioning ability to manufacture change within ourselves. Remember: Sylvie had had no shortage of cognitive programs to help her to focus more and harness her seemingly bad behavior. But what was preventing her absorption and implementation of these programs (all of which had as their goal more conformity towards ostensibly productive outcomes) was that all her psychic energies were being consumed trying to block from consciousness how frustrated she was. She was an independent, inflexible little girl stuck in a rigid home and school system, and it was just too much for her. She had not wanted to know how frustrated she was, preferring to exist instead in a semi-conscious la-la land, unable to focus on any one given thing for long, increasingly trying to block her parents out.

Sylvie's mind, in fact, was taking shape the same way all our minds originally take shape: according to the unique (albeit sometimes unfortunate) confluence of nature and nurture which, for whatever reason, may require us to ignore what feels bad inside ourselves. In needing to conform or adapt to our inadequate environments, we unwittingly lose touch consciously with perhaps any number of possible thoughts, impulses, desires, memories, wishes or emotions we may in fact be having. In Sylvie's case, the reason for her difficulties was not readily apparent. She came from a loving, attentive family, and was in a great school system with good teachers and all the privileges of a fantastic set of after-school activities. Her anomalies made no immediate sense.

Sylvie's problem represents what is unfinished, unresolved and puzzling in each of us; everything that, for whatever reason, haunts us inexplicably because we also had to bar from consciousness something we didn't want to know or feel, perhaps because we didn't think that anybody would be able to cope with it. And just like Sylvie, it's sometimes hard to understand ourselves.

The truth is, emotions, more often than not, don't even have a language. They are simply energies that land here and there, often without a cohesive or reality-based narrative, and which can feel exceedingly uncomfortable and challenging for no good reason. And how change typically happens, as it did in this case, is also below the level of conscious awareness. That is to say, Sylvie was no more aware of how she was originally creating herself as a kid with ADD than she was aware of how she was improving and evolving through treatment into a calm, creative, productive person who didn't have to submerge entire factions of her distinct personality.

As long as we can get curious about challenging behavior, thoughts and feelings, we stand a chance of being able to work on how best to prepare our own and other people's minds for self-discovery, which makes it possible for new synapses to form in the brain so that healthier, more effective narratives can be created and discerned. In turn, three things each serve to prepare our patient's minds sufficiently for self-discovery: 1) there is a shift in drives; 2) a new form of *object relations* emerges that are based more on trust; and 3) our patients can finally tolerate their most unwanted thoughts and feelings. When any one or more of these three things is achieved in treatment, change feels natural and not forced: an addiction will abate, a depression will lift, a good habit will be born, unhealthy symptoms like ADD will naturally dissolve, and it all happens without much conscious effort, just like the terrifying Wicked Witch melted in the *Wizard of Oz*, after Dorothy threw a bucket of water on her.

Over the years, many has been the time when a patient of mine has grown disheartened by the process of psychoanalysis, particularly at junctures where things became uncomfortable, where there did not seem to be anything new coming up and when the levels of hope were at an all-time low that anything could ever improve. At these times, when I recommended the patient stay in treatment anyway, even though they said it didn't seem to be helping, I said, "What have you got to lose? Do you have any other options?" This, more often than not, would make it possible for the patient to stay. And this is also what I want to say to our society. I want to encourage greater curiosity about our mental condition and to instill hope that twenty-first-century psychoanalysis can help create change, as long as we can learn from its most recent discoveries, including: *joining, following the contact* and designing effective *emotional communications*. I want to ask: Why don't we try to get more interested in our unconscious? What have we got to lose?

Certainly, I can appreciate that it is totally counter-intuitive to become deeply curious about people around us when they are dominated by distorted, depressed, anxious, unproductively angry and even paranoid narratives. No parent wants to see these things in their child. And yet, when we can allow ourselves to get curious enough about someone, to deeply recognize that person emotionally has endless merits. Now more than ever, while our society is so open emotionally and, yet, so disillusioned by current therapeutic modalities, I believe twenty-first-century psychoanalysis has a powerful contribution to make by helping us leverage curiosity towards new depths of well-being and satisfaction in life.

Perhaps, with this book, I will have fostered the hope that simply becoming more curious about our mental health struggles, however challenging or frustrating they may be, can be extremely effective in creating change, particularly when we know how to prepare the mind sufficiently for continued self-discovery. And I hope to have sufficiently identified what I believe goes into that preparation, according to the most recent discoveries in the methods of twenty-first-century psychoanalysis, including, most notably:

1 Following the contact and joining people in their psychological world (Chapter 3).
2 Applying specific models of the mind to serve as compasses to inform our curiosity (Chapter 4).
3 Designing effective emotional communications (Chapter 5).
4 Using our own emotions as instruments to both assess and intervene (Chapter 6).

We are certainly more in need than ever of a method that recognizes how limited we can be in our ability to act grown-up; a method that succeeds in restructuring energetic systems and creating new forms of connectedness so the mind can truly get to know itself. When Sylvie could finally know herself, she could say "NO!" to some of the interruptions her external environment made to her creative focus. She could know, without any internal conflict, that she was mad, and she could say it. She could be helped, if not to live in a more comfortable world, to at least understand her positive place in it.

If society continues opening up to how irrational, unreasonable and mentally disorganized we can all be sometimes, and if we can shift paradigms from the more cognitive and behavioral methods to this emotion-based method founded on curiosity, then I believe the future of psychoanalysis looks good, and a place for it is guaranteed. Because if there is one thing I believe more than any other, and to which I have devoted my entire life, it's this: when you can bear to know the hidden truth about yourself, things do get better.

Notes

1 This is known psychoanalytically as 'symbolic communication.'
2 The feelings people expose you to are known as 'induced feelings.'

3 A 'diagnosis,' usually, is not determined by a set of specific criteria gleaned from a formal interview, but by using our emotions, mostly, to gauge the level of psychic disorganization in tandem with the level of tension we experience in the room with the patient. The greater the disorganization and tension, the greater the pathology.

4 Isabella's fantasy that I was Jewish was positive, since she was also Jewish— it possibly meant I could be trusted. This is *transference*. When a person's transference reveals that they are identified with you, it's called the 'narcissistic transference.' If they imagine, however, that you are mean like their mother, or dismissive like their father, it's called the '*negative narcissistic transference*.' We don't correct these transference communications, primarily because they give us information about the patient's internal life; the way they project their own internal states. Secondarily, fostering the narcissistic transference makes it easier to enter into the patient's mode of thinking, because we are willing to join the patient in their version of reality rather than trying to introduce our own.

5 In essence, Isabella was developing, with her husband, a negative transference to Sylvie.

Postscript

Dear Student,

Most of the stories in this book, you may have noted, have happy endings. And while it is true that the right kinds of emotional experiences do lead naturally to change, what you have experienced here is a form of time-warp photography, snippets of real life strung together in a new way that make change seem instantaneous.

In truth, it can take season upon season of searching inner terrains and external ideas before you land on something that feels different, that has the right elements of discovery—that creates a shift that changes someone forever, even as old parts of them remain the same.

And in truth, change can be invisible—observable mostly in retrospect, where you can readily discern a distinct before and after, since in the moment, people are usually busy living life.

I'm telling you this to try to address any potential future discouragement. Sometimes, even as we read stories that lift our spirits and inject a necessary dose of hope and inspiration, we turn back to our own life and find it only in the shadows of that story's bright light, where it pales by comparison.

My main hope for this book is that you become more curious. Not only about your own condition, but that of people around you, especially the ones you care most about. Curiosity is at the heart of all scientific investigation, even when the science, as is always the case with psychoanalysis, has no hope of ever being able to re-create a controlled experiment or predict one person's destiny on the basis of someone else's successful analysis. Human beings just do not lend themselves to those aspects of science.

The one thing a method of investigation can offer is an exciting way to stoke your curiosity and to engage your seeking brain. If any of your present dissatisfaction, restlessness, or sometimes despair and frustration can bring you to that seeking, I will be pleased. That is the goal. And my job will be done.

So now, be curious. Put yourself out there, into words. Seek experiences that will help you to be heard, to see things in a new way and then to land upon a new thought or feeling...something you'd never realized before.

Glossary

Analytic transparency   I coined the term 'analytic transparency' to describe the attitude a twenty-first-century psychoanalyst must adopt in place of a position of 'analytic neutrality' usually espoused by classical analysis, since today, neutrality could be construed as distancing (and therefore off-putting) to some patients. The term 'transparency' better captures, to my mind, how the twenty-first-century psychoanalyst must aim to be with the patient: someone who will not get in the patient's way. This is achieved by resonating emotionally with the patient, including, when appropriate, expressing an emotional attitude, and being what feels "real" to the patient.

Conflict theory   The premise of conflict theory is the belief that we are dominated by unconscious conflicts that create emotional and professional stagnation. One or more of the hidden aspects of the conflict may often reflect the opposite wish from the conscious wish. For example, a desire not to be angry anymore may reflect a hidden desire to find people to be angry with. A fear of a child hurting himself may reflect an understandably repressed impulse to do harm to a child. According to conflict theory, once the hidden aspects of a conflict can be accepted into consciousness, the personality will become free from the immobilizing shackles of the conflict. It will no longer be necessary to ward off dangerous impulses, thoughts and feelings, thus allowing the psyche to move forward.

The contact function   Also known as 'following the contact,' the contact function is a term used to describe how the analyst allows the patient to take the lead on what to talk and think about. The patient's contact may be read through verbal as well as non-verbal cues, including the analyst's own emotions, which, provided they have been analyzed and are therefore free of their subjective elements, can become the most useful tool for the analyst to use in gauging what the patient can and cannot yet comfortably address verbally in treatment.

Countertransference   Thoughts and feelings the analyst is having. **Subjective countertransference**   Thoughts and feelings the analyst is having that have little if anything to do with the patient, but which are being triggered by the patient. **Countertransference resistance**   Subjective countertransference thoughts and feelings that impede successful treatment, usually resulting from unresolved issues on the part of the analyst. These resistances are typically managed by the analyst in private supervision or analysis when they become obvious enough, either because the patient wants to leave treatment or because the analyst is uncomfortable with the session material.

Drive theory Drive theory holds that we have two drives: aggressive and libidinal. When the drives are fused properly, they work in tandem to promote health and well-being, leading to healthy ambition and fulfilling love. Excessive aggressive energy that is not fused with enough libidinal energy, however, becomes destructive, like in cases of addiction or abuse. On the inverse, libidinal energy can become depleted holding too many dangerous aggressive energies in check, as with depression. The analyst works to help the patient become integrated emotionally, neutralizing the destructive potential of the aggressive impulses and freeing up libidinal energy. This is achieved by helping the patient be able to become increasingly more comfortable with a wide variety of impulses, wishes, thoughts and feelings simultaneously, without having to ward things off.

Ego The psychoanalytic conceptualization of 'ego' may be likened to the modern-day understanding of 'mentation.' It is the part of the mind that mediates between the conscious and the unconscious and enables us to think rationally and maturely and to understand and mitigate the realities posed by the outside world. It is not to be confused with the Buddhist conceptualization, which defines the ego as the body of thought that contains all of our illusory states of suffering.

Emotional communication Emotional communications are interventions the analyst makes that address the underlying thoughts, feelings, wishes, longings and impulses that the patient expresses directly and non-verbally. The goal of emotional communication is in sharp contrast with the goal of 'interpretation' to make the conscious unconscious. Instead, emotional communications prepare the patient for their own self-discovery by 1) liberating libidinal energy or neutralizing the destructive potential of aggressive energies, 2) creating shifts in how relationships are experienced (object introjects) or 3) exploring the hidden side of an intrapsychic conflict. With the goal of preparing the patient's mind for self-discovery, emotional communications effectively address the problem of rigid defense systems that usually stand in the way of self-discovery and mental health.

Inductions Emotional induction occurs when interaction with another person arouses similar feelings in us. If someone comes towards us in an angry, irate state, chances are we will soon experience those feelings. We use our inductions, in psychoanalysis, to better understand and examine what the patient may be experiencing emotionally.

Interpretation Interpretation was one of the primary clinical interventions originally used in psychoanalysis. By stating his hypotheses about the patient's unconscious thoughts and feelings, the analyst intended to make them conscious. Now, the intent behind an interpretation is to provide language for the patient who is deemed ready to connect to unspoken dynamics, thoughts and feelings which the analyst is able to discern and sense in the session.

Joining   Joining is a clinical technique that enables the analyst to enter into the psychological universe of the patient. Whatever the patient's feelings may be, even if they include unjustified anger, distorted sadness or grief, or other irrational impressions, thoughts and feelings, the analyst nevertheless 'joins' the patient by reflecting their compassionate understanding of the patient's emotional universe without any thought to correcting, analyzing, or otherwise changing the patient's mind.

(The theory of the) mechanisms of defense   The theory of the mechanisms of defense (or defense mechanism) explains how we build walls around our consciousness in an attempt to prevent disturbing thoughts, feelings, sensations, impulses and wishes from being known to us. These defenses, however maladaptive, unconstructive or otherwise unwieldy, nevertheless provide a mental organization that enables us to avoid conscious conflict or anxiety.

Modern psychoanalysis   Modern psychoanalysis, developed by Hyman Spotnitz in the early 1950s, pioneered the innovative technique of leveraging the psychoanalyst's own emotions as a tool for the design and delivery of emotional communications and of working emotionally to reverse the patient's patterns of self-attack and self-sabotage.

Object and ego-oriented questions   By monitoring tension levels in the room, the analyst is able to design and implement ego or object-oriented questions that ensure that the patient will be sufficiently comfortable to continue talking.

Ego-oriented questions are deeply personal, such as "Did you love your mother?" or "Did that scare you?" Object-oriented questions are of two types and are designed to protect the patient's fragile ego. Object-oriented 1 questions are personal, but do not explore the patient's emotional reactions. For example, "How many siblings do you have?" or "How many years did you spend in Alabama?" Object-oriented 2 questions are the least intrusive and explore nothing that is directly about the patient. For example, "Will it rain tomorrow?" or "Did you like that movie?"

Ego-oriented questions are typically employed when the patient has developed greater ego strength and is not regressed in treatment to high levels of tension. More regressed patients and new patients who have not yet been sufficiently diagnosed would be asked more object-oriented questions.

Object relations   Object relations refer to internalized relationships between the self and significant others (objects), particularly parents and other significant individuals. We form a mental representation of the object as perceived by the self as well as representations of the self in relation to the object. We may for example carry images of other people who we can't trust or people who will hurt us, or people who are intrinsically good, and so on. We call these mental representations 'object introjects.' Therefore, when we speak of a person's object-relatedness, we are referring to the images they have in their heads, and the relative relationship of those images to a realistic recognition and appraisal of the other person.

Projection and projective identification Projection occurs when unwanted thoughts, feelings, wishes and impulses are displaced onto another person and become recognizable and discernable in the other person. For example, a person projecting their own murderous impulses onto another person may think that person is out to kill them. Projective identification is when the contents of your own (usually unconscious) mind become erroneously perceived and identified in the thoughts or behavior of another person.

Regression An emotional return to an earlier developmental period.   A 'regressed' person is someone who is re-living, emotionally, an early dynamic.

Structural theory In his structural theory of the psyche Sigmund Freud conceived the mind as consisting of three parts: the ego, id and superego. We think as structural theorists when we study defense patterns, and how the different mental structures work together to defend against unwanted thoughts and feelings. We study the development of the patient's ego strength as well as how the id strives for pleasure and gratification. And we consider the effect of the superego reflected in the patient's ideas of right and wrong: the "shoulds" and "should nots."

Therapeutic action Therapeutic action is a term used to describe the significant interactions that take place between the patient and analyst over the course of the analysis that lead to change in the patient's personality, that is, the process by which patients get better.

Transference Transference refers to the redirection, often unconsciously, of thoughts and feelings we have for someone else onto another individual. In therapy, the patient may, for example, have a positive or negative transference to the analyst based on feelings he experienced with a parent or other significant person in his life.

There are various types of transference. For example, a **negative narcissistic transference** describes the negative projections we may have toward someone based on unresolved feelings we may have had toward early objects in our lives; feelings that keep getting triggered and re-aroused in relationships with people who have similar attributes to that original person or who arouse similar negative feelings.

An **object transference** is a transference toward another person that is based on reality. Object transference makes it possible for us to discern the 'object' (person) without discoloration from our internal representations and projections.

Countertransference is the term used to describe the transference feelings the analyst has toward the patient, and which similarly may be **subjective** (emanating from the analyst) objective, or negative narcissistic, and so on.

Index

a real break 20–1
addiction 161n2, 179, 184
admiration 22
advice 13, 25, 61 74; *see* fixing
    problems; practical solutions
amygdala 2
analytic neutrality 46, 60; *see* neutrality
analytic relationship 3, 5, 31, 35, 46,
    55, 62, 63, 65, 77, 83, 109n1; *see*
    friendship; therapeutic relationship;
    transference
analytic transparency 60–1, 65, 183
anger 101, 103, 107, 131, 175; as
    a defence 81; children's 154;
    facilitating expression of 44, 97
autonomic defense system 27
awareness 2, 28, 46, 52, 53, 54, 55–6,
    59, 120, 158, 179

balance 12, 17, 23, 38; *see* imbalance
behaviorism 64, 168, 174, 180
Boston Graduate School of
    Psychoanalysis 53
breakdown 28, 41, 43; *see* a real break

catharsis 31, 79, 80
children: building a bridge to 147–58;
    coaching 149; code of emotion in
    163–6, 170, 175, 180n1; feelings
    in 169; getting curious about, 169;
    method for raising 145; who are
    struggling 169
classical analysis 3, 31, 183
clinical technique *see* technique, clinical
code of emotion 163–6, 169, 170–3,
    175–6, 180n1; cognition 105, 107,
    177
commands 32, 105, 174, 177
conflict 28, 47n2, 82, 98, 105, 137,

145, 180; hidden 105; in marriage
    97–8; intrapsychic 30, 72, 105;
    marital 89, 97–103; of interest doing
    treatment 106; *see* unresolved conflict
conflict theory 28, 29, 81, 82, 183
confusion 12, 30, 175; benefits of 59,
    65; in countertransference 133, 170;
    in marriage 97
connectedness 63, 158
consciousness 79, 108, 109, 117, 123;
    chasm between patient and analyst
    134n3, 161n4; in avoidance mode 43,
    179; investigation of 28; new states of
    32, 64, 65; protective mechanisms to
    preserve 63, 81, 178; regressed states
    of 27; tickets to 83; words of the
    collective 113, 115
contact function 30–3, 43, 46, 60–5, 180
couch: use of 10, 18, 38, 39, 41, 46
countertransference 30, 33n2; knowledge
    of 32; resistance 33n8, 61, 65n2,
    33n9, 84n4, 84n9, 132–3, 134n1,
    159; use of in treatment 33n10,
    34n12, 109n1, 113, 131, 178, 180;
    see hair insecurities; impatience; using,
    your own personality
critical mother: becoming a 148, 178
criticism: of children 138–9
curiosity 28, 62, 130, 175, 182;
    importance of for parenting 179–80

defence: 33n11, 19, 63, 118–20; against
    feeling 25; mechanisms 26, 31, 85n7;
    pushing against 30; respect for 23,
    33n7; walls 2; *see* perfectionism
defense structures 33, 63, 107
demands: environmental 177, 11; in
    marriage 92, 93; in treatment 64
denial 62, 87; *see* repression

depression 1, 11, 13, 17, 25, 27, 44,
    154, 179; medication for 23
diagnosis 80, 101, 113, 164, 166, 167,
    181n3
discovery 56, 77, 112, 129, 133, 158,
    174; psychoanalytic 179–80; *see* self-
    discovery
distortion: psychic 25, 62, 106
drive theory 23, 28, 29, 36, 82, 105,
    116; *see* tension
drug use 141, 153, 171

early trauma 37, 109n4; resolving 84n6;
    see trauma
edginess: in marriage 14
education: about optimal states of
    wellbeing 39; psychological 26;
    requirements for psychoanalytic 53
ego strength 2, 62, 63, 131; *see*
    strengthening
ego-oriented: exploration 30; questions
    30, 57, 60
emotional ally 17, 106
emotional communication 30, 31, 32,
    33n7, 43, 45, 105–6, 108–9, 132;
    159, 161n6, 180; *see* faking it
emotional contagion 37, 46; *see* induced
    feelings
emotional depth 52–3
emotional induction 46, 47n1, 85n9,
    132; *see* induced feelings
emotional insulation 63; *see* defenses
emotions: as instruments for doing
    treatment 30, 31, 32, 45, 57–8, 60;
    see countertransference; induced
    feelings
emptiness 140, 141
enactments 46
exploration 29, 44; *see* ego-oriented,
    questions; object-oriented questions

failure 11, 154, 159; learning from 54,
    64; treatment 3, 177
faking it 150–1, 156, 161n5
fear 21, 30 60, 85n8, 88, 107, 117,
    174; as a challenge to psychoanalysis
    177; of unconscious 177
fight or flight 39
fixations 84n6
fixing problems 102, 143, 168; *see*
    advice; practical solutions
FlyLady 156
following the contact *see* contact
    function

foundations: of belief 21–3; of
    competency 21, 24; of connectedness
    24
freak: feeling like 55, 56
friendliness: towards children 145–6,
    150–8, 163
friendship: in analysis 40, 42, 51–9,
    60–5, 72, 77, 84, 87; in families 128,
    145–6, 150–7, 163; in life: 72, 77,
    84, 87
frustration: ability to talk about 178;
    in treatment 44, 45, 108, 182; with
    children 172–5
future of psychoanalysis *see*
    psychoanalysis, future of

Gilbert, Elizabeth 127
gratification: in marriage 107; in
    treatment 44, 159, 186
grief 80, 103, 129, 185
guilt 97, 173, 175

hair insecurities 19, 23
higher cortex 2, 3
hope 38, 39, 77, 93, 165; about
    treatment effectiveness 61, 70, 75,
    84, 176–7, 179–80; for my readers 5,
    182; from normative standards 40

illusion 32, 119, 141, 177
imbalance 2; *see* balance
impatience 22, 40, 71, 76, 95, 98, 119
implicit memories 80, 131
impulsivity 44, 108
induced feelings 26, 33n11, 61, 64,
    85n9, 85n14, 132, 160, 163, 180n2;
    see countertransference; emotional
    contagion; hair insecurities
initial stages of treatment 29, 47n2, 60,
    63, 175
insight 3, 27, 31, 68, 79, 82, 106, 178
insurance: and psychotherapy 41, 53, 86
interpretive method: failure of 2, 3
internal object representations 28, 109n5
internalizing aggressor 148
interpretation 3, 19, 25, 27, 60, 63, 68,
    74, 81, 85n15, 105–6, 108, 118,
    134n5; limited use of 25
interventions 64, 83, 105–6, 115, 158;
    as emotional communications 31;
    choosing 83; design of 29, 45; *see*
    emotional communication
intrapsychic conflict 28, 30, 72, 105,
    184

irreconcilable differences: in marriage 98–101, 109

jealousy 16, 22, 112
joining 29, 30, 33n3, 33n4, 33n6, 63, 73, 84n3, 85n13, 161n4, 161n5, 170, 179, 180, 185; *see* strengthening

language: for experience 81, 101, 109, 111–12, 115, 124, 169, 179; of psychoanalysis 4, 110
lay analysis 53–4
Lesser, Elizabeth 127
libidinal energy 82–3, 105, 185; liberating 28–31
limits 163
loving-kindness meditation 89, 108
manufactured change 177
marijuana use 137, 140–2, 152, 157
marriage 41, 71, 74, 91, 93–104, 106; completion in 107; reasons for 93; *see* negative union

meanness 144–5
medication 51, 167, 177; stopping 23
memory 79–80, 87
mental health: crisis in 2; future of 4; in society 1, 177, 180, 184
mental illness: rising rates of 1–2
mental murder 88, 108; *see* loving-kindness meditation
mental organization 29, 63, 69–70, 85n7, 185
mental structure *see* mental organization
mentation 2, 184
metaphor 43, 149; *see* symbolic communication
metatheory 3, 28–30, 82, 84, 105, 157
methods: 41, 63, 88; 118–19; behavioral and cognitive 180; clinical 27, 32, 54, 65; interpretive 2; investigation 2, 54, 182; of treatment 2–3, 3, 27, 75, 180; parenting 145–6; research 62, 158; *see* treatment, methods of
methodology *see* methods
mindfulness 108
mirroring 82; *see* mirrors, becoming for people
mirrors: becoming for people 74, 86, 124; for the soul 60, 74
missing experiences 81
models of the mind 180

mothers 17, 154–5, 170; as change agents 158

narcissistic tendencies 26
narcissistic transference 84n5, 85n12, 134n3, 161n5, 181n4, 186; *see* friendship; negative feelings; negative feelings, in transference; negative introject
narratives 26, 39, 79, 81, 82, 131; construction of 178–80
negative feelings 148; in countertransference resistance 112, 174; in families 147–8; in transference 72, 84, 85n12; knowledge of for doing treatment 33n2, 57, 84, 85n8, 186; projected 85, 93, 112; negative introject 85n11, 85n17
negative path 72
negative transference *see* negative feelings, in transference; narcissistic transference
negative union 107
negativity *see* negative feelings
neutral questions 52; *see* object-oriented questions
neutrality: analytic attitude of 114, 183; emotional 121; 109n1
normalcy 2, 31–2, 67, 78

object relations 28, 82–3, 105, 179, 185
objective countertransference 85n14
object-oriented: exploration 29, 52; questions 52, 57, 60, 62, 65n1, 84n1, 185; *see* neutral questions
observation 52–5, 57, 60, 69, 93, 166, 169, 173–4, 178
organization: models for 146, 156
overlooked: feeling of being 149, 161n3

pain body 113, 116–19, 126, 127
paranoia 85n8, 142
parenting 145; confusion around 175; consistency in 11; contemporary solutions for 168, 170, 173, 174; expectation around 76, 172; models of 169
perfectionism 11, 13, 25, 26, 28, 29, 33n11
personal analysis 54, 64, 132
Pink, Daniel 156
playground of emotion 64
pleasure principle 85n16
positive attitude 69, 151, 157

power struggles 53, 168, 173
practical: life 165; matters 40, 43, 63; ways 56, 75
pre-analytic patients 39, 43–7
pre-oedipal problems 80; *see* early trauma
pre-verbal states *see* pre-oedipal problems
problems 12, 15, 16, 24, 33, 38, 40, 43, 62, 77, 80, 168; children and 166; ethical, in treatment 106; in contemporary society 1–2, 39, 177; in marriage 97, 100; unresolved 107
projection 45, 63, 74, 80, 84n2, 84n4, 85n13, 106, 107, 119, 133, 186
projective identification 4, 84n2, 109n3, 186
promise of psychoanalysis 4, 41, 85n6, 177
psychic distortion *see* distortion
psychoanalysis 30, 43, 54, 62–3, 74, 85n10, 89, 111, 114, 118, 124, 125, 134n5, 182; as a research method 62; careers in 53–5; challenges to 25, 27, 47, 67, 131; classical 3, 31–2; contemporary role of 2–3, 4, 27; experience of 40, 112, 124, 131, 159; future of 25–7, 177–80; innovations in 25, 31, 78, 105; love for 4; relevance of 1, 5, 160; training in 51, 52, 53, 60; treatment population for 32, 64; *see* promise of psychoanalysis
psychoanalytic observation *see* observation
psychology 40, 53, 83, 110, 146

questions 13, 17, 27, 30, 74, 105, 106; developing for treatment 43, 55, 105; in psychoanalysis 42, 60–1; *see* ego-oriented, exploration; ego-oriented, questions; object-oriented, exploration; object-oriented, questions

reality 2, 26, 28, 51, 61, 63, 64, 67, 72, 80, 97, 101, 106, 161n3, 166, 179, 181n4, 186; zone of 13
regression 33n5, 46, 105, 186; *see* spaced out zone
relationship: to defenses 33n10
relationships 2, 14, 68, 69, 85n6, 85n17, 93, 94, 102, 107, 150, 160, 184, 185, 186; in a family 106, 158;

to self 102; with supervisor 61, 131; with words 111–12
repetition compulsion 120
repression 63, 79–81, 87, 120, 178
research adventure 64
resistance: resolving 32, 72, 118, 134n5, 72; to treatment 42, 47n2; working with 73–5
resonating emotionally 64
respect: for defenses 81
restlessness 71
revelation 79
rules: for couples therapy 91

sacrifice: in parenthood 154
schizoid personality disorder 85n7
schizophrenics 55
scientific investigation 182
scientific revolution 1
seeking 182
self-destructiveness in children 153
self-discovery 31, 63, 72, 81, 82; preparing the mind for 3, 24, 28–33, 44, 62, 70, 81, 82, 105, 106, 158, 161n2, 161n4, 179, 180, 184; preparing other people's minds for 106, 131, 132, 179
self-help 67; *see* advice; solutions
self-improvement 35; *see* advice; solutions
self-love: in marriage 93
sex therapy 89
sibling rivalry 161n1
society 180
solutions 13, 38, 43, 170; *see* practical, matters
soul: of psychoanalysis 4; mate 17, 96; to-soul-connection 46, 60, 63, 111
spaced out zone 18
Spotnitz, Hyman 54
stalemates: in treatment 37–8, 39
strengthening 17–19, 29, 118, 132, 161n3, 161n6
structural theory 28, 29, 105, 186
subjective countertransference 33n1, 33n9, 34n12, 47n1, 65n3, 85n12, 85n14, 132, 133, 134n1, 134n2, 134n4, 134n6, 159, 183, 186
superego 13, 25, 186
supervision 112–16, 122–6, 127, 128, 132–3; importance of 32, 134n2, 184; need for 112, 131; requirement 53, 133, 134n2
symbolic communication 44, 180n1; *see*

code of emotion; metaphor

tabula rasa 114; *see* neutrality
talking 15, 133, 149, 153–4, 158, 163, 168, 175, 185
technique 88, 129, 161n4; clinical 29, 185; innovations in 30; theory of 25, 28, 29; *see* contact function; emotional communication; joining; mental murder; methods, clinical; methods, of treatment
tension 18, 29, 62, 97, 107, 138, 149, 157, 158, 174; assessing, for diagnosis 113, 174, 175, 181n3; levels of, in treatment 30, 44, 57, 63, 70, 80, 91, 185
theory 15, 29, 118, 160; curriculum for 53; of repression 87; of technique 40; of the mind 25, 28–9, 30, 79–84, 157, 160; purpose for 83–4; *see* conflict theory; drive theory; object relations; structural theory; technique, theory of
therapeutic action 2, 27, 31, 34n13, 72, 78, 133, 186
therapeutic relationship 32, 63; *see* analytic relationship; friendship; narcissistic transference; negative feelings, in transference; soul-to-soul connection
Tolle, Eckhart 113, 116–17, 118, 123
transference 27, 44, 45, 47, 80, 84, 84n2, 84n5, 85n10, 85n12, 115, 119, 161n3, 181n4, 186; and resistance analysis 44; working with 73–7, 85n10; *see* countertransference; narcissistic transference; negative transference
trauma 37, 43, 84n6, 128; *see* early trauma
treatment 1, 2, 24, 25, 29, 32, 33n5, 44, 46, 47, 64, 65, 84, 106, 114, 177; challenges to 2, 38, 43, 53, 80, 133, 134n2; Claudia Luiz's 4, 21, 54, 57,

114, 131; early stages of 26, 29, 43, 45, 64, 150, 163–6, 175; efficacy of 1–3, 40, 62, 160, 179; failures 64; methods of 2, 30, 60, 61, 83, 108; plans 52; resistances to 64, 72–5, 131, 159–60, 167
treatment destructive resistance *see* resistance, to treatment

unconscious 3, 32, 44, 46, 85, 107, 117, 119, 120, 121, 178, 183, 184, 186; current therapies and 2; dynamics 26, 40, 74, 106; insight and 79, 184; method of working with 3, 4, 27, 28, 43, 60, 64, 81, 82, 84, 85n13, 177; motivation 26–7, 82, 120; psychoanalysis and 2, 78; psychoanalysts and 3, 31; resistance to knowing 33, 43, 46; schizophrenia and 55; struggle 25, 179
understanding 11, 15, 27, 29, 31, 32, 52, 61, 63, 71, 133, 156, 158, 161; of clinical theory 160; marriage and 92, 101, 103, 109; parenting and 165, 171, 175
unresolved: conflicts 178–9; dynamics (problems, issues, feelings) 26, 31, 43, 64, 84, 106, 107, 132, 133, 177, 184, 186
using: emotions 4; your own personality 114, 161

virtuosity as an analyst 159–60

working through 109n2, 134n5; *see* therapeutic action

zone of the ego 57

Taylor & Francis eBooks

Helping you to choose the right eBooks for your Library

Add Routledge titles to your library's digital collection today. Taylor and Francis ebooks contains over 50,000 titles in the Humanities, Social Sciences, Behavioural Sciences, Built Environment and Law.

Choose from a range of subject packages or create your own!

Benefits for you
>> Free MARC records
>> COUNTER-compliant usage statistics
>> Flexible purchase and pricing options
>> All titles DRM-free.

Benefits for your user
>> Off-site, anytime access via Athens or referring URL
>> Print or copy pages or chapters
>> Full content search
>> Bookmark, highlight and annotate text
>> Access to thousands of pages of quality research at the click of a button.

REQUEST YOUR **FREE** INSTITUTIONAL TRIAL TODAY

Free Trials Available
We offer free trials to qualifying academic, corporate and government customers.

eCollections – Choose from over 30 subject eCollections, including:

Archaeology	Language Learning
Architecture	Law
Asian Studies	Literature
Business & Management	Media & Communication
Classical Studies	Middle East Studies
Construction	Music
Creative & Media Arts	Philosophy
Criminology & Criminal Justice	Planning
Economics	Politics
Education	Psychology & Mental Health
Energy	Religion
Engineering	Security
English Language & Linguistics	Social Work
Environment & Sustainability	Sociology
Geography	Sport
Health Studies	Theatre & Performance
History	Tourism, Hospitality & Events

For more information, pricing enquiries or to order a free trial, please contact your local sales team: www.tandfebooks.com/page/sales

Routledge
Taylor & Francis Group

The home of Routledge books

www.tandfebooks.com

For Product Safety Concerns and Information please contact our EU
representative GPSR@taylorandfrancis.com
Taylor & Francis Verlag GmbH, Kaufingerstraße 24, 80331 München, Germany